BEST NEWSPAPER WRITING
1989

Best Newspaper Writing 1989

EDITED BY DON FRY

Winners: American Society
of Newspaper Editors
Competition

KASCHT

Copies of *Best Newspaper Writing 1989* are available for
$10.95 each from The Poynter Institute. Earlier editions are
also available in limited quantities. See order form at the back
of this book for details.

**To Gene Patterson,
who started all this.**

About this series

SEPTEMBER 1989

The Poynter Institute for Media Studies proudly publishes the 11th volume of its series *Best Newspaper Writing*, valued since 1979 by students, teachers, and professionals as an indispensable text on clear, effective, and graceful newswriting.

This year's volume is dedicated to Eugene Patterson, editor emeritus of the *St. Petersburg Times*. It was during Gene's 1977-78 term as president of the American Society of Newspaper Editors that ASNE made the improvement of newspaper writing one of its primary long-range goals. Under Patterson's leadership, the society inaugurated a contest to select the best writing in several categories from newspapers in the United States and Canada, and to reward the writers with $1,000 prizes. The Institute volunteered to spread the gospel of good writing by publishing the winning entries along with notes, commentaries, and interviews. That first volume, *Best Newspaper Writing 1979*, sold out long ago and has become a collector's item.

As in past years, *Best Newspaper Writing* is a joint venture of ASNE and the Institute. Each spring, a panel of ASNE editors meets in St. Petersburg for two days to screen more than 500 entries and choose the winners. The first six volumes of *Best Newspaper Writing* were edited by Dr. Roy Peter Clark, dean of the faculty at the Institute.

Clark was one of the first newspaper writing coaches and has been a national leader in the growing movement to make American newspapers more readable, more interesting, and more accurate. Trained as a Chaucer scholar at the State University of New York at Stony Brook, he came to the *St. Petersburg Times* in 1977 from Auburn University. He joined the Institute, then known as the Modern Media Institute, to direct its writing programs.

Clark conducted writing seminars for newspaper professionals and for advanced liberal arts graduates seeking careers in journalism. He also worked with high school students, college journalism teachers, school newspaper advisers, and their student editors. Clark has developed a pilot program for fourth- and fifth-graders, which has had remarkable success in teaching elementary schoolchildren not only to write well, but also to love writing. Clark describes his philosophy and methods in his book *Free to Write: A Journalist Teaches Young Writers* (Heinemann, 1986).

In 1985, Clark was joined on the writing faculty by Dr. Don Fry, his mentor and former colleague from Stony Brook. Fry graduated from Duke University and the University of California at Berkeley. He is a distinguished scholar of early English literature and an outstanding teacher of writing. He serves as a writing coach and consultant to many newspapers, and lectures frequently at universities and national meetings. He has published a number of articles on the qualities of good writing, coaching, and ethics.

Clark and Fry co-edited the 1985 volume of *Best Newspaper Writing*, and Fry has edited the subsequent volumes. The 1986 edition added a new feature, a bibliography of the best articles and books on newswriting. Jo Cates, the Institute's chief librarian, compiles an annual bibliography of newswriting, editing, and coaching.

The 1989 award categories included deadline writing, non-deadline writing, commentary, editorial writing, and state and local government reporting, and the committee increased the prize to $2,500. A committee of 15 editors, chaired by Eugene L. Roberts, executive editor of *The Philadelphia Inquirer*, judged this year's entries:

Richard Aregood, *Philadelphia Daily News*
John Carroll, *Lexington* (Ky.) *Herald-Leader*
Judith Clabes, *The Kentucky Post*
Colleen Dishon, *Chicago Tribune*
John Driscoll, *The Boston Globe*
Earl Foell, *The Christian Science Monitor*

Timothy J. Gallagher, *The Albuquerque Tribune*
Ellen Goodman, *The Boston Globe*
William Hilliard, Portland *Oregonian*
Karen Jurgensen, *USA Today*
Saundra E. Keyes, *Philadelphia Daily News*
David A. Laventhol, Times-Mirror Company, Los Angeles, Calif.
Jean Otto, *Rocky Mountain News*, Denver, Colo.
Howard Simons, Nieman Foundation
Frank Sutherland, *The Times*, Shreveport, La.

The Institute wishes to thank these judges for their fine work, and to compliment them for their dedication to good writing.

The Institute notes with great sadness the death of Howard Simons, who was one of the judges of this year's contest. As managing editor of *The Washington Post*, curator of the Nieman Foundation, and a member of ASNE, Howard was one of the great champions of telling the truth and telling it with style and grace. Journalism is better because of Howard.

***

Founded in 1975 by the late Nelson Poynter, chairman of the *St. Petersburg Times* and its Washington affiliate, *Congressional Quarterly*, the Institute was bequeathed Poynter's controlling stock in the Times Publishing Company in 1978. It invests its dividends in educational activities in four areas: writing, graphics, management, and ethics. The faculty teaches beginning and mid-career professionals, publishes teaching tools such as this book, and conducts educational and research projects, all of which seek the same goal: to raise levels of excellence in newspapers and the communications media generally.

The Institute congratulates the winners and finalists of the ASNE Distinguished Writing Awards.

Robert J. Haiman, President
The Poynter Institute

Acknowledgments

The Des Moines Register and Ken Fuson
The Hartford Courant and Lynne Tuohy
The Miami Herald and Arnold Markowitz
The New York Times and Francis X. Clines
The *News and Observer,* Raleigh, N.C., and
    Michael Skube
The Sacramento Bee and Pete Dexter
The *St. Paul Pioneer Press/Dispatch,* Ann Daly
    Goodwin, and James Lileks
The *St. Petersburg Times* and Thomas French
The Tampa Tribune and Mark Davis
The Washington Post, Henry Allen, Robert Barnes,
    and David Jay Remnick
The Washington Times and Samuel Francis

    We wish to thank the following people for their generous assistance in producing this volume: Jo Cates, Roy Peter Clark, and Joyce Olson of the Institute staff, editorial assistant Lisa Schoof, and of course, the authors and their editors. *Best Newspaper Writing 1989* was produced entirely on a Macintosh II computer and typeset on a Linotronic 300.

Book design and production by Billie M. Keirstead
Cover art by John Kascht, Washington, D.C.

Contents

Introduction

A young bureau reporter called me, saying she had endured a rough performance evaluation that day and needed help. Her editors had told her, among other things, that her writing needed "brightening." She asked them what that meant, and they replied huffily, "Brightening, you know, brighten your copy." She asked them to show her some brightening in someone else's work. They said they couldn't, but would know it when they saw it. She asked, quite properly, "If you can't tell me what brightening is, and you can't show it to me, how can you expect me to do it?" And they replied, "Go ask Don Fry."

What do we mean by "brightening"? Bright writing would include some, maybe all, of the following characteristics:
- Punchy sentences
- Interesting characters
- Lots of voices
- Graphic description
- An author's voice
- Witty surprises

Ideally, all newswriting would include all of those virtues, but we have accepted a tradition of flat prose. The ASNE started its Distinguished Writing Awards to change that dull tradition, so let's illustrate bright writing with examples from this year's winners.

STARTLING SENTENCES

Nobody writes punchy sentences like Francis X. Clines of *The New York Times*, this year's co-winner in the deadline category. He leads a piece on death in Belfast like this:

> Beyond the coffin, out in the churchyard, red-haired Kathleen Quinn was full of fun and flirting shamelessly for all her eight years

of life. "Mister, I'm to be on the TV tonight," she told a stranger, squinting up happy and prim. Kathleen had taken her brother's bike and skinned her knee bloody, all while people were praying goodbye inside the church to another rebel body in another coffin.

Soon the cameras were watching the coffin being carried out from the windowless fortress of a church, down the curl of the street in the simple hamlet, and on to the ever-filling grave-yard patch devoted to republican rebels.

Clines places the girl "beyond the coffin, out in the churchyard," without cluttering his sentence with either the name of the coffin's occupant or the location and affiliation of the churchyard. He has Kathleen "squinting up happy and prim," rather than "happily and primly." Clines uses repetition for ironic rhythmic effects in "all while people were praying goodbye inside the church to another rebel body in another coffin," surprising us with "praying goodbye" rather than "saying goodbye." Instead of having the street "curl," he turns the verb into a noun, "down the *curl* of the street." And the phrase "on to the ever-filling graveyard patch devoted to republican rebels" plays the di-minuitive "patch" against the grandiosity of "re-publican."

All these tricks make the sentences pop.

But punchy sentences need not run so poetic or so complex, as in this stark example:

There was more macabre violence at an Irish Republican Army funeral today as two armed British soldiers in civilian clothes drove their car into a crowd of panicked mourners and were seized, beaten, and finally shot to death.

Clines told me: "I wanted to use the words 'macabre' and 'finally.' That word 'finally' was important to me, to imply that the people who shot them had time to think about it. And I was surprised that you could coil all that into a sentence now and not look too foolish." Maybe Frank Clines writes punchy sentences with ease because he speaks punchy sentences.

LIVELY CHARACTERS

Nothing brightens prose like sharply etched characters readers can see and hear. James Lileks, a staff writer at the *St. Paul Pioneer Press/Dispatch*, won the non-deadline prize for his savage humor columns full of Minnesotans, especially this most famous one:

> And there he is. A sequoia in a room full of saplings.
> Keillor is unmistakable: he towers over all others, to the extent that he should have aircraft warning lights attached to his tux. For the first time, I wonder how much of Keillor's legendary reticence is simply a reaction to being so damn big. If Keillor had a personality to match his size, he would have to be from Texas. In a quieter state, it is wise to behave like Paul Bunyan's bookish brother.
> He doesn't look like he is enjoying this. Nor does it seem to be particularly unpleasant. If you want to know what he's thinking based on his expression, practice on the Sphinx.

Readers can see Garrison Keillor because Lileks does not describe him much at all. This description contains a notion of relative height, a tux, and an unspecified facial expression, but no more physical detail. Most readers know what Keillor looks like, and Lileks evokes him with just a few touches. We also see Keillor through Lileks's reactions; people are the sum of other people's impressions.

Lileks rounds out the characterization by letting the reader hear Keillor:

> "I came here with my father when I was 11," he begins slowly. The gears of his story-

telling machinery begin their comfortable mesh. "I hadn't been anywhere else, not even the Black Hills. It was a different place in 1953, still very much a city of the '30s, of pushcarts and peddlers. I saw the Empire State Building, Radio City.

"It was a time of hot weather...."

Lileks lets us hear Keillor's rhythms and Minnesota-isms ("not even the Black Hills"), and he frames the quotation with indications of manner. Keillor looms up out of the page.

VOICES IN THE RUBBLE

Bright stories teem with voices of real people, not just careful politicians. David Remnick, a Moscow correspondent for *The Washington Post*, shared the deadline-writing prize with Frank Clines. Remnick's graphic descriptions of the Armenian earthquake devastate the reader, but their real terror comes from the voices of the Armenian survivors:

A young woman, wrapped in a torn, dank blanket, wandered the streets of this ruined town the other day, by shattered factories and schools, past the coffins of her friends and families. "We Armenians," she said, "we have always lived under a black cross."

To visit Armenia now is to meet with a people who are often on the brink of despair. "Sometimes we feel as though even the heavens are against us," said Larissa Margachyan, a woman whose children were killed when a nursery school in Spitak collapsed.

Remnick frames the speakers in landscape and situation, and lets them speak simply.

Reporters tend to clutter up their stories with too many quotations, plus all the necessary baggage of attribution. Remnick lets the reader hear a multitude of voices, keeping the apparatus simple. A sampler:

"In this town, it used to be that when one

person died, we all cried," said Artavad Kogosyan, a sugar worker who was still looking
for his daughter today. "But now only a few
can cry. We have no more tears left."

"It all happened in an instant," she said. "A
noise, a terrible swaying, and then there was
no one."
All she salvaged from the debris were her
pictures and, strangely, a pair of high-heeled
shoes, a kind of memorial of long-past family
events. "I have to leave this place," she said.
"There is no life here anymore."

"This is what the end of the world must
look like," said one factory worker.

"So few are left," one old woman said, "and
a lot of us who made it now cannot stand to be
alive."

Bright writing makes grim subjects bearable.

DESCRIBING A ROAD
All the writers above excel at description, but
Mark Davis of the *Tampa Tribune* succeeds in the
daunting task of brightening up road building.
Mark won the government reporting award for a
series on the construction of an overpass on U.S.
Highway 19, at perhaps the worst intersection in
Florida. He simplifies complex description by in-
voking human scale:

A football team could play on the largest
bridge, a 420-foot-long, six-lane creation. At
its zenith, it would allow almost 17 feet of
clearance for the traffic passing below. The
108-foot Whitney bridge, by comparison,
could hold a basketball team but would be
hard-pressed to find room at either end for the
cheerleaders.

Every reporter has compared something to a
football field, but Davis puts people, a whole foot-

xviii

ball team, on the bridge for comparison. And they
don't just stand up there; they "play."

Davis lets the reader experience a roadroller
through Richlene Young, a newly hired worker:

> They went through the instructions as Bar-
> ney pointed the levers that controlled the ma-
> chine. He also noted that it had a control that
> shook the 15,000-pound roller. When it vi-
> brated, the roller banged moisture out of the
> earth so asphalt would adhere more readily to
> the roadbed. Young was entranced.
>
> They put the roller in gear, and it lurched as
> it chugged toward the southeast corner where
> workers dodged cars as they followed a barri-
> cade trail. Barney showed her where to use
> the roller, and she uncertainly aimed the behe-
> moth toward the roadbed and curbing. Sitting
> eight feet in the air, her hard hat dazzlingly
> white in the canopy's shadows, she watched
> the traffic pass by.
>
> She began to feel at home atop the clatter-
> ing machine as she pushed levers and the ma-
> chine, miraculously, responded to her direc-
> tions. It tickled the bottom of her boots, and
> she enjoyed the sensation. It felt like home.

Readers see very little of the actual machine, but
they feel it as they watch Richlene react. People
make description live.

THE RIGHT VOICE

Bright writing brims with people, plus one more
person, the author, experienced as a distinctive
voice. Samuel Francis, deputy editorial page editor
of *The Washington Times*, won the award for editorials, a form most people think of as essentially
faceless and voiceless. But Francis chisels a voice
for himself resonant with intelligence and an edge
of meanness, as in this attack headlined "A Brief
History of the L-Word":

> The signers assure the reader that they paid
> for the ad themselves and that it "has not been

authorized by any candidate"—although you don't need a Ph.D. to know which candidate most of these eggheads are supporting. Nor do you need an advanced degree to see through the transparently fallacious argument that an attack on liberalism is an attack on the principles upon which the American republic was founded. We thought you weren't supposed to deal in labels this year, but whatever name you want to give to the ideas and principles that informed the American founding, they bear scant resemblance to what travels the world under the passport of liberalism these days.

An author's distinctive set of habits and devices induces a sense of a voice "heard" by the reader from the page. Francis writes long and complicated sentences, with slightly elevated wording. He creates a tone of intellectual superiority by lecturing the "eggheads" on American history, and smacks them with the indirect allusion to "fellow traveler" in the last clause.

Sometimes he lets that voice get downright snotty, as in this comic blast:

If you thought Mikhail and Raisa were a stitch, just wait til you meet Fidel Castro. According to Sen. Claiborne Pell, recently returned from a boondoggle to Cuba and a three-hour chin-wag with the Cuban strongman, Mr. Castro is "a man of great personal vitality and vivacity" and "as an individual he had, I think, a good deal of charisma." From these insights, Mr. Pell concludes that the United States should start "normalizing" relations with Mr. Castro's unreconstructed communist government.

Francis uses slang ("stitch," "chin-wag") in his characteristically long sentences, emphatically ending with a right-wing tag: "unreconstructed communist government."

Such a voice, such writing, clearly has a real person behind it.

SURPRISE!

Finally, bright writing often shines with witty surprises. Michael Skube, book page editor of the Raleigh *News and Observer*, won the commentary prize for his trenchant reviews. In the following paragraph, he keeps surprising the reader by getting progressively meaner:

> James Michener's new cinderblock of a book, *Alaska,* is 868 pages long, and I think I began reading it sometime toward the end of the last Ice Age. I have been chipping away at it, in any case, for what seems an awfully long time. *Alaska* (Random House, $22.50) is not a book to be read so much as got through. Events move along at glacial speed, an inch at a time, until the dinosaurs are gone and the oceans have receded and the landmasses have emerged and at last something we might recognize as Alaska comes dimly into view. When you've not read one in a while, you forget just how long a book James Michener can write.

If you call a book a "cinderblock" in the first line, you have to have a quiverful of wit to write the next line. Skube startles his readers with a series of zingers, such as:

> Everyone knows, of course, about Michener. He writes woodenly, he appeals to people who move their lips when they read, and his books sell by the truckload, like so many boxes of bran flakes.

> In Michener's case, the temptation is always strong to fire a few well-aimed BBs at the barn door and knock off for the day.

> There's a sex scene—I guess that's what it was—that made me think of two sawhorses.

Michael Skube is no slouch in the voice department either.

BRIGHT PEOPLE
So bright writing comes from bright sentences, bright characters, bright voices (including the bright author's) bright descriptions, and bright surprises. But who has time and space for all that shining on city hall or night cops or the school beat? You do. Any reporter does, who's willing to bring back people in the notebook and not just data.

Writers win the bright prizes by writing about people.

Don Fry
September 1989

BEST NEWSPAPER WRITING
1989

James Lileks
Non-Deadline Writing

JAMES LILEKS left his hometown of Fargo, North Dakota, the minute he graduated from high school and headed for the University of Minnesota. He studied architecture, humanities, secondary education, art history, journalism, and English for eight years without earning any degrees. He began writing humor for the *Minnesota Daily*, and eventually stopped bothering with such trivialities as going to class. He wrote food and restaurant reviews for a weekly called *City Pages* until he was sued for libel for accusing a Chinese restaurant of using too much MSG. In 1988, he published his first novel, entitled *Falling Up the Stairs* (Dutton, $19.95). Then the *St. Paul Pioneer Press/Dispatch* hired him as a features writer, what James calls "lifestyle infantry."

He'll take Manhattan

APRIL 3, 1988

This is the news from New York City, the little town where time is money, that the decades cannot impress, where all the women are busy, the men are busier, and a lot of the children are being tried as adults.

It's a messy, noisy town of style and exuberance—Calcutta designed by Bill Blass. It's also the home of Minnesota's modern myth maker, Garrison Keillor. One might wonder what Keillor—slow-talking storyteller and professional Shy Person—is doing in a city founded on speed, sound, and fury. After all, this is as far from Lake Wobegon as you can get.

Which might be the point.

Keillor left St. Paul last summer, hinting that he found his celebrityhood claustrophobic. He was tired of being a famous person in a town where there are few of the famous, he said; he wanted blessed anonymity, a place where he could be just another guy, to "live the life of a shy person." He moved to Denmark with his new wife, where, apparently, anonymity stretched as far as the eye could see.

Recently, he returned to the States, but not to the land of birth: he reappeared in New York City. He took an office at *The New Yorker*, the vehicle of the finest American humorists of the 20th century. He began to pop up in magazines and newspapers, forswearing his taciturn nature for leisurely discursions on life. A month ago, *The New York Times* wrote an article about having dinner with Keillor, reporting his comments on the decor and the food. His New York celebrityhood was established for certain on March 20, when the *Times* fashion supplement delivered Keillor's cogitation on his lucky red socks.

This would all seem to be the antithesis of the

Keillor who left a year ago. Endless mash notes from the press asking what he put on his feet, confiding what he put in his mouth. From a distance—say the distance between St. Paul and New York—one might think that Keillor had changed, that New York had brought out a different side of him. Perhaps the press was treating him differently, eager to be nice to a fresh celebrity. Or perhaps Keillor now has the blessings of celebrityhood among those who matter, while enjoying the anonymity of the big city.

Conjecture is hard; distance makes it harder. Compounding matters was the Hatfields-vs.-McCoys approach to human interaction that has characterized this paper's relationship with Keillor. But I decided that the only thing to do was to go to New York and find Garrison Keillor and ask him certain questions, observe him in his environment before he returns for his Orchestra Hall concert on April 7.

I would have to be cautious, stalking my prey, living in the shadows. I'd know him when I saw him, for we'd met once before, four years earlier. He'd given me advice. "If you want to be a writer, go to New York," he said. I supposed the same thing applied if you just wanted to look for one.

FRIDAY

The bellboy drops my luggage in my room, opens the windows, and shows me where the bathroom is. Thirsty work, and certainly worth the healthy gratuity I am obligated to produce. As I slip him a dollar I ask, "Ever had to show a room for Garrison Keillor?" He thinks for a second, then asks who Keillor is. I say he's a writer.

"He write Westerns?" says the bellhop.

I give him the tip, wondering if, in time-honored detective fashion, I should peel off bills until he tells me what I want to hear. Two of the larger denominations, and he would probably admit to Keillor banging out all his works in this very room. Three bills, and he'd confide that Christopher Marlowe actually wrote *Lake Wobegon Days*.

This is going to be harder than I thought. I

4

know, based on press clips, three things: Keillor's neighborhood, his favorite cafe, and that he is appearing Monday at a benefit for Attorney General (and aspiring senator) Skip Humphrey (staged in New York to tap the funds of exiled Minnesotans). Anything else is up to me.

Friday night is spent prowling Greenwich Village, looking for an approximation of Keillor's Sidetrack Tap, a homey bar run by kindly people, with archaic music on the jukebox and hoary bromides tacked up over the bar. A place serving two-bit beer. The closest I could come was a place called Hi-Tech Mex. By the time I leave, the beer tab is 136 bits.

I hail a cab. As we bound through into midtown at speeds normally reserved for the Bonneville Salt Flats, we pass the Algonquin Hotel. In the 1920s, the Algonquin was home to the fabled Round Table, the brightest wits and humorous writers of the day. You needed a large ego and a loud voice to survive there. By working at *The New Yorker,* Keillor was assuming the mantle of Thurber, Benchley, Parker, others who had come to New York and found success as humorists. I wonder how a shy person would have done at the Round Table.

I ask my cabbie if he's ever heard of Garrison Keillor.

"Garrison Keillor." Pause. "What is that, a hotel?"

SATURDAY

Chelsea is a district on the southwest side of Manhattan. The north is Clinton, or Hell's Kitchen, which would make Chelsea Hell's Drawing Room, I suppose. To the south is the unruly tangle of streets known as Greenwich Village.

In between is Keillor's neighborhood, a part of town that never had the bad reputation of Hell's Kitchen or the enduring cachet of the Village. But Chelsea had its vogue toward the end of the 19th century; in 1872, it was home to the city's most oft-raided vice den, as well as the city's liveliest entertainment district. By the end of the century, Chelsea was home to the city's silent-movie indus-

try, and some of the city's largest department stores
lined its streets.

The entertainment district shifted north, and
commerce faded; Chelsea settled in for a half-cen-
tury of decline and senescence. But since Manhattan
real estate pressures ensure that any neighborhood
that's not a smoking pile of bricks with radioactive
waste sluicing down the gutter will eventually be
reclaimed, Chelsea is being gentrified. For the moment, it is caught between incarnations. A glance
through one set of windows shows abstract art and
spindly halogen light fixtures; in another window,
one sees the back of an old tube radio. A lot of
people have lived here for a long, long time.

Keillor lives in a triplex on 22nd Street, Chelsea
at its quietest and finest. There are trees, all with the
scrappy, ravaged determination of any plant outside
the parks. And you don't get the feeling that if you
opened any door, money would gush out. The cars
are modest. The mailbox wears a few inscrutable
slashes of graffiti, calling cards from New York's
tireless army of vandals, but otherwise the street is
unscarred. A little more time and a little less money
and Chelsea would not be as pleasant a place to
live, but that hasn't happened, and it won't.

There's even an old Lutheran church near the
middle of the block. No one has spray-painted his
bid for immortality on the nameplate. You can still
read the church's name: St. Paul.

All of these things make Chelsea a pleasant afternoon walk, but I am here to find Keillor. A walk
up the avenues that cut through Chelsea—wide,
nondescript, crammed with small stores—proves
equally fruitless. I eventually feel overcome by the
need for a cup of coffee that costs a dollar and will
never be refilled, even if my life hinged on the
matter, so I go into a neighborhood cafe, the
Lemon Tree.

Duty intervenes. When the waitress comes by to
present the check, I say, "Garrison Keillor lives
around here, I understand."

Since none of my words involves an item on the
menu, the waitress pays no heed and ambles off.

But a couple at an adjacent table look over at me.

"Excuse me," says a woman in her late 30s. "Did you say Garrison Keillor lives around here?" In her mouth, the name is Gawrisun Keuyluh.

"It says so in the *Times*," I reply.

"I thought he lived in, what, Minnesota?"

"He did, but he moved here. Do you live around here?"

"No," says the woman. "We're looking at a place today." She looks at the gentleman sitting across from her and bats his hand. "See? I told you this wasn't such a bad neighborhood."

SUNDAY

No one does anything on Sundays here. Laundry, maybe. Long phone calls. I have a few of those to make, a few questions to ask.

The perpetual question: How does Keillor feel about New York? But now that he's been here a while and the locals have had a chance to look him over, it seems appropriate to ask how New York feels about him.

New York, of course, never has a unified opinion about anything.

Bryan Miller, a food writer for *The New York Times*, saw Keillor close up. He invited him to be the subject of a Dining Out column, the *Times* version of "Esquire Goes on a Date."

"He was, ah, how should I say, a man of a dry sense of humor. Not the raconteur I had expected. You'd expect non-stop stories. But he was thoughtful; when he had something to say, he said it."

As for how New York perceives His Lankyness, Miller sounds somewhat amazed. "People here always wonder why anyone who doesn't have to move to New York would do so. They're curious why he would be a celebrity in his hometown and yet want to come to a crowded, congested, less healthy city and pay three times the price for everything."

Does Miller have any theories?

"He was quite clear about why he came. He said this was the place for a writer to be. Said there's a camaraderie in the writing community he didn't feel out in St. Paul."

Emily Prager, media columnist for *The Village Voice* and novelist—her recent Vintage Contemporary novel, *Clea and Zeus Divorce*, examines the questions of celebrityhood and embracing public scrutiny—finds Keillor's emergence in New York slightly curious.

"His whole draw seems to be that he lives in the Midwest. I don't know how he's going to keep going if he lives here. I mean, this is *not* the Midwest. Why would he live in New York? They don't know who he is."

Well, he said that was why he was moving here. To be anonymous. Prager chuckles.

"Writers want to be a little bit anonymous, not completely. You want anonymity, move to Canada."

But people do know who he is. According to a spokesman for the publicity department of Viking Penguin, Keillor is one of the most requested authors for public appearances, such as benefits and book signings, averaging four requests per week.

Perhaps the sagest observers of Keillor's transplantations are his fellow Minnesotans. Cheryl Brama, a creative assistant for an advertising firm who has lived in New York just five months longer than Keillor, predicts Keillor will miss the serenity of a smaller city's pace. In addition, she said, "If Powdermilk Biscuits did exist, he wouldn't find them here. He'd find Powdermilk Bagels."

Do people bring up Lake Wobegon when they discover she's from Minnesota?

"Only if they're also from Minnesota. Then, it's like a code word for sanity."

Wesley Ellenwood, head of the video production department at New York University, grew up close to Keillor's Anoka, and says he found *Lake Wobegon Days* entertaining and accurate.

"He basically set down a record of my upbringing, right down to the boiled potatoes and tasteless meat."

But the knowledge that Keillor, like him, is now a New York resident, doesn't enhance the parallels.

"I never run into him. Probably because he doesn't take the D train to Brooklyn."

Do his students, upon finding he is from the land of Keillor, ever bring up the Wobegon connection?

Sigh. "Yeah. But in my social circles, there's no concern where you're from. New York is just too big to be concerned about where you're from."

MONDAY

I contact the Skip Humphrey campaign to get admission to Humphrey's reception. I am told it's at the Algonquin. Somehow, I'm not surprised.

First, however, supper. Keillor had mentioned in *The New York Times* that he enjoyed eating at Miss Ruby's Cafe, a restaurant at 135 Eighth Ave. It's the sort of restaurant you find in that part of town—decor assembled according to the vagaries of the owner's tastes. A coat of rust-brown paint, a few framed pieces of art, some battered stars perhaps liberated from an old Texaco station. The food falls into the category of Whatever the Chef Feels Like Cooking. American roadhouse favorites side by side with Caribbean curiosities.

A Minnesotan's skull would rise and revolve upon greeting the bill; you can just hear someone named Elmer saying, "I am *not* paying $45 for a meal in a place where they can't even panel the walls over." But the food is good, the coffee pot bottomless. Keillor's plug was well-deserved.

It seems reasonable that the staff would know him, and indeed they do. The waitress says she's waited on Keillor often, and while her smile indicates she found him a pleasant customer, it is hardly reason to rush to the phone and remake Page One. He was a customer, which meant food to be served, plates to be cleared. Still: he sounds like a regular, an old friend.

A few minutes after the queries are launched, a manager who identifies himself as Michael appears at the table. He explains that the staff will not be answering any more questions about Keillor.

"We respect his privacy," he says. "We have a lot of people who come here because we respect their privacy. He's a good customer, and he comes in with an assortment of people, and I'd prefer to just leave it at that."

I have no quarrel with any of that. He makes some suggestions for the meal, smiles, and departs.

In the middle of the chicken-fried steak he returns. "I just spoke with Miss Ruby," he says, "and she agrees that we can't really say anything." Pause. "He does seem to like ham and redeye gravy, though. Does that help?"

MONDAY NIGHT

I'm early for the reception. The Oak Room, where the Round Table began 68 years before, is as empty as a museum at midnight, a few white-coated waiters joking among themselves before work begins. I decide to wait at the bar on the other side of the lobby.

Tending the bar is a young man named Fran. I ask Fran if he is tired of people asking about the Round Table, and his expression says yes; it also says he's tired of being asked if he's tired of being asked. He has heard of Keillor.

"He's gotten a lot of play," Fran says. "The things he talks about are alien to this town, and people love that. But, you know, I read the book, and I can't make up my mind whether he was expressing scorn or admiration toward this Lake Wobegon."

But he read the entire book.

"I'm an anthropology major," he says in a New Jersey voice. "I like to read about foreign cultures."

By now, enough people in tuxedos and formal gowns have filed past the door of the bar to indicate the reception is about to start. I decide to give the party time to start firing on all cylinders before I elbow my way in and start asking questions. As a woman in Humphrey's campaign had warned me, there are a lot of people who had paid $250 to be in the same room as Garrison Keillor, and journalists were not about to be allowed to monopolize the evening's star.

After a few minutes, I pay my tab and walk into

the Oak Room. And there he is. A sequoia in a room full of saplings.

Keillor is unmistakable: he towers over all others, to the extent that he should have aircraft warning lights attached to his tux. For the first time, I wonder how much of Keillor's legendary reticence is simply a reaction to being so damn big. If Keillor had a personality to match his size, he would have to be from Texas. In a quieter state, it is wise to behave like Paul Bunyan's bookish brother.

He doesn't look like he is enjoying this. Nor does it seem to be particularly unpleasant. If you want to know what he's thinking based on his expression, practice on the Sphinx.

For a moment, there is no one else queued up to claim their $250 worth of attention, and I slip in and introduce myself as a writer from the *St. Paul Pioneer Press/Dispatch*. If that rings any warning bells, it doesn't show; he is perfectly cordial. I have, of course, several questions: Do you know people think you're a hotel?

I settle for asking what he thought he might have written had he been born here, instead of Minnesota.

"I don't think I've considered the possibilities," Keillor says. "I'm satisfied where I'm from."

Well, what's the attraction to New York, then? If the Lake Wobegon stories came out of love, why move away to their antithesis?

Keillor stands still for a second. His foot is tapping and the hand that holds his drink rolls the wine back and forth in the glass, almost as though his extremities were steam vents for nervousness.

"I came here with my father when I was 11," he begins slowly. The gears of his storytelling machinery begin their comfortable mesh. "I hadn't been anywhere else, not even the Black Hills. It was a different place in 1953, still very much a city of the '30s, of pushcarts and peddlers. I saw the Empire State Building, Radio City.

"It was a time of hot weather. We were in Brooklyn. Families in the apartments had taken bedspreads and pillows and were sleeping in the

park. To look, to see children sleeping in the grass
in a huge city, the grown-ups smoking, convers-
ing.... It was a different city then. New York was
always in my imagination after that."

But people sleep in the park today because that's
all they have. They sleep there when it is a time of
cold weather, too.

Keillor knows this, of course. "Those things
have changed, and they are to be mourned. But
what struck me then is still present. All the life is
on the street. The streets are full of conversation in
Manhattan, and to a person from the Midwest, that
is amazing. Minnesota is a culture of small towns,
a culture suspicious to large cities. Cities like Minneapolis have changed, too—the freeways, the
skyways now isolate people from one another."

Now that he's in this new world, away from the
source of his material, does he fear his material
will change?

"I hope it does. But moving here was, in a way,
not that much of a change—it's actually a simpler,
quieter life. We live in a section that feels like a
neighborhood. Has a church.

"I keep running into Minnesotans here. They
transplant well. Something to be proud of—industri-
ous, conscientious, honest, and intelligent people.
Living out here, I feel proud of where I come from."

There are more questions, but there are more
people; I thank him and move away.

None of this—the opinions of strangers, the look
of his neighborhood, his answers to a few questions—adds up to anything conclusive; you can
read them all according to your preconceptions. As
with most celebrities, those preconceptions are inevitably more entertaining than the truth.

Enigmas fascinate, and Keillor makes for a perfect enigma. His writings seem to take place in
some comforting dusk of everyone's past, and his
voice is as warm as the fire in the hearth—yet the
man stands apart with a reserve that is simultaneously Olympian and pained.

The truth about Garrison Keillor is like that jot
of white material on an egg yolk you can never get

with your spoon. Whether it is an unintentional function of a shy personality or a calculated construction matters less in New York than the effect. It is best to keep people guessing.

As for why he went, he doesn't owe us explanations. It's the delusion that our celebrities are our personal friends that makes us think everything needs to be set out for our approval. He can live wherever he chooses. But the choice of New York is telling. New York nowadays does not easily give comfort for the asking, but there is a certain level of money and fame at which the city becomes malleable.

Keillor's work has given him the means to keep the city reasonably hospitable, to keep the New York of his imagination alive. When he tells the story of coming here as a child to a magical place of great power and promise, there is no disappointment in his voice to suggest the city has turned out differently than that child of 11 thought it would.

One quote stands out: "Living out here, I feel proud of where I come from." That is the exile's catechism. To be proud of where you come from and not stay there implies, after all, a greater pride in where you happen to be now. And on the night I found Keillor, he had landed at the Algonquin, a place the best and wittiest had called home. No, it's not the Sidetrack Tap, but again: that just might be the point.

Observations and questions

1) This piece turns on contrasts, especially of Minnesota versus New York expectations. Follow these contrasts throughout, noting how Lileks uses them for structure.

2) Lileks also structures this piece as a search for Garrison Keillor. Why does he take so long to find him? Why does he ask people unlikely to know Keillor?

3) "I slip in and introduce myself as a writer from the *St. Paul Pioneer Press/Dispatch*. If that rings any warning bells, it doesn't show; he is perfectly cordial." Lileks told me that "warning bells" refers to Keillor's animosity toward the paper, adding, "I think anybody who had followed the paper, seen the letters from the editor, and read the quotes would know." Can we assume that readers read the opinion pages?

4) "None of this—the opinions of strangers, the look of his neighborhood, his answers to a few questions—adds up to anything conclusive; you can read them all according to your preconceptions. As with most celebrities, those preconceptions are inevitably more entertaining than the truth." This passage seems to attack journalism's basic method, telling the reader what's out there rather than what's in the reporter's head. Is Lileks right?

5) Lileks comments: "He doesn't owe us explanations. It's the delusion that our celebrities are our personal friends that makes us think everything needs to be set out for our approval." If a celebrity, who is, after all, the creation of the media, "doesn't owe us explanations," how can reporters justify intruding on his privacy?

6) The lead and the ending of this piece reflect each other's wording, suggesting that Lileks has solved the enigma of Keillor. Has he? Could he?

Riding the rails offers more than rest and relaxation

JUNE 19, 1988

The following, I think, is typical. I took a sleeper-car train to New York City, following the old routes, living the old rhythms the jets have tried to kill. The experience taught me three things. One, the trains aren't dead. They're coming back. Rarely on time, granted, but coming back nonetheless. Two, I never want to go over a high bridge in a train again in my life. Three, nothing equals what a train provides. Nothing. That says a lot for jets, but it says more for the trains.

ST. PAUL TO CHICAGO: COACH CLASS

"But what if someone puts a penny on the tracks?" the guy across the aisle whines. He has a voice best suited to walking up to the table and announcing that he would be your waiter tonight. "What if we derail?"

This is not likely. Put a penny on the tracks, let a train pass over it, and you will have a thin penny to show for your efforts. What is more likely is that I will take the hard little pillow Amtrak provides for my comfort and hold it over this guy's face until he quiets down, for he has been blathering on without cease since we left. Compounding matters are two precocious members of the My Little Pony set who amuse themselves by jumping up and down in front of strangers and demanding that you guess the names of their cousins. "Starts with X!" "Xavier." "No!"

It is eight hours to Chicago, and it feels like one interminable taxi down a runway in a plane, never taking off. The tracks are in such bad shape the train has to tiptoe through most of Wisconsin. Go ahead, put a penny on the rails. It'll double their maintenance budget.

I have a headache and I'm hungry and I already miss my girlfriend and let's just not talk about this leg of the trip.

CHICAGO

We change in Chicago, the town known to toddle. The train station was built in 1926, and that also appears to have been the last time it was swept or painted. I drag my belongings to the baggage department and show them which bag contained the breakables, so they won't have to waste energy throwing all my bags around at careless velocity. As I have had nothing to eat but my own cuticles —the train was late, and I feared missing my connection—I purchase a small boiled mailing tube masquerading as a hot dog, slather it with red mucilage, and wolf it down. My comfort thus assured, I look for a place in the station where I can sit down and get up without sticking to my chair.

I spend my layover in Amtrak's first-class lounge, where the lure is apparently hearing a better class of baby wail its lungs out. The lounge looks like a dentist's office, circa 1959; in the center is a gnarled tree cowering under a blast of fluorescent light; in one corner, a TV bolted high on the wall in the mode favored by mental institutions.

To my left sits an old man. He has reached the age when pants naturally crawl up to the sternum, and he wears a hat mashed down on his head. He studies the room in silence for 10 minutes, then says to no one in particular, "Perhaps the money is going into improving the tracks."

There is no information board in the lounge to tell you when your train is due, the gate from which it departs, whether it even exists. You have to depend on your Amtrak employee. They're not hard to identify—all wear uniforms left over from some cocktail lounge's attempt to celebrate the Bicentennial. But the depot is not exactly overrun with them. When you find one, the wisest thing to do is nail his feet to the floor and charge other passengers a fee to speak with him. When half the coach-class waiting room rose and shuffled out, I actually found one of the Scarce and Uniquely Attired individuals and inquired if they were boarding the train to New York. They were. I schlepped my baggage down to the tracks, got in line, stepped through the gate—

CHICAGO TO NEW YORK VIA SLEEPER

—I step through the gate, and something changes. There is a blast of cool air with the tang of diesel; the train stretches ahead into the distance, engines throbbing. This is a different train. This isn't the train that takes you to your connection; this was the train that takes you all the way to where you wanted to go, the train that was waiting for you all this time.

My car was called the *Pacific Queen,* a refurbished sleeper built in 1948 but looking new and polished. There was a slight trouble boarding when everyone attempted to get into the car at the same time, a feat equal in ease to shoving cashew nuts down a funnel. The hallway of the car is wide enough for two people to pass if one of them doesn't show up. Unfortunately, between me and my room stood an adherent of the Pavarotti diet. How he was going to get through his narrow door without a lot of grease, good will, and a battering ram, no one knew. But I try to pass him. We perform a little dance. He glares at me for having the gall to be average weight for my height. I slip past, winded, and find my room; I drop my baggage, slide the door shut, and look around.

It doesn't take long to look around the room. Six feet long, 3 feet wide, 8 feet tall. A coffin with great head room. The rooms are masterpieces of ergonomics—every square inch serves a function. The sink folds into the wall. The bed folds into the wall. You're surprised the wall doesn't fold into the wall. You've one comfortable seat, and a personal commode. The important items, like the reading light and the ashtrays, are located at a height accessible from the seat and the bed. Everything is painted a regrettable shade of beige, but the novelty and the echoes of a past era are so pronounced you expect a butler to be lying prone on the bed when you pull it down.

There are men in the corridors, all wearing spoiled-cranberry-colored Amtrak jackets, talking into walkie-talkies and getting furtive crackles in response. I suspect they are telling the engineer that the majority of the people on the train are standing up, and hence this would be a good time for the train to lurch forward and knock everyone back into his seat. The engineer apparently agrees; the train shudders and coughs, the wheels squeal, and the train begins its halting pull out of the station.

We were still chugging through Chicago when my porter delivered the first-class amenities. These included a packet of stationery, a small bottle of wine, and the famed Amtrak Snak Pak, which contains everything from French cheese to a Slim Jim. I am given my meal tickets—first-class tickets include free meals—but that, as we are about to see, was not exactly an act of friendship.

DINNER

They seat you European style, which is a fancy term for Forced to Eat With Strangers. My table companion this evening is an engineer from Illinois who sells drill bits to the Japanese. He has not only participated in the drilling of huge tunnels, he has done so without getting one interesting anecdote out of the experience.

The menu describes the food as though it were a gourmet's dream, and the waiters serve it with cheer. If I were the waiters, I would serve it and hide. Here, alas, is food that makes you wish you were on an airplane. Microwaves are the culprits. The New York strip tasted like a horse's bit; the cheeseburger had all the aroma and flavor of particle board. The meatless entree, manicotti, looked less like a meal than a murder scene.

The coffee is good. You have to fire signal flares to get a second cup, but it is hot and tasty—two adjectives not found in close proximity to one another in the Amtrak kitchen. The days of white linen tablecloths and china are gone, and where once the dining car was an oasis of civility, it is now a forced labor camp. There's no escape. You can't order out. The general attitude was best expressed by a waiter's reply to a customer's request for a substitution.

"The cook," he said, "don't make no alternations." Bingo.

THE BAR CAR,
OR DEATH STOPS AT TOLEDO

In the double-decker cars, the bar car is down-
stairs, giving it the air of a speakeasy. The chairs
face each other, encouraging confabulation. East of
the Mississippi the car is a strange beast—a long
bar in the middle of the car, a few rows of seats
pointed toward the front. Everyone sits in his chair,
drinking, looking forward. It looks like an audience waiting for its hallucination to show up and
take the stage. There are two businessmen, hover-
ing like zeppelins around the mooring post of a
solitary blond woman. They are talking and telling
jokes, and she, to their delight, is laughing in all
the right places.

We also have a crazy on board, a genuine bozo
muttering a long and rambling account of his dis-
pute with the White House. It seemed to be a matter of money and a lack of respect.

"So I call the president. And he gets mad, if you
can believe that. Says it's a bad day, can I call him
later. Well, I've had enough."

I turn to the blonde in the seat across the aisle,
jerk a thumb at the mutterer.

"Uh...," she says, "some people *are* different." I
am about to nod agreement, but she continues. "I
mean, I'm pretty bizarre myself."

"You *are* bizarre," says one of the businessmen.
"But I mean that in a positive sense."

Well, I've had enough. I go back to the bar. Our
bartender tonight is named Nick, a twitchy sliver
of a man with a laugh like a hacksaw working on a
metal pole. There is a sign over the bar that says,
ASK TO HEAR OUR TRAIN WHISTLE. I ask.

"There's no whistle," says Nick. "I just reach under the bar and make like I'm pressing something. I
say, 'You hear that?' and they say, 'Yeah...yeah, I
do.'" Nick shakes his head. "The things I do to
amuse myself."

I ask Nick what sorts of things he has seen

working this bar.

"Life, death, you name it." Death? "New Year's Eve, three guys had a heart attack here in the bar. While we were stopped in Toledo."

An older couple with grave Slavic faces have come in to order vodka; death they understand. They pay attention. Particularly since Toledo happens to be our next stop.

"A guy had a heart attack as we were pullin' in. Nothing much you can do but keep them comfortable. I closed the bar, but you always got some morbidites walking over the body and saying, 'Ya gotta beer?'" He frowns. "We radioed ahead, and there was an ambulance waiting. Just as they're rolling him off, another guy kicks. Had to get the ambulance back for *him*. Half an hour later, we're pulling out of town, *another* one gets it. Had to stop again to pull him off."

A conductor comes through to catch the end of Nick's disquisition on the way of all flesh.

"New Year's Eve?" he says. Nick nods. The conductor looks around the bar as if to tell us not to even think about having a heart attack. Then he announces we are pulling into Toledo.

"Wha're we doin' in Taledo?" shouts one of the businessmen from the darkened bar. His voice sounds like red meat and Winstons.

"No one," says his buddy, "shoul'live 'n Toledo."

Nick shrugs.

GOOD NIGHT

I undress in my room. I realized that I cannot take the bed down without standing outside of the room. I put my clothes back on, as I do not want to be caught in the hall in my underwear, struggling with a wall. The bed comes down with a clunk; I climb up, slide the door closed, undress with something less than the grace of a snake shedding a skin, and stow my clothes in the closet. I put my shoes in the shoe locker—which, as my porter reminded me, was accessible from the hallway, so I'd best not put anything valuable there. I had wondered why my shoe locker was open to the world, when I realized that in the old days, the porters came by and *shined your shoes while you slept.* My porter hadn't mentioned that. Of course, I'm sure that in the heydays of trains, they didn't go around slinging Slim Jims with abandon, either.

I get into bed. It's not bad—imagine a very thick doctor's examining table hooked up to the World's Largest Magic Fingers machine, and you have a bed on a moving train. I like the idea of hurtling headfirst towards New York City at 95 mph, on my stomach, riding this arrow fired at the heart of Manhattan. If we have a crash, of course, my socks and my brains will be indistinguishable. I take off the covers and remove my socks. Just to prevent confusion.

But a crash is my last worry, or anyone else's, probably; a train at night on good tracks feels like a beast running for the sheer pleasure of running, sure-footed over favorite terrain.

And a train at night cradles you, rocks you back and forth. The familiar clack and slap of the wheels against the rail marks the miles and the minutes until neither matters, and you are ushered gently into smooth slumber.

The last thing you hear before you sleep is the whistle, the most haunting sound ever made by man. If that sound came from a wild animal, primitive man would have ascribed great wisdom and sadness to it, and they would have feared it. We know what a train whistle is when we hear it, but we don't know what it means. No one can hear it without feeling the sudden thrust of melancholy against the heart: *something is passing by, going to where I am not.*

It doesn't feel any different to be on the train, riding the whistle; then it speaks of the places you are passing and leaving, not the places you are heading toward. But the emotion on both sides fades with the whistle. The sound opens the air and lets the train behind it stitch it back together again. Behind you the fates swing up and traffic lumbers over the rails. By the time you wake up, the train will have made a neat and seamless suture of all the land you traveled while you slept, and if you dreamed of the whistle, it will be the part of the dream you can never quite fit into words.

TOPPLING INTO THE RIVER

Breakfast looks like something for which you would blame your dog. I am playing a game with the eggs: I swallow them, they want to come back up. It is a frisky and playful thing, this breakfast. It doesn't help matters that we appear to be approximately three inches from falling into a river. The train is barreling along at a disconcerting angle, taking turns I am certain are going to dunk us in the drink. I begin to feel the sensation I used to get on planes before I swore off flying—the feeling of one anxious rat gnawing on the rope that holds closed the cage containing hundreds of anxious rats. I tell myself that this is crazy.

I do not know, of course, that on the way home, on a different train that threads along a thin path along a mountain in West Virginia, that my steward will confess to a horror of the route. "Derailed the last time," he will say. "The train just hung there. I thought we were going to go down the hill and into the river." I don't know this yet, and I think I'm being silly for entertaining thoughts of the D-word. Derailing. It doesn't sound so bad, anyway; planes CRASH, a word that sounds like it probably feels. But *derailing* sounds almost civilized. *Pardon, sahr, but we will be derailing at eight, if you would care to join us.*

But we are running right along the banks of the Hudson, and I am a little unnerved. Prior to our certain and gurgling demise, however, we are at least treated to scenery. Old bridges, full of rough and ugly grace; houses built high on bluffs; a ruined castle on an island. This is old America, and the land no longer looks as though it has grudgingly agreed to be civilized. We are soon joined by other tracks, and suburban train stations appear. The posters advertise the New York that is just an hour away.

I go back to my cabin and watch the world slide by. Like most trains, the *Lake Shore Express* crawls in through the back door of the city, making a slow, clanking trip through the industrial section. We see old factories, abandoned warehouses, ramshackle homes with back yards full of all sorts of urban flotsam. There's much colorful graffiti, courtesy of the boroughs' roaming bands of aesthetically minded Visigoths. Then the city disappears. Completely disappears. And we are in hell.

Hell, in this case, is an eternal tunnel caked with soot, dimly lit, ancient. The presence of light bulbs tells you that this is a place in New York so bad that no one will come here to steal the light bulbs. Tracks are visible on either side of the train as far as the dim light permits me to see, and I hear a faint groaning of wheels and tired steel.

Up above, my porter tells me, is sunshine, and Manhattan.

The train slows, stops, and a voice cries, "Grand Central Station." I step off into a blast of cool air. My porter hands me my bags. "They used to roll out the red carpet for the *20th Century Limited,*" he notes. But it's bare concrete all the way to the stairs. I thank him, pick up my luggage, and struggle toward the exit, miles down the platform. Up the stairs. Up a ramp, past people with the grim New York look of great and indifferent importance, that lemming-with-an-MBA look. They bump into my baggage with extra zeal.

Upstairs is Grand Central Station, newly polished and painted. I put down my bags and look up at that magnificent ceiling. The ceiling, unlike the abstract heights airplanes reach, is high enough to dazzle and awe. But if you could jump as high as it makes you feel, you could touch it. I look like a tourist, standing there looking at the ceiling, my mouth probably open. But I don't live here. I can do that. That's the whole point of the trip—to ride a narrow box across the country and be spilled into a room whose height outreaches every dream of height you've had on the train. If people walking by want to snicker at the rube, well, I have earned this.

This trip had started in the Midwest, at a place where trains merely stopped; it ends where trains had begun, at a place where trains have always mattered. There was nothing of home left in me by now—the motion of the train had shook home out of me a long time before.

But it put something else in its place, something besides miles. When I lay down to sleep in my hotel room, I could still feel the rhythm of the train, as if I were still riding the rapids of that long metal river. The train ebbs from your blood, slowly, leaving just an aftertaste of the whistle and the iron. You savor that taste until you board a train again.

Observations and questions

1) In the opening sentence, "The following, I think, is typical," what does "the following" refer to? Don't decide too quickly.

2) Lileks presents himself in this piece as an irritated jerk and a somewhat mean-spirited smart ass. Think about the poses we adopt in columns, and the hazard that readers will miss their point. Does a columnist need a consistent persona over time?

3) This piece consists largely of a series of quips. Study how Lileks uses various structures, especially chronology and geography, to keep it flowing.

4) What color exactly is "a regrettable shade of beige," or "spoiled-cranberry-colored"? Reporters seldom use color at all, much less such an emotionally tinted color vocabulary. Why not?

5) More than halfway through, Lileks casually drops this bit: "...before I swore off flying." Would you be tempted to move that piece of information higher?

6) This column turns from nasty to nostalgic, and back to nasty and ends nostalgic. Think about the hazards of subjecting readers to such an emotional seesaw, even when the point is Lileks's ambivalence toward train travel.

War is heck

JUNE 24, 1988

CAMP RIPLEY, Minn.—I belong to the Reporters' Reserve. Once a year, we take time out from our normal jobs to go and do our civic duty: writing a feature story about the National Guard. There are the monthly weekend meetings, sure, where we have such classes as "How's the Chow: Questions Not to Ask" and "Getting Full Names From Guys Conditioned to Answer in Rank and Last Name." But it's the annual field maneuvers, held here at Camp Ripley, near Little Falls, that we really look forward to.

National Guard maneuvers are held throughout the summer and winter at Ripley; up to 6,000 men and women at a time are here to hone their skills. For two-week stints, they train for the usual disasters that plague the land: fire, flood, riots, chemical spills, citizens lost in the woods. But they're also staging maneuvers that simulate the rigors of combat in foreign lands.

Reveille sounds at 0500 hours, cruel as ever, the soldier's bane. I groan, roll over, pick up the phone, and thank the desk clerk. I orient myself and recall that I am bivouacked at a motel in Little Falls. Rising at 5, hungry and uncomfortable, makes me one with the men who will be out in the field. As I shower I get in the mood for the task by imagining what it would be like if I had skipped the shower, or had smaller towels.

Camp Ripley, the state's main military training center, is seven miles north of Little Falls, 10 miles south of Brainerd. The entrance to the camp is a huge, glowering pile of rock. You leave your first name and your individuality at the gate with the guard. He doesn't give you a receipt.

Beyond the fence are tin barracks and brick buildings, lined up for miles in rote formation, looking like a Spartan vacation spa. We are met by our guides for the day, all wearing fatigues and camouflage paint. They hand us our helmets, which are A) heavy, and B) ugly and heavy.

I travel with Capt. Lucy Kender and Capt. Steve Schmitt, who pilots the WWII-era jeep along the road at a neck-snapping 15 miles per hour, so as not to raise dust. (The roads are kept unpaved to simulate enemy terrain; apparently we are soon to be at war in Guadalajara.)

As we poke up the road, Capt. Kender describes the morning's mission. We are to proceed to a field—I forget the technical term, probably AREA, GRASSY, OPEN—to observe Company B, 2nd Battalion, 135th Infantry from Pipestone-Marshall practice landing and evacuating in helicopters.

"They've already had a busy day," she said. Remember: it is 6 in the morning. "They got up at 4 to put on their MOPP suits." The suits are lined with charcoal to keep out chemical poisons. Add the rubber-lined shoes and gloves and your NBC mask (the merry trio of Nuclear, Biological, and Chemical), and you're dressed for the end of the world, if not a sweaty morning.

Talk soon turns to the personal stuff you share in the uneasy peace before battle. I ask my companions what they do back in the world.

"I'm a homemaker," says Kender. "Make that Engineer, Domestic." She lives in Shoreview, has a 9-year-old daughter, and also volunteers as a tour guide at Walker Art Center. Here, she captains the Guard's public relations efforts. Schmitt manages an insurance agency in New Ulm; here, he handles what he cheerfully calls "paperwork."

We arrive at the Area, Grassy, Open. Schmitt steers the jeep off the road and into the trees. He points out that we had driven over an area designated as a minefield a while back, and that "technically, we're dead." Having had but one cup of coffee that morning, I agree.

There are already members of the 135th here, standing in the trees, waiting for the choppers. They are to practice evacuation and invasion in hostile territory. Say that the hills are alive with en-

emy troops, the choppers the only way out. They
must learn how to get to the choppers fast, or dis-
embark with equal speed, avoiding in either case
the whistling blades above their heads. There have
been no casualties in this sort of exercise in the history of the Minnesota Guard, but since it is not exactly a spin in the pickup into town, the mood of
the troops has a certain charge.

My Op Man (Operations Manual) for Writers,
Features, Ironic, says I should ask these guys how
they feel about going up in the helicopters, but one
look tells me how they feel, and I leave them
alone.

It is a gorgeous morning for war. Fog hangs on
the land, and the morning sky is cloudless. No
sound. Then—

chudchudchudchudchud. You hear them before
you see them. One, then two, then two more, floating over the trees, airborne tadpoles with a mad
whirring blur over their cockpits. They hover over
the field, the grass beneath them trying to flee but
held in place by the roots.

A shout, and the woods come alive—men
stream from the trees, crouching, and pile into the
choppers' open doors. Another shout, and the
Hueys lift off one by one, form a file in the sky,
and disappear over the trees again.

This is an exercise, and it has to be repeated.
When the helicopters return, the troops who got on
jump out and hug the earth, their packs making
them look like some race of large turtles. A new
batch rushes from the trees and the copters roar off
again. You can feel the rhythm of the rotors in your
gut long after the sound has died away.

I could give you a technical description of the
operation, delivered to me by a man auditioning
for the role of Sergeant, Grizzled, Stogie-Chomp-
ing, but I couldn't understand a word he said. He
had a mouthful of sunflower seeds, and he spoke in
a level of jargonese that would baffle a four-star
general. Better to talk to the men.

Not that they were lounging around, trading jokes
—there was still work ahead. After their helicopter

trip, they were back in the woods, assuming the posture appropriate for invading hostile territory—gut-first in soggy gullies, crouched behind trees. The next step was to secure a portion of the road wide enough for the unit to cross. On the other side of the road lay territory tainted with chemicals, and if the troops couldn't find a safe route through, they'd have to don the NBC masks.

After that, the best part—combat. But we'll get to that.

These guys are infantry. The infantry's lot is dirty, hot, and hard, and the men who sign up for this sort of duty are not lawyers and surgeons in real life. Spec. 4 Todd Taylor, stockboy at a supermarket in Marshall. Spec. 4 Andy Przybilla, grain elevator worker. One guy works as a barn straightener, righting old farm buildings. Another is a night manager at a convenience store. Meat cutter, loading dock worker. None of them seems to think he's deserving of any particular glory for doing what he's doing here today.

"The worst part of this," says Spec. 4 Andy Brevik, "is that you're required to go at any time." So what's the best part? "The esprit de corps."

A medic, busy splinting a private who sprained his leg jumping from the copter, says he joined "to use my brain, to learn something I could use. Like, if a kid gets hurt on a playground, I can do something to help."

You get the sense that civic duty, ingrained so deep it is a given, has something to do with why these guys are here. Bring it up and you'd soil it somehow by asking them to comment on it.

But ask if they'd enlist if there was a war on, and you get different answers.

"Probably *not*," says Pvt. Kevin Guttormsson.

"I'd have to think about that," says another. He leaps up before I get his name—he has his orders to move, and he is gone without another thought.

Guardsmen are often thought of as imitations of the real thing, weekend warriors. That idea doesn't hold with 1st Lt. Louis Utleras, a regular Army adviser sent along to evaluate the troops and offer

advice. Lt. Utleras is unsmiling, cordial, and probably knows 30 ways to kill me. An unnerving man.
He is preparing to lead the men across the road.

"This unit is very good," he says. "It started really weak. After more training, it got better, more
precise, and now, these guys are OK."

Battle ready? Would he go into combat with
these men?

"With this unit, I would go. No problem."

Capt. Kender is standing by the road. She
watches the first pair of soldiers cross the road into
the woods. It is hostile territory.

"They're dead," says Kender. No comment on
the men's ability. But this is war, and hers is a reasonable assumption.

Up the road, they are sitting around the camp,
waiting to be killed, again. This is the endpoint of
the morning's exercise. The troops who have
jumped off the copters, made it over the road and
through the poisonous woods, now have to take
this camp. It will be a "hasty attack," which is mili-
tary-speak for "We didn't know it was there, but
we stumbled across it and succeeded in shooting it
to pieces."

The objective is hardly Hitler's bunker. There's
a communications tent and an officer's tent, both
smelling heavily of old wet canvas. A single foxhole guards the area. Thin black communications
wires slither through the forest. It doesn't look like
much, but it can yield many secrets. After the
troops have killed or captured the opposing forces,
they note which radio frequencies the enemy em-
ploys and gauge their strength from their munitions
and transport. Then, with the aid of plastic explo-
sives, they blow the entire mess into Manitoba.

Well, not really. There's no sense in blowing up
perfectly good U.S. Army trucks, nor will anyone
actually be killing anyone in the assault. The guns
carry blanks, with flash suppressors at the end of
the muzzles so no errant sparks ignite the forest or
blast powder at a fellow soldier.

We wait for the first wave. A couple of soldiers
man the LPOPs, a euphonious acronym for the

Listening Post/Observation Posts at the perimeter of the base. It's their duty to A) watch for the enemy, and B) die after a valiant fight. Bad duty. The guys back at the base, ready for battle, are relaxed; until they hear the gunfire at the LPOPs, there's little to do. Talk turns to ammo, munitions, and the soldiers' perennial obsession: chow.

We're all hungry, and the invading force is late. *Let's get this war going.* A few soldiers touch up their war paint. A hearty officer walks around distributing ammo like a new father giving out cigars. We wait. Noon crawls around, settles in the air. You can hear bird song in the distance, and the woods start to look less like a place of lurking menace than a friendly tangle of trees and weeds, a place where you could walk and think, perhaps take the kids. Camp out. Fish. Sleep under the...

Gunfire. M-16s, popping like firecrackers, with throaty interjections from the M-60s. Everyone at the camp tenses, melts into the bush; a few run for the tents, one dives for the foxhole, and the rest dash off to the path. In seconds, the woods are full of confusion—rattling weapons sound from all directions, smoke wafts from unseen rifles, green-and-brown figures flow between the trees, evaporate, release a burst of fire. If you've never seen combat or know only the choreographed version of television, it is, for a moment, startling and frighteningly convincing.

Almost.

"Bang!" someone shouts. "I'm out of ammo. But you're dead."

"Missed me," his target answers.

It is over in minutes. Now it is time for the sweetest tandem life in the field offers short of sleep and a dry bed: food and mail.

Chocolate milk on raisin bran, reconstituted eggs, bacon, and white bread. Everyone lines up, takes his portion, finds a tree to sit under, and begins to eat. The lucky ones have letters waiting; they spill from a bag on the ground, the envelopes written in feminine hands.

The eggs and bacon are especially welcome; the

standard field ration is something with the appetizing name of MRE. It comes in bulky plastic packs, and there is general assent that you should avoid the Pork-and-Beans MRE. Stamped on the side of this meal, they say, are the words NOT FOR FLIGHT OR PREFLIGHT.

"The beans make you nauseous," says the medic. "It's that bean component."

I think he's speaking in jargon, of course. Bean Component. Really, guys. Someone hands me the Pork-and-Beans MRE. Stamped on the front: CONTAINS BEAN COMPONENT.

The soldiers finish their food and stretch out for a few minutes. No one is barking at them. No one is asking them to do this or climb over that or jump in this. It's cool in the shade, and their stomachs are full. It's too good to last, and it can't: it's only noon. The day is just beginning.

Back at the hotel, I strip and clean my pen. Then I check my operations manual for instructions on how to end this piece. It's under Conclusions, Subjective. It instructs me to note that the notion of a local militia is almost a quaint and antiquated holdover of the Revolutionary War mentality. But the idea of training the citizens of a community for such duties, of keeping the National Guard a matter of local pride and initiative, is a refreshing change from the coast-to-coast homogeneity of most things American.

I am also required to note that the participants are serious about their duty, not paid great sums of money, and put through substantial inconvenience. There is a box at the bottom of the page, and it says, WARNING: AVOID EXCESSIVE SENTIMENT AND/OR CYNICISM IN CONCLUSION.

I will. It's enough to note that there's a guy on a loading dock, a Guardsman back in civilian clothes, and he's throwing boxes into a truck. Every so often he probably thinks about the day he learned how to escape hostile territory in a helicopter. That, he might think, makes him different. And he'd be right.

Observations and questions

1) Lileks told me: "As a newcomer, I had been saddled with every perennial assignment there is, one of which was National Guard training maneuvers." Beginning reporters can impress their editors by doing such perennial stories brilliantly, as Lileks does here. Of course, you might then get all of them!

2) The first two sentences led me to think that Lileks actually belonged to the National Guard, so I asked him if he did. He replied, "I invented that, probably because I had to get up real early in the morning to do this piece, and I was angry about that." How could he revise those two sentences to avoid confusing the reader? Should he? When is confusion appropriate?

3) Lileks plays with military jargon, especially inverted descriptions, for example, "AREA, GRASSY, OPEN." Normally reporters translate jargon for the general reader. Study how Lileks translates the jargon as he makes fun of it.

4) We hear the helicopter: "*chudchudchudchudchud.*" Columnists get to use such comic onomatopoeia, or imitated sound. How could beat reporters use this technique?

5) Turning a comic piece suddenly serious and even appreciative takes skill. Watch this: "You get the sense that civic duty, ingrained so deep it is a given, has something to do with why these guys are here." But notice how Lileks undoes each serious moment as fast as the reader gets absorbed in it.

6) Study Lileks's ending, which begins, "Back at the hotel..." He mocks the traditional endings of such stories at the same time he writes one. What all is getting parodied here?

Finally, there's a cure
for cultural illiteracy

OCTOBER 9, 1988

According to all the recent surveys of high school intellectual aptitude, every American under the age of 18 is, and I quote, "dumb as pound cake." Perhaps that overstates the case a bit, but you've read the news stories—high-schoolers who couldn't place World War I in the proper millennium without hints; kids who, when asked to find Vietnam on a map, circle Manitoba.

The reports indicate that this will have far-reaching consequences for Western civilization, and they're right; those who don't know the horrors and mistakes of the past are doomed to repeat them. Consider that ABC recently completed casting for *The New Charlie's Angels*, and you'll see what we mean. Senselessness like this *can* be avoided, but it will take a return to basics.

Before we beat the whelps over their empty little heads with a few volumes of Plato, though, we should examine ourselves. Most of us are no longer threatened by compulsory education, and all of those calling for a War on Idiocy are well past the draft age. Before we get too smug, we should ascertain if we are as smart as we'd like to be.

Anyone curious to know just what they have forgotten, what they never knew in the first place, and what the next generation should know must immediately read *Test Your Cultural Literacy* (ARCO, $7.95) by Diane and Kathy Zahler. The Zahlers have put together a compendium of things every well-educated person should know. Painting, literature, geography, history, philosophy—it's all here, all the remedial knowledge necessary for membership in Western civilization.

Best of all, it's a multiple-choice quiz.

Here's an example, taken from the Art and Architecture portion.

Question 37: What is this statue? A) *The Sleep-*

ing Muse; B) *Adam;* C) *The Recumbent Figure;* D) *The Thinker.*

(Hint for our readers: there is a picture of a man thinking.)

If you answered D, you're right!

Few questions in this book are this easy; most require specific knowledge or enough general savvy to make an educated guess. *Which of the following nations is not an island chain? What are the typical architectural elements of a Gothic cathedral? Who was Enrico Caruso? Where did I leave my keys?* (Just kidding about that last one.)

Fascinating stuff, and somewhat daunting, no matter how literate you consider yourself. But what about the culturally illiterate? What happens if our schools do not improve? If the future leaders of tomorrow have the intellectual candlepower of a wet shingle, how will cultural literacy be gauged? This test, after all, is unfairly biased against the stupid. There's no way we can expect the Brave New Cretins of Tomorrow to know this stuff.

In the interests of a more egalitarian approach to cultural literacy, I have devised the test below, which simultaneously expands and contracts the definition of culture. By which I mean, of course, less history and more TV. The various subjects are all mixed together, to simulate flipping around the channels with a remote.

1. Which of the following is a continent? Think carefully.

A) Al Jolson

B) North America, Which Is Certainly A Continent, Oh Yes

C) A sack containing sticks and old phone books

2. Literature: What is the correct name of Harvey Mackay's book?

A) *Swim With the Sharks Without Getting Eaten Alive*

B) *Swim After Eating Without Getting Cramps*

C) *Tag Along With the Sharks Until They Give You a Blurb*

3. Which was the cutest of the sisters on *The Brady Bunch*? Pick the season of your choice.
A) Jan
B) Cindy
C) Marcia

4. Which of the following was never referred to as "the fifth Beatle"?
A) Billy Preston
B) George Martin
C) Cardinal Richelieu de Plessis

5. Which of the following is a painting in the Modern style?
A) *Big Pointless Blobs of Paint*, Robert Motherwell
B) *Looks Like Someone Had An Accident*, Jackson Pollock
C) *My Kid Could Do That*, Wassily Kandinsky

6. When Louis XVI said, "L'etat, c'est moi," he was:
A) Speaking in, like, French
B) Played by Laurence Olivier in a BBC series
C) Absolutely serious

7. In the classic Doors song "Riders on the Storm," what does the singer *not* feel like?
A) Like an actor out on loan
B) Like a dog without a bone
C) Like facing up to the self-destructive behavior which would, ultimately, lead to his early death

8. Which of the following is not a Martin Scorsese film?
A) *The Last Temptation of Roger Rabbit*
B) *Who Framed Pontius Pilate?*
C) *Raging Bull Durham*

9. Donald Trump is noted for:
A) Introducing the fresco painting technique to Northern Europe in the 14th century
B) Buying all the fresco paintings of Northern Europe in the 20th century

C) Actually looking good, if the alternative is Leona Helmsley

10. Liposuction is:
A) Teen-age slang for kissing
B) The only possible explanation for Cher
C) Latin for "too rich to diet"

11. The greenhouse effect is caused by:
A) Too many heat-trapping substances floating in the atmosphere
B) Too many tenure-seeking scientists floating in the universities
C) Natural disasters, such as volcanic eruptions, melting polar caps, and the reappearance of Richard Nixon on the political scene

12. Radon is:
A) Just what we here in the media needed to sell some papers
B) The creature soundly defeated by Godzilla
C) A colorless, odorless substance you cannot see or taste

13. A presidential candidate is:
A) A colorless, odorless substance you cannot see or taste
B) A creature who, when confronted by Godzilla, would consult with his Large Mutated Lizard PAC before advocating action
C) Somehow, by sheer coincidence, always a white male

14. A quark is:
A) A theoretical particle whose existence can only be hypothesized, not proved (see "Cathy Lee Crosby, Talent of")
B) The Appalachian pronunciation for an idiosyncrasy, as in "making hogs squeal out lawd fer fun is just one'a his personal quarks"
C) Part of this important breakfast

15. Dick Clark looks perpetually young because:
A) He sold his soul to the devil

B) The devil does all his makeup and handles the lighting

C) He is the devil

16. The Van Allen belts are:

A) Bands of radiation surrounding the planet

B) Rapidly being replaced by the more stylish Van Allen suspenders

C) What any sensible hard-working Van Allen has at the bar after a hard day

17. Which of the following is not a catch phrase taken from television?

A) "Nanu-nanu"

B) "Dy-no-mite!"

C) "Unstrap that careless butter salesman, Agnes."

18. How many amendments are there to the Constitution?

A) How many do you want?

B) Fourscore and seven

C) $33\frac{1}{3}$

19. In the event the president is incapacitated, who becomes president?

A) Ed McMahon

B) Doc Severinsen

C) Tommy Newsom

20. What is the point of cultural literacy?

A) Not being shown up by geeks at parties who actually studied in school

B) Smug pride in your collection of arcane facts

C) Having a basis of shared knowledge and ideas that facilitate advancement of intellectual discussion

ANSWERS: There are a few correct answers scattered around, but most questions and their answers are bogus. If you went all the way through the test, diligently marking what you hoped was the correct answer—even though you had no idea—you are culturally illiterate.

Pick up your high school diploma at the door.

Observations and questions

1) List all the targets in this satire. Your list might be longer than the column. And you thought columns had to concentrate on just one thing.

2) In the third paragraph, Lileks says: "Before we get too smug, we should ascertain if we are as smart as we'd like to be." Satirists often make points by insulting their readers, as in this piece. Does satire have a place in newswriting, which regards the reader as god? Is satire hazardous to our circulation?

3) *Test Your Cultural Literacy* is a real book, unlike most of the stuff in this column. Is it fair to slam the book indirectly by associating it with all this wild parody?

4) This piece actually depends on quite a bit of "cultural literacy" to understand the jokes, as, for example, in question five. Is this column a condescending shot at the less educated, or an attack on the reader who might read such a piece? Or both?

5) Question 20 has three different points of view, each marked by a different level of vocabulary. Why is this question last?

6) This piece insults any reader who reads it to the bottom, making it the ultimate "inverted pyramid." Print journalism may have just peaked.

Hallowed nights

OCTOBER 29, 1988

Pay attention to people's Halloween costumes; they're telling you something. The couple that shows up dressed as a pair of parentheses, for example, wants the whole world to know that they have a relationship so insular and exclusive that they view the entire world as being teamed against them and perhaps have resorted to Amway to strike back. Then again, when they are standing in a way that forms a) (, perhaps they are advertising for new partners.

All I know is that if someone dresses up as Gilligan, you should take his word for it. And if someone comes dressed as a product of Appalachian inbreeding, replete with corncob pipe and Li'l Abner clothing, you should keep him away from the couple dressed as Salt & Pepper, lest he start an argument about miscegenation and God's intentions. And when someone shows up as Death—and someone always does—you should be wary.

I knew Death at the last costume party I attended. He had a room upstairs. He made for a hearty Death, as though he regretted making Last Call but knew a great after-hours joint. Still, there is something unnerving about knowing that the gentleman dressed as the Grim Reaper works, in real life, as a repossession man. You wonder if he's been promoted and these are his new work clothes.

He laid a hand on the shoulder of everyone he passed. "You are next," he said. He'd turn to someone else and say, "Your time is soon." Everyone laughed. He was, after all, not entirely Grim. More like the Three-Sheets-to-the-Wind Reaper.

He took up residence around a keg of beer and granted a few more years of life to all who approached the keg with an empty glass. Later, he took to the dance floor and did the usual spasmodic twitch to "Burning Down the House" by the Talking

Heads. People worried about whether Death was fit to drive but were reassured that Death lived here. When I left the party, Death was sprawled in the corner, talking to one of the parentheses. They seemed to be hitting it off.

I had spent the night dressed as a 1920s society figure—tux and top hat, walking stick and white gloves. A tape player and a set of small tinny speakers in my jacket played old jazz, but the din of the party was too loud for the music to be heard.

When I left the party and stepped outside, I heard the music for the first time in hours, a thin thread of gaiety unraveling inside my costume. I looked up at what was left of the Halloween night—a calm, half-finished moon in the sky, a few rough drafts of clouds, the trees still and untroubled by wind or gusting spirits. Nothing on the street but empty shadows, indifferent darkness. It was an adult's Halloween. Oct. 31. Rent was due tomorrow.

I don't believe that everything was better when you were a child. Holidays are usually stacked in favor of adults. Most holidays mean tight clothing and the small table with the rest of the kids. No matter how much you enjoyed it, adults always had a corner on the Real Meaning, and they kept to themselves; the Adults in the Living Room, with their smoke and amber potions, owned the holidays. They doled them out to you in generous, indulgent doses, but it was their name on the mortgage. You sensed that.

But Halloween was yours. By definition. There was no church attached, which was your first clue; the purpose was candy, which clinched the deal.

You knew it wasn't a holiday on the order of the big ones, for school did not cease to let you enjoy it. But school recognized its importance and made room. When art period came, it was not block prints with carved potatoes or crayon drawings, but Ghosts. Orange and black appeared in the schoolroom, colors the world was assuming on its own, now given a delicious shiver of mystery. You carved pumpkins, let the seeds dry, ate them, their

salty taste almost the taste of the leaves you kicked
on your way to school each morning.

Somehow you sensed a natural progression to
life—the anticipation of Halloween, the sober duty
of Thanksgiving, the deep delights of Christmas.
That was how it was last year; that was how it was
always going to be.

A decision was due: your costume. A hobo? Too
obvious. Someone else was always a hobo. Dracu-
la? Good, good, but like Frankenstein's monster
and the Wolfman, they were year-round figures, always there. You went down to the store—the Ben
Franklin, if you had one—to see what had come in.

There was always a seasonal row at Ben Franklin, a hall of worthy merchandise. In a few months,
it would be full of silver baubles and tinsel and, after Halloween, there'd be nothing but stupid
turkeys in buckled hats. But for now, it was just
right. Forbidden things: fake scars, fake blood,
fake faces of disfigurement and horror. All those
things that happened for real out there, somewhere
beyond the Living Room of the Adults, were here
for you to wear and use to reap your treats.

The great debate of childhood: homemade or
from a box? A costume from a box was the height
of cool. There was no feeling like toting that box
home and looking at it each day, waiting, waiting.
You were going to be the most meanest superhero
or the most beautiful princess. But, after school
one day, you tried on the mask that came with the
box—just for a few minutes, so as not to spoil
it—and, well, to be frank, it lacked. Your breath
was hard to draw; the air you took in had a plastic
tint, and the edge of the mask was sharp and un-
friendly.

The demands of the profession, you figure.

The days pass with the infuriating deliberateness
of all things designed by adults. When Halloween
comes, there is no rain to keep you inside—it never rains on Halloween.

One year I remember. I was Spider-Man—store-
bought mask, homemade costume made from old
blue pajamas. Cousin Keith was a hobo, homemade

all the way. In the photos in the scrapbook we are hoisting the pumpkins in the air, grinning, the neighborhood still unplundered. With the floating circle of the flash bulb still drifting in our eyes, we set out to Trick or Treat. He has a cool plastic pumpkin; I have a bag with a cackling witch on the side.

There is, if I remember the night, a pumpkin in almost every window. Paper ghosts and cats, backs arched in warning, hang in the windows. Scary old neighbors who never wave when you pass them by don't put out pumpkins and we pass them by. But the rest of the street is ours. Dark by choice. Every house with a jack-o'-lantern is another promise kept. All that remains is to pretend to scare them.

We arrive at the doorstep with other kids from the block, judge their costumes, cast quick looks at the depth of the booty in their bags. We ring the bell. When the door opens, we say the word—TRICKATREAT!—and the adult is properly horrified. We know we don't scare them. But there is that moment when they open the door, when our voices combine, when we all know we have a moment of anonymity and power, and that makes us believe in the fierce determination of our little masks. We are rewarded, and we scamper away. We say thank-you first.

None of us believes in the faces, the witches, the ghosts; that's for babies. But we all agree there is *something* out there. Something between Dad in the car down the block and the cold sliver of the moon. There is something scary in the leaves in the gutter, the sharp command of the wind, but no one knows quite what. There is the sense that if you take Halloween on the terms you've made for it, it's just kids' stuff, and if you imagine there's something else, you don't get it. Yet.

Adults have Halloween rituals of their own. They show us what they want to be, what they can't be, what they fear, or an exaggeration of how they think the world sees them. It is dress-up, and it is harmless. Some religions celebrate Halloween; others condemn it as devil's work. Most of us note its arrival and departure through the displays in greeting-card store windows.

It's one of those times that does not profit from being measured against childhood. It is something so germane to being young that no one ever measures an adult Halloween against those of years long ago. We even manage to believe it is more fun to go to a party than scurry through the dark to strange houses; we probably tell ourselves that all that candy is bad for you anyway.

But it's not all a cozy, happy memory. There is always one Halloween in your life when you realize that the house at the end of the block is dark, and you are not certain whether those headlights at the other end of the street are Dad's. For one moment, the mask matters little, and the bag of treats is heavy. At that moment, something is planted inside you, a seed that will blossom years later and make you laugh at the repossession man when he enters the party, laugh and give him a drink and try to get on his good side. That seed tastes pulpy and salty, strange, like the taste of fallen leaves you kicked through with great determination.

Observations and questions

1) Again, Lileks does a "writing job" on a perennial assignment. List all the traditional ways of doing Halloween stories, and then study how Lileks has transcended them. What do you suppose he might do with the new telephone book, or with daylight-saving time?

2) This piece would benefit from subheads. What would they say, and where would you put them? You may have some problems with tone in writing them.

3) The lead on this column may take several readings. In a craft based obsessively on clarity, when can we explain complex things complexly?

4) Notice the use of second person, a rarity in newswriting. Study how Lileks moves across the three persons (I, you, he, etc.), spelling out the effects he achieves. The second person runs the hazard of striking the reader as tedious. Do you think Lileks overuses it?

5) Notice how easily Lileks moves between past- and present-tense storytelling, and how the present tense promotes a sense of presence and intimacy. But like the second person, too much present tense can annoy the reader. How does Lileks avoid this trap?

6) At the end, Lileks inverts all the earlier fun and spookiness in a frighteningly suggestive turn. What's the subject of the last paragraph? Does he prepare the reader for this turn?

A conversation with
James Lileks

DON FRY: How did you land a job at St. Paul?

JAMES LILEKS: I had been talking with the other newspaper in town for some time, and they had *not* said, "Come in, we love you." But after one interview, Deborah Howell hired me.

She told me that she interviewed you for four minutes and said to herself, "I've got to hire this guy, no matter what!" That must have been one hell of an interview. [Laughter]

I would like to know what I said in those four minutes. I don't know if I matched her cuss word for cuss word or what [Laughter], but something must have clicked. She hired me as a general assignment features reporter, sort of lifestyle infantry.

Your feature articles read like columns.

They're not columns, but some of them really want to be. There isn't a great deal of space in daily newspapers nowadays for long essays, but some of my pieces are just that.

You seem to have learned newspaper writing by just doing it.

Yes, pretty much. I have never done the classic news story. I've had to do a couple of items for the paper when some local people were up for national awards, and some architectural reporting, but I never took any classes to do it.

EDITOR'S *NOTE: I have edited these telephone interviews very heavily for clarity and brevity; in some cases, I have rearranged passages and recomposed questions.*

Have editors helped you?

Yes, I've had editors who found ways to shoehorn me into the appropriate style in an objective mode. But it really isn't that difficult, and what I like about features is that it isn't necessary to adhere to the traditional scripture of journalism.

Do you negotiate space ahead of time, or do you just write and let the desk adjust?

No, I usually write in excess by a factor of five. Half the time, I try to write the pieces in sort of modular construction so you can take any part out. Someday I would love to publish just the scraps that have fallen on the floor.

You're a novelist, and that's your material. Save that stuff.

Believe me, I'm saving it for my bitter invective against the newspaper industry. [Laughter]

Let's walk through your writing process. First, do you mostly take assignments, or do you come up with your own ideas?

Half and half. The assignments they give me are ones they know I can have fun with, and the other half are things I want to do.

How do you find your story ideas?

Just stuff I bump into, or sometimes things that just interest me, I try to figure out why and explain it to a larger audience.

Sounds egotistical to me.

Well, I suppose it is, but it's just saying, "Here's something I liked, and I liked it so much I want to tell you about it." For example, I love train travel so much that I wanted to write a piece on it.

Do you do a lot of interviewing?

Depending on the story, sometimes a piece will need ten times more interviewing than I thought it would. For the Halloween piece, I didn't have to interview anybody; I just cranked it out. The train piece was pretty much showing up and letting it happen. The New York piece was going out and trying to find as many people as possible to interview.

Do you tape these long quotations?

No, I use a completely illegible scrawl that, unless I transcribe it within about a day or so, becomes nothing but dissected insect entrails. [Laughter]

How do you know when you've reported enough?

I never think I've reported enough. I'm always convinced I've missed something, and it's generally true. You just have to cut yourself off and say, "No more." The outline is usually in my head, but I don't write it down. Without even consulting my notes, I just start to write.

How early in the process do you have a tentative outline?

Probably after I have written about two paragraphs and figure I'm going nowhere. [Laughter] After I've rewritten it 30 times over, I construct an outline just to make me feel better. I don't know if I adhere to it that much because I'm just putting down what I intend to do anyway.

So you just start typing?

Yes, I turn the machine on and walk away, and three hours later there's a piece. [Laughter]

"Just writes itself," as they say. Do you write from the top, or do you write bits and pieces?

For instance, I write the lead last.

Really? If I can't get in the door, I can't write the piece, and a lead is always the way in. Sometimes it's oiled hinges, and sometimes you have to take a battering ram to get into the piece.

How do you come up with leads? Or do they just write themselves, too?

Kind of. I just sit there and toy with it until I get something arresting.

Toy with words or ideas?

Words first and foremost. You've got to get the reader in the first line, because if you can't come up with a good first line, there's no incentive for somebody to read the rest. That's your foot in the door. It usually has to be somewhat startling.

What's next? Do you just keep writing until you come up with an outline?

A couple of graphs, then a cup of coffee, then eventually the outline will present itself, and I'll try to keep to that.

Are you aware of the blocks of the outline, or do you just knock it out sentence by sentence?

I sort of write until I get the feeling that the idea is exhausted, and I go back and try to clean it up. I have a great tendency to say the same thing several times in different ways.

Do you revise as you go along, or do you revise at the end?

Not very much. A lot of it gets revised before it comes out my fingers.

Talk about that.

I'm not sure how it works. When I'm writing a piece and it's going well and I'm enjoying it, every image that you have in front of you is essentially more or less the way it came out. If it stayed on the screen for more than five minutes, then it probably is going to make it into the paper. Stuff that I don't like is just gone.

I also revise before the words fall out of my fingers. I speak a sentence to the screen, and if I like it, I type it. If I don't like it, I speak it again and again until it comes out right. Do you have the ending in mind when you start?

Half the time. It usually presents itself before I get there. The ending is really a problem, because I'm not exactly sure of the essence of the story. Or I don't know how to say it. Late at night, I desire an ending a great deal.

What are endings for?

They leave an impression. If the opening line is your little trick to get readers in, an ending should be a payoff in a way that lets them take something away that's greater than the sum of any words you have written. I try to make the last line more evocative so you hear overtones of the rest of the story, so it has more resonance.

Do you work on your endings a lot once they're typed?

They probably have to get toyed with the most. Some of them just sit there like a large incontinent opera singer you can't do anything with. It's getting them to slim down and behave. [Laughter]

After you type the last word, do you let it sit for a while?

I read the whole thing through once and do a spellcheck, and if everything goes nicely, I ship it off to the office.

Oh, you write at home?

Yes, that's another thing I love about this job, the
fact that they do not insist that I show up at 9:00 in
the morning with a tie on, which I do sometimes
just to confound them.

**How can you tell if humor works? Do you try it
on other people?**

If it doesn't make me laugh, it doesn't go in. After
doing it for a number of years, you figure out that
your instincts are as good as anyone else's. I try
things out on my fiancee, and I can tell the difference between a geniune laugh and the appreciative
"I'm-your-spouse-until-death" laugh. [Laughter]

So she has a good sense of humor.

Yes, *she* does, but a few editors are an awful lot
like comics watching other comics competitively.
Instead of laughing, they say, "That's good."
[Laughter]

**Was the Garrison Keillor piece your idea or the
desk's?**

It was my editor's idea. He knew that I was looking
for any pretext to go to New York City. He decided
that we should see exactly what Garrison Keillor
was doing. It was shortly after he had moved, and
there was still a bit of public resentment toward this
guy for having changed addresses.

Is there a lot of resentment in Minneapolis?

No more so than in St. Paul. It's a hard story to do
because there are so many different little issues.
This man does not have to apologize to anybody,
or to explain to anybody where he goes, but there
was the feeling that he was one of our own, and
that he had to go away because he thought we were
too small.

There was a lot of bad blood between Keillor and our newspaper. Part of it had to do with an old friend of his who is one of our columnists who reported on how Keillor's personal life was affecting the show. That incensed Keillor to such a degree that it turned all of the friendship right on its head. There was a long and bitter feud as to how much people are permitted to see into his private life. Then we made the mistake of publishing his home address so people could look at his house.

Ouch!

At this time, Keillor was feeling he could not do anything without getting stares from somebody. He was an uncomfortable figure here, and he left for New York. Some of this continued to fuel a number of letters to the editor, and pieces from Keillor. So, showing up in New York and saying I was doing a piece on Keillor if I ran into the man would make me the devil incarnate at that time.

Did you know him?

No, I met him once at the *Minnesota Daily* years before. I had asked him if his success had opened the door for other Minnesota authors, and he said, "Well, I think the thing to do is get an agent, go to New York, and write a novel." I never listened to the radio show, and I had no opinion about him one way or the other.

Here's your lead: "This is the news from New York City, the little town where time is money, that the decades cannot impress, where all the women are busy, the men are busier, and a lot of the children are being tried as adults.

"It's a messy, noisy town of style and exuberance—Calcutta designed by Bill Blass. It's also the home of Minnesota's modern myth maker, Garrison Keillor. One might wonder what Keillor—slow-talking storyteller and professional Shy Person—is doing in a city founded on speed,

sound, and fury. After all, this is as far from Lake Wobegon as you can get.

"Which might be the point."

You say you don't listen to the radio program, but that first paragraph parodies it.

I know his style. I sat down and listened to a couple of things. I knew he started out with these monologues, and the first line parodies that. I was trying to cram as much as I could into that lead. I had to start the beast with something familiar to the Garrison Keillor fans. By appropriating his tag phrases, it parodied him without being hostile toward him.

What are you trying to do in this lead?

I am going to tell you a story about Garrison Keillor, but I am going to tell you my way. My style with my jokes. Not trying to slay the king. My perspective is different from his. By showing you how I am rewording his perspective, you get an idea of where I'm coming from. Does that make sense?

Indeed. One of the things I like about your pieces, particularly about this lead, is the distinctive voice. Do you work at that?

The person who probably got me doing this was Fran Lebowitz. I read a couple of her books and said, "I could do this. I, too, can be archcynical." And I was, until I got tired of being archcynical. Then I read a lot of S.J. Perelman, who could use words nobody knows. Somewhere in that, my original style came out, and I got feedback from people that they liked the arresting nature of it. But I wasn't self-consciously trying to develop a style; it just happened. And when I write in that voice, the pieces work the best.

Can you describe that voice?

It's hard.... I have heard it described more accurately than I have been able to do it. I think it's...hmm.

How would you want it described?

As one of most brilliant literary voices to burst upon the scene! [Laughter] I think it has a cynical edge without that moral aridity, that dryness you find in cynicism. There is a slightly self-deprecating tone to it, too, as if the author is willing to turn the same voice on himself as on other people. A voice that is willing to step away from the mainstream discussion to make an offhand observation.... Well, it's a hard thing to describe. It's like describing your back. I know it's there, and if I look in the right variety of mirrors, I can probably see it, but it is hard for me to tell you the topography of it.

You use the first person in this piece. Talk about writing in the first person in a newspaper.

I love it. In news reporting, I am not concerned what reporters have to say about the city council meeting or anything else. I just want to see what they see or say has happened. I don't really see why it should be taboo in a features section to use the first person, and as a columnist, I got used to using it.

So you're not self-conscious about it at all.

Oh, no. When the reporter refers to himself in the third person, he becomes sort of a disembodied entity. How many *New York Times* stories have I read where someone says, for example, "A reporter was struck on the head by an iron bar." You are describing an assault on a *Times* reporter, and the person writing is that person. Say: "I was hit on the head by an iron bar, and I didn't like it!" [Laughter]

But I don't feel I have to be present for a piece to be good. I can write a third-person piece where I am obviously present, and never use the first person, and it works just as well. For a piece like this where I am on a search, it seemed that I would give the audience a character through which to observe all this stuff.

You also write part of this piece in the present tense. Talk about writing in the present tense in a newspaper.

I like it. In the past tense, the piece kind of sits there, typical and normal by newspaper standards. But in the present tense, there is a little bit more immediacy. Even though you are writing from the perspective of the event being over, you can plant little clues and hints to what is coming up. And when you finally get to what is coming up, it is almost as though the world has miraculously ordered itself to the way you wanted it to be. That's just a trick.

Listen to this bit about the bellhop: "I give him the tip, wondering if, in time-honored detective fashion, I should peel off bills until he tells me what I want to hear. Two of the larger denominations, and he would probably admit to Keillor banging out all his works in this very room. Three bills, and he'd confide that Christopher Marlowe actually wrote *Lake Wobegon Days*."
You and I are English lit types, so we get the Marlowe reference. But what kind of reader will get it?

I don't know. Somebody who has a nodding acquaintance with some of the cultural touchstones. Somebody who wouldn't necessarily know that some befuddled scholars think Marlowe had nothing better to do, so he wrote Shakespeare's works. But they would get the general message that this bellhop would get paid until he told me what I wanted to hear. And if they didn't exactly get the reference, it would not be as amusing to them.

How do you keep the copy desk from adding "a 16th-century English playwright best known for..."?

By frequent brandishing of firearms and crossbows. [Laughter] If you pull up a stepladder, crouch down on it like a gargoyle, and cradle a big rifle, it keeps them in line. Sometimes you have to insist, "Don't be so damn literal; let some things go out there unexplained." I try to put a few things in, hoping that somebody will get the reference. But I try not to make it the focal point of a joke.

Here's a passage I liked: "Chelsea is being gentrified. For the moment, it is caught between incarnations. A glance through one set of windows shows abstract art and spindly halogen light fixtures; in another window, one sees the back of an old tube radio. A lot of people have lived here for a long, long time."
I admire that passage because it's simple and very nicely selected. You don't show us too much.

One of the reasons that newspapering is good for me is that it has limitations. I'm not sure how I would have approached that passage if I were writing a novel and had a lot more space. I might have gone on longer and ruined it. This is not a piece about Chelsea, so I did not have to go into any greater detail.

You have a number of New Yorkers speaking in this piece. But you don't use dialect or any of the standard stage devices to make them sound like New Yorkers.

In dialect, unless it's like "dese," "dem," or "dose," or a couple of words that you immediately know are signal words, if you try to contort everything to look phonetically correct, it's usually more of an impediment to the reader. It looks like you're trying too hard. It also makes the people sound like they're out of a Mark Twain novel. If you've set the scene well enough, readers can generally hear them talk when they read the voices. And not everybody I met in New York talked with that kind of accent.

When you finally come face to face with Keillor, you show yourself asking him questions: "I settle

for asking what he thought he might have written had he been born here, instead of Minnesota."

I do that a lot. I have to have some means for explaining why an answer is there, of not pretending that this person is spontaneously speaking the words I want him to speak. Also, I want to give readers an idea of what is going on in Keillor's mind and in my mind, why he's saying what he's saying. I don't use quote marks for my part because I have slightly reconstructed the question, not in order to make the answer any different, but sometimes you can bring out an extra aspect of the answer by phrasing the question another way.

My yellow caution light just started blinking. Maybe you need a warning at the front: "DANGEROUS HUMOR FOLLOWS."

Sometimes it's needed, but I don't get many angry letters.

Some of these quotations are quite long. How did you record them?

Desperately scribbling away. I could hear him speak when I started to do this, especially the line which made this trip worthwhile. I did not know where he was going to be when I went out there, and I lucked into meeting him at the Algonquin Hotel through many frantic phone calls. When he said, "It was a time of hot weather," I knew I had the story. That was as "Keillor" a thing as I ever heard in my life. I knew that I would be coming back with that line as a trophy.

When you take notes, how much of a quotation do you write down?

Illegible little squiggles for conjunctions and stuff, but the entire quote. Somebody will go four or five words into a sentence, and then shut it down and start onto the next one. When you try to take down every word, you end up with sentences like wrecked freight trains.

A little later, you say: "Enigmas fascinate, and Keillor makes for a perfect enigma. His writings seem to take place in some comforting dusk of everyone's past, and his voice is as warm as the fire in the hearth—yet the man stands apart with a reserve that is simultaneously Olympian and pained.
"The truth about Garrison Keillor is like that jot of white material on an egg yolk you can never get with your spoon. Whether it is an unintentional function of a shy personality or a calculated construction matters less in New York than the effect. It is best to keep people guessing."
Every once in a while, your humor column turns serious.

I'm trying to do it as quickly and efficiently as possible. I was trying to find out a way to explain to everybody what I found, summing up the piece. I think it gives the humorist some grounding.

Do you see these pieces as educative?

That's not the intention. The intention is to amuse. I think they may occasionally enlighten someone. Sometimes they may just confirm somebody's ideas or prejudices, but I'm not trying to educate.

Here's your kicker: "No, it's not the Sidetrack Tap, but again: that just might be the point." You picked up the wording of the lead there. Did you decide that at the end, or did you plan it that way?

The ending ought to refer back to the beginning in a way that comments on the beginning. It provides a nice closure, gives you the sense that you have read something instead of just a series of words. It's less making a point than suggesting one.

Indeed. How did the railroad piece come about?

After I had taken company money to go to New York, I felt obliged to turn out at least three pieces about the experience. I wanted to see what it's like nowadays to take a sleeping car to New York. It's something I always wanted to do because I love trains. So I just got on board and went, and sat down one night and wrote it up. This one was a delight to write, because it just wrote itself.

How long did it take it to write itself? [Laughter]

About three-and-a-half hours.

Let me read the lead: "The following, I think, is typical. I took a sleeper-car train to New York City, following the old routes, living the old rhythms the jets have tried to kill. The experience taught me three things. One, the trains aren't dead. They're coming back. Rarely on time, granted, but coming back nonetheless. Two, I never want to go over a high bridge in a train again in my life. Three, nothing equals what a train provides. Nothing. That says a lot for jets, but it says more for the trains."
What messages are you trying to send to the reader in that lead?

That this is not going to be the most specific piece you've read in the newspaper, but it's probably going to be more evocative than a compilation of Amtrak's budget for the last fiscal year. Also there's drama coming up, and humor. I knew I had room with this one.

I want to look at one of your quotations, in the passage about train food: "There's no escape. You can't order out. The general attitude was best expressed by a waiter's reply to a customer's request for a substitution.
"'The cook,' he said, 'don't make no alternations.'"

We have problems here with grammar and the word "alter*n*ations." Talk about *not* cleaning up that quotation.

I would have to sandblast this quote to make it normal English. The wrong word gives you an idea as to exactly whose hands you're in. Here you have somebody who thinks "alternation" is something you can do to the menu. I know what the guy means, but that's a pretty funny way of putting it.

How about the phrase "don't make no"?

That's the way people speak. I just left it as it was. It just seemed natural to do that.

Do you mark these oddities for the copy desk so they won't mess with them?

No, my editor does that. He runs interference for me more than I ever see. But I have a feeling that one day the desk is going to have an aneurysm. [Laughter]

This piece has wonderful subheads, such as "THE BAR CAR, OR DEATH STOPS AT TO-LEDO." I assume you wrote them, but how do you get the copy desk to let you do that?

Yes. Again, I'm sitting on the ladder with a shotgun in my lap. I know it grieves them no end, but how many times has death stopped at Toledo? I think they just let it go.

I always write my own subheads. And my subheads refer to each other, making them harder to revise, so editors usually leave them alone. That way, the desk knows where I want the breaks to fall, even if they whack the subheads out later. I hate that idiot key on some editing terminals that boldfaces the first three words of every fourth paragraph, producing such meaningful markers as "IN AN OLD..." or "AND THEN THE..."

Later, you say: "The last thing you hear before you sleep is the whistle, the most haunting sound ever made by man. If that sound came from a wild animal, primitive man would have ascribed great wisdom and sadness to it, and they would have feared it. We know what a train whistle is when we hear it, but we don't know what it means. No one can hear it without feeling the sudden thrust of melancholy against the heart: *something is passing by, going to where I am not.*"

I grew up in Raleigh, North Carolina, with omnipresent trains, and those whistles in the night make you wish you weren't in Raleigh.

Yes, that's the reason I wrote the piece, that feeling, and what makes me love these things, and explaining why.

Did you have that idea in mind when you started this graph, or did it just come out?

It just came out. I had to figure out how I was going to structure the piece, and I figured I'd do it blow by blow. I thought that the section on sleeping in the room was going to be something out of a Marx Brothers movie. But the more I wrote it, the more I started thinking about how I felt when I lay down to sleep. That's the joy of writing, just letting everything flow out, and finding things you obviously believe because they're coming out of you, but you hadn't seen expressed in that way.

In the Halloween piece, you mix first-, second-, and third-person narration. Listen to this: "I don't believe that everything was better when you were a child. Holidays are usually stacked in favor of adults. Most holidays mean tight clothing and a small table with the rest of the kids. No matter how much you enjoyed it, adults always had a corner on the Real Meaning...But Halloween was yours....You knew it wasn't a holiday."
We talked about the first person. Can you talk

about the second person in newswriting?

People get tired of it, and they think you're trying
to use it as a hip convention. I use second person
when I'm saying something that I believe or that I
have experienced, and I'm trying to make it general. Sometimes I use it to say that any reasonable
person in this situation will have this reaction.

**Newspapers rarely use second person. I like the
way you violate traditional forms all the time and
get away with it. You do it so gracefully that it's
not noticeable.**

Every once in a while, it hits me exactly how different this is from other stuff in newspapers, and I
have to thank God I have editors who let me do
this. Otherwise, these are not pieces I would be
able to publish easily.

**Most of them would go into good magazines.
Now, a general question: who are your idols as
humor writers?**

I don't think I have any idols any more. When I
started, I read contemporaries like Fran Lebowitz
and Woody Allen. Then I went back to S. J. Perelman, who was probably the worst influence I could
possibly have, because no one can do what he
does. If anything, I learned from him a sense of the
ridiculous possibilities of language, how you could
make words themselves be funny. Then I tried
reading some Benchley, but it never made me
laugh. Then I started reading humorous novelists,
Anthony Burgess, whose tremendous style had an
influence on me, and Peter DeVries, who has a
punning streak in him, which I did not appropriate.
His word play is tricky. The funniest guy writing in
newspapers today, just on a simple gut level, is
Dave Barry. I enjoy reading P. J. O'Rourke, who
has taken over for Hunter S. Thompson in the Wild
Man Beat. Even though he can be the epitome of
the Ugly American, he says what he believes with

unapologetic relish. He's the master of the unfair observation that sums up what you really want to think.

But it's hard for me to see exactly what lessons I learned where. I was never up to their level, so I gave up on idols and just kept writing as much as I could.

Do you find newspaper writing confining or freeing?

Both. I thought I would find it tremendously confining when I started. I found the insistence on fact in every piece just infuriating, because I had been making things up my whole career, and I didn't think I had to put facts in to make them good. And then I learned that you can have fun with facts. The challenge of presenting information to people and not making everybody snooze is something I never had to do, and I love doing it. The newspaper never says that I can't do pieces like the ones you have before you, and if I'm allowed to be incredibly indulgent, as in the train piece, I can't see that it's confining. When they rein me back, it's usually judiciously done and for a reason.

Do you think you'll ever find newspapers confining, and leave?

No. There are so many other things that I'm doing right now that are fun, but even if my second novel makes $874 million, I can't see a situation where I would leave the paper. There's nothing as immediate as daily journalism. I wrote a piece on John Tower in one day, and bam! It's in the paper three days later while the issue is still hot. I would go nuts if I didn't have that link.

Newspaper writing is fun, isn't it?

It's a gas. You expect pieces you publish in a book to be book quality. In a magazine, if it's printed on glossy paper, it must be good. There's something dispensable about newspapers. People are not surprised when they find the ordinary there, and they are surprised when they find something out of the ordinary there. But no matter what it is, they're going to toss it at the end of the day.

Not your stuff. I'm going to preserve it in *Best Newspaper Writing 1989*.

Francis X. Clines
Deadline Writing

FRANCIS X. CLINES grew up in Brooklyn and
finished one year at St. Francis College in New
York before a two-year stint in the Army. He talked
his way into *The New York Times* as a copy boy in
1958. He became a reporter in training for six
years, covering police and general assignment in all
five boroughs, and even wrote copy for the mar-
quee in Times Square. He worked his way through
the following beats: real estate, Eastern Long
Island, New York City welfare, and state legislature
and the governor. From 1976 to 1979, he wrote the
"About New York" column. He covered the
presidential campaign of 1980, and was assigned to
the Washington bureau from 1980 to 1986. He
served in the Philippines before going to London
for two years, where he wrote these prize-winning
stories. He has recently joined the Moscow bureau.

Gunman terrorizes Belfast crowd gathered at funeral

MARCH 17, 1988

BELFAST, Northern Ireland, March 16—Three people were killed and dozens wounded today as an assailant threw grenades into a screaming crowd at a funeral and then fled across the graveyard from enraged mourners.

Panic broke out and grieving families dived for cover by the mud of the open grave as four grenades exploded amid thousands of mourners gathered for the burial of three Irish Republican Army guerrillas. The guerrillas, unarmed but on a bombing mission, were slain March 6 by British undercover agents in Gibraltar.

"Kill the bastard!" came cries from the crowd as dozens of mourners ignored the gunshots fired by the retreating assailant and chased him a quarter-mile to an adjacent expressway.

CROWD IS STUNNED

Families, clergy members, pallbearers, and gravediggers watched stunned on the cemetery hill as the wounded mourners, who had been saying the rosary moments before, staggered bleeding among the headstones.

The collective screams of shock and panic soon changed to cheers when the crowd of more than 5,000 saw the blue-coated invader finally collared and pummeled after he coolly turned and threw the last of his grenades and fired bullets at furious pursuers.

"We beat him unmercifully," said George McMurray after racing down the hill toward the gunman, who was widely suspected of being on a terrorist mission for one of the paramilitary Protestant gangs. The gunman was rescued and arrested by officers of the Royal Ulster Constabulary.

Beyond the three dead men, four mourners were listed as seriously wounded among the dozen who were hospitalized. More than 30 others were treated and released, according to the hospital.

The attack on the eve of St. Patrick's Day in Milltown Cemetery pushed this city toward a fresh cycle of the sectarian vendetta and street violence that has marked the last two decades of Northern Irish life. Cars were hijacked and set afire by youths as anger built at nightfall in the heavily policed ghettos of the Catholic minority.

The grieving families back on the hill arose and completed the burials amid the emotional uproar even as the bodies of the newly slain were carried off bloodied in one of the waiting hearses.

POLICE FORCE ACCUSED

"God, we can't even bury the dead in peace," one woman declared, her Belfast lilt hard-edged with terror. She watched above the tombstones for more danger to the skewed and scrambling crowd where children screamed at parents covering them protectively on the graveyard earth.

Sinn Fein, the political arm of the outlawed IRA, accused the Royal Ulster Constabulary of collusion in the attack and of notifying Protestant terrorists that the cemetery service would be unusual for its lack of any police presence.

The constabulary dismissed this as an "outright lie," saying it had decided to keep its patrolmen away in response to complaints from church and Irish nationalist leaders that so many of their past funerals had degenerated into sacrilegious brawls because of the heavy presence of the police. The constabulary, which has long denied charges of bias and brutality, limited its presence at the midday funeral to two helicopters that hovered overhead.

A white van parked on a highway during the attack could be seen suddenly driving off as the gunman darted back down the hill. This fueled the charges of police conspiracy by Gerry Adams, the Sinn Fein president. The constabulary later said the van was part of a police patrol that was uninvolved in the incident.

PROTESTANTS DENY INVOLVEMENT

The police also announced that a second suspect had been taken into custody, but they offered no details. Leaders of several Protestant paramilitary gangs denied that the marauder represented their factions of Northern Ireland's violence.

The police statements only fed the suspicions of IRA leaders. They have been incensed in recent months by the British government's decision not to prosecute police officers found to have obstructed justice in a special inquiry into charges that anti-terrorist police engaged in "shoot to kill" attacks on unarmed IRA suspects.

This mood was only heightened by the manner of death of the three Irish rebels being buried here in the Catholic enclave of Andersonstown. Knowledgeable IRA figures have said that the three unarmed rebels were making plans to plant a powerful bomb at a public military parade in Gibraltar when they were shot to death by the undercover men.

In contrast to the IRA's portrayal of them as martyrs, British officials have hailed their demise. They say it avoided another of the civilian atrocities that have marked the modern era of the Irish rebels' age-old attempt to drive British authority from Ireland.

Protestant politicians also quickly pointed out after the cemetery attack that the IRA had exploded a bomb at the graveyard entrance to a Protestant funeral on March 13 last year. But Sinn Fein leaders insisted there was a qualitative difference because only police officers and no civilians were injured.

Today, until the intruder appeared and began lobbing a half-dozen grenades into the throng, the funeral had been remarkably serene. With the police absent, the IRA, in turn, had backed down from its usual defiant paramilitary displays, which anger officials.

Thus a moment of minor progress seemed at hand on the gray cold day as the breeze sweeping the humble cemetery was cut by the bagpipers' skirl of "The Minstrel Boy." The hearses and mourners were arriving after a peaceful Mass and procession from nearby St. Agnes's church.

BRITISH PRESENCE DENOUNCED

Then came the prayers for the dead preceding burial and another vociferous denunciation by Mr. Adams of Britain's presence in Ireland. He stood in the special IRA burial ground, surrounded by two centuries of rebel remains.

The coffin of one IRA insurgent, Mairead Farrell, was lowered into the common grave. Her father and five brothers, after accepting the Irish tricolor and the black beret and gloves of a fallen IRA guerrilla, each threw a shovelful of red earth atop her coffin.

Then, as the coffin of Sean Savage was brought forward, the first grenade thump startled the crowd and a blot of black smoke arose only about 20 yards away.

People were confused, some wondering whether this might signal a harmless IRA military display. But then a young woman staggered toward the green-fenced IRA plot, her face bathed in blood, and three more grenades were calmly thrown by the man. The crowd cried out at the sudden menace amid their grief.

Mourners ducked down behind tombstones. "Jesus!" came a cry. "What? What?" shouted another.

A PLEA FOR CALM

"Be calm! We must bury our dead!" Mr. Adams pleaded as people toppled out of the range of the gunman. He seemed slow and careful in exploiting the mass surprise for his mission.

"A big burly fellow he was," said John Jordan, a 60-year-old van driver for one of the many foreign television news crews in the cemetery. "He had on a blue anorak with these bombs in the pockets, like black eggs they looked. The bombs made me duck, otherwise he would have got me." Mr. Jordan pointed to a bullet hole dead center on the driver's side of his van's windshield.

The attack left the crowd looking in two directions. They looked toward the grave where first Mr. Savage and then the third IRA guerrilla were eventually put safely to rest at the feet of their appalled survivors. "Let us bury Danny McCann in dignity," pleaded Mr. Adams as the third young insurgent was lowered to final rest.

But even more than the funeral, the throng looked to the retreating gunman as he ran a bit, then wheeled to crouch and fire a dozen shots at his pursuers.

"Get him! Get him!" shouted a watching boy balanced atop a tombstone.

The gunman ran out from under his tweed cap as he fled out onto the motorway. Unable to stop a car, he was brought to the ground and a cheer went up across the hillside, as if a goal had been scored in some deadly contest.

A chant began: "IRA! IRA!" and the wounded were hurried off to the Royal Victoria Hospital's emergency ward, long a battle-hardened depot in the troubles.

Tom King, the Thatcher government's chief minister in Northern Ireland, denounced the assault as "insane and depraved" and called for calm.

Earlier, at the funeral Mass, the Rev. Tom Toner spoke sympathetically of the three who were killed in Gibraltar and said murder was a question of ethics. By Christian ethics the three had been murdered "just as the killings of soldiers and police were murdered" by the IRA, he carefully declared.

More emphatically, the priest pleaded for communal peace and urged his people to observe the "special" young people who brought the Eucharistic sacramentals of bread and wine forward past the three coffins. The youths were children with Down's syndrome. They smiled honestly amid the church gloom, walking past the kneeling, praying, and in some part, angry, people.

"Gentle prophets in a violent world," Father Toner said, pointing to the youngsters. "They testify to the infinite value of every human life," he told the people shortly before they arose, walked outside, and headed with the three coffins toward Milltown Cemetery.

Observations and questions

1) Clines begins with a hard lead: "Three people were killed and dozens wounded today as an assailant threw grenades into a screaming crowd at a funeral and then fled across the graveyard from enraged mourners." But the lead is not so hard as it looks: no specific who, where, why, or how. Rewrite the lead including all five Ws and the H. Why is Clines's version better?

2) Although Clines had the good fortune to observe these events firsthand, the general confusion deprived him of such basic information as the names of the new dead, the exact number of injured, etc. Study how he writes around these gaps without hiding the sketchiness of the information from the reader.

3) Clines waits until the eighth paragraph to tell us that this attack happened "on the eve of St. Patrick's Day in Milltown Cemetery." Would you be tempted to move the name of the cemetery and this ironic date a little higher? Why didn't Clines put them up there?

4) Just past the middle of his story, Clines retells the action chronologically from the beginning. Think about the advantages of this "champagne glass." form. What do you have to leave out to tell the story twice?

5) Clines tells us the names of the three people being buried almost two-thirds of the way through, and even then gives us only two and holds the third for five more paragraphs. He must have an understanding and restrained copy desk. How can we train our own copy editors not to make everything float up to the top?

6) "The gunman ran out from under his tweed cap as he fled out onto the motorway. Unable to stop a car, he was brought to the ground and a cheer went up across the hillside, as if a goal had been scored in some deadly contest." List the visual details in this paragraph, and study how Clines gets very graphic effects out of very little. Selection is the key to our art.

British soldiers killed at IRA rites

MARCH 20, 1988

BELFAST, Northern Ireland, March 19—There was more macabre violence at an Irish Republican Army funeral today as two armed British soldiers in civilian clothes drove their car into a crowd of panicked mourners and were seized, beaten, and finally shot to death.

Their bloody bodies were discovered a short while later in a garbage patch. The military authorities denied the two men were undercover agents observing the funeral.

The two were trying to flee quickly when challenged by a neighborhood security watch, according to local residents, and they then drove directly into the cortege. A spokesman for the British army said the two men were not on duty and were merely on the way to new assignments outside Belfast when they came across the funeral.

MANY AT WEDNESDAY FUNERAL

Many of the frightened and enraged mourners had been at a funeral Wednesday at which a civilian threw grenades and killed three mourners. The authorities are holding Michael Stone, 33 years old, in that incident and say they have arrested a second person.

The bloody funeral scene today made this one of the grisliest weeks in the last two decades of violence in Northern Ireland.

Prime Minister Margaret Thatcher of Britain denounced the slayings of the soldiers, who apparently were taken away and executed, as "an act of appalling savagery," saying: "There seems to be no depths to which these people won't sink."

But officials of the outlawed IRA said the shootings were carried out in defense after the men drove into the cortege and fired weapons as the crowd converged. A news correspondent in the funeral march reported that an occupant drew a pistol after the car approached the cortege at about 40 miles an hour, shrieked to a stop just short of the hearse, and sought unsuccessfully to reverse direction as the crowd moved in.

CROWD SURROUNDS CAR

A shot was heard as members of the crowd surrounded the car. Someone was heard to shout: "He's got a gun!"

The two soldiers were dragged out, beaten, and driven off in a taxi, according to witnesses. They said shots were soon heard a short distance away where the bodies were found later.

Three West Belfast civilians were arrested for questioning soon after the authorities found the bodies of the men, who had been strip-searched, beaten with bars, and finally shot, according to witnesses.

Angry local residents contended the men were provocateurs, not murder victims. They said the three IRA insurgents who were killed while unarmed on a bombing mission March 6 in Gibraltar were murder victims. The three were killed by British undercover agents who said they considered themselves threatened.

BURYING WEDNESDAY VICTIM

The mourners today were burying Kevin Brady, one of the victims of the funeral attack Wednesday. They were stunned as a marauding Protestant gunman with suspected paramilitary ties killed three people with grenades.

Catholic residents accused the security forces of creating trouble with undercover intrigues.

The army denied that the soldiers had driven at high speed toward mourners, but local witnesses said that this was the case. The army also denied charges that the men belonged to the Special Air Service, the elite British army unit that specializes in anti-terrorist operations. The army insisted it was not unusual for soldiers to be armed and in civilian clothes.

But neighborhood residents said it would be highly unusual for disinterested soldiers to stray from nearby main roads to drive by the cemetery here in the Andersonstown enclave, a known center of Catholic resistance to British authority.

Aside from the killings today, the small community has been a crossroads of grief and death this week. After the three burials Wednesday, mourners attended a funeral Thursday, two on Friday, and faced three today, with all of the dead consigned by violence, most as innocent victims, some as active Irish rebels.

IRA APOLOGIZES

In the middle of today's fury, the IRA issued an apology to the survivors of a woman shot to death last night in County Farmanagh, saying the killing was a mistake and the intended victim was her brother, whom the IRA suspects of pro-British activities.

This evening, rumors spread through the anxious and angry neighborhoods. Police of the Royal Ulster Constabulary, who had been observing a new low-profile sensitivity to IRA funerals, flooded back into the embattled sectarian ghettos, alert for fresh rounds of the nighttime arson and vandalism that has occurred most of this tense week.

As on Wednesday, the shaken mourners resumed the Brady funeral, heading into the grimly familiar Milltown Cemetery, some of them weeping as their mission was heightened by shock, anger, and fear.

The gyre of death, mourning, and fresh death underscored a growing crisis for the government of Prime Minister Thatcher.

Catholics here and officials of the Irish republic have accused London of ignoring increasing evidence of civil rights abuses of Catholic civilians by anti-terrorist forces of the police and of the British army charged with keeping the peace. Security officials insist they generally stay within the law in attempting to combat armed IRA operations against their forces.

Tonight, British officials sounded as enraged as the Catholics here. Tom King, Mrs. Thatcher's secretary of state for Northern Ireland, ordered a full inquiry into the soldiers' deaths, describing them as an act of "barbarous animal savagery."

Gerry Adams, a member of Parliament from West Belfast and leader of Sinn Fein, the political arm of the IRA, said the provocation to the mourners was such that there was no chance to rescue the two soldiers.

"I did my best to restore calm," said Mr. Adams, who led the procession to the nearby cemetery after the two soldiers were dragged off to apparent execution. "What were they doing there?" he asked repeatedly.

This bizarre and deadly occurrence heightened the already severe tensions of the latest dark turning in the centuries of British-Irish struggles and violence. Many in Ireland and Northern Ireland were outraged last month when British officials confirmed that the police had obstructed justice in some shootings of unarmed civilians. But the Thatcher government said they would not be prosecuted because of the overriding need of national security and the public interest.

The killing of the soldiers marked the Thatcher government's turn to express outrage. Clearly the deaths will exacerbate foundering British-Irish relations, with London officials again preparing to turn an angry eye to the increasing troubles, and the IRA vowing renewed armed resistance.

Observations and questions

1) Clines told me that he felt particularly fond of two words in his lead: "macabre" and "finally." Cut them and see what happens, not just to the lead, but also to the whole piece.

2) This article abounds with unnamed sources. Examine each one and think about why Clines chose to be less specific than he might have been. Do these unnamed sources undermine the credibility of the article?

3) "Three West Belfast civilians were arrested for questioning soon after the authorities found the bodies of the men, *who had been strip-searched, beaten with bars, and finally shot,* according to witnesses." Should the italicized clause come higher in the story, perhaps replacing "were seized, beaten, and finally shot to death" in the lead sentence?

4) "In the middle of today's fury, the IRA issued an apology to the survivors of a woman shot to death last night in County Farmanagh, saying the killing was a mistake and the intended victim was her brother, whom the IRA suspects of pro-British activities." I could not report that fact without screaming privately, yet Clines writes it perfectly flat. Think about how traditional newspaper style enables us to handle outrages and outrage.

5) Clines takes some liberties that lean toward editorializing, for example, "This *bizarre and deadly* occurrence heightened the already severe tensions of the latest *dark* turning in the centuries of British-Irish struggles and violence." Do you find other wording in the article that might need flagging? Where are the boundaries between interpretation and opinion?

6) Notice how Clines weaves new and recent events with history in a breaking news article. He does not assume that readers have read any of his previous pieces.

In Belfast, death, too, is diminished by death

MARCH 20, 1988

BELFAST, Northern Ireland—Beyond the coffin, out in the churchyard, red-haired Kathleen Quinn was full of fun and flirting shamelessly for all her eight years of life. "Mister, I'm to be on the TV tonight," she told a stranger, squinting up happy and prim. Kathleen had taken her brother's bike and skinned her knee bloody, all while people were praying goodbye inside the church to another rebel body in another coffin.

Soon the cameras were watching the coffin being carried out from the windowless fortress of a church, down the curl of the street in the simple hamlet, and on to the ever-filling graveyard patch devoted to republican rebels.

As it turned out, the television ignored Kathleen and missed a classic Irish truth, a sight for sore eyes. She climbed back on the bike and headed off in a blur, oblivious of a piece of nearby graffiti that seemed about all of life's withering dangers: "I wonder each night what the monster will do to me tomorrow."

Eventually there was woeful monotony in what became a week of mourning and parading and dying. At a funeral for three slain republican agents Wednesday, a grenade-throwing intruder had killed three people. There was another republican funeral Thursday, then two on Friday, and three more on Saturday. The dead were produced by assorted violence—some were innocent victims, others were zealous aggressors. Yesterday, at a cortege for a victim of Wednesday's funeral, two British soldiers in civilian clothes drove into a crowd of mourners and were dragged from their car, beaten, and shot to death.

The best hometown poets wisely retreat from Northern Ireland once their sense of mortality is honed to piercing, so this dark progression was left to be described in the prosaic catchall "the troubles," as if Job had called his plagues "the unpleasantries."

The deaths were handled by Gerry Adams, the eerily placid, black-bearded leader of Sinn Fein, the rebellion's political arm, as if he were the Osiris of his people, the king rallying souls to the underworld, to the plain slant of Belfast hillside called Milltown Cemetery. Mr. Adams, whom police officials suspect of being deeply involved in rebel violence, exhibited the demeanor of a parish curate in adapting almost instantly to expressions of fresh official grief for bodies freshly felled in Wednesday's attack.

The earth had not been closed on their predecessors before the newest victims went from praying for the dead to being dead. Asked what he thought of it—the brazen intruder exploding the grief—Mr. Adams replied rather gently, "It was one of those things." He cited it as a demonstration of the state of war he prefers as a description of life here, as opposed to the state of criminal terrorism the British government, trying to rule this place, attributes to the rebels of the Irish Republican Army.

There is at least as much fighting over words and symbols as over flesh and earth. Most metaphysically absurd was the attempt by Mr. Adams's enemies in the paramilitary gangs of the Protestant loyalist majority to portray the grenade attacker as a genuine eccentric among the hundreds of modern Irish gunmen who have stalked their fellows in all imaginable lethal manner. The attacker was somehow being rated as beyond the bounds of the "normal" killers of Belfast, "rejected" by the main paramilitary organization, said one quasi-brigadier, as if denying the vendetta wildness of the historic gangs of Ireland—the Peep O'Day Boys and their nasty counterparts.

"You, the people of Belfast, have won the battle of the funerals," a Sinn Fein official told a graveside crowd. He spoke not of quantity of casualties but of the police's finally deciding to stay away from the cemetery and overlook the rebel rhetoric and paraphernalia. This victory of the funerals was proclaimed in a booming brogue across the gravestones by a speaker who seemed intent on listing each outrage in eight centuries of Anglo-Irish violence.

But this hoary tower of calibrated grievance seemed to crumble at the sight of placid Irish women suddenly made to suffer here and now. Here was a young woman, a Catholic nationalist, staggering back from a grenade, bleeding from her face onto gravestones proclaiming the certainty of final peace. "Why would anyone want to do that?" she asked so simply later. And there was an older Protestant loyalist woman asking virtually the same question the morning after as she stood with singed hair by the ashes of her house after it was gasoline-bombed in a random, retaliatory raid by nationalist vandals. "Some poor Catholic woman will get it done to her," she said of the vengeance.

One point of rare agreement among nationalists, loyalists, and the British authorities is that atrocity tends to be layered like slag here, not woven linearly. So the latest sensational deaths at a funeral instantly diminish the importance of the preceding outrage. Thus the Sinn Fein mourners, in feeling newly violated, could also feel freer of the pall of the rebel explosion last fall that killed 11 Protestant civilians.

Comparable rubrics seem to underpin the postmortem morning television news shows as they assemble the usual balance of partisan analysts. In this, the London government often leaves the nationalists livid by assuming the role of the sad, bewildered referee among these unruly Irishmen.

The same leaders from a score of civic and church institutions come forward each time to the television cameras with capsules of concern and recriminations that can seem, with each new funereal cue, as horrendous in their own good way as the inevitable deaths to follow. More was the hopeful comfort, then, in the death-defying sight of redhaired Kathleen as she happily skirted the latest funeral.

Observations and questions

1) This piece, presented as a news story, has an indirect lead of three paragraphs. In deciding whether to use a hard or soft lead *on this piece*, what factors would you consider? Why would Clines choose the indirect lead?

2) Clines ends his lead with a bit of graffiti: "I wonder each night what the monster will do to me tomorrow." Might you be tempted to use that quotation as an ending? What effects would you produce? Would you injure the lead by doing so?

3) This article has a tone of weariness. Locate all the wording and devices that create that tone. Try eliminating Kathleen and see what happens to the tone.

4) I would call this passage poetic: "The best hometown poets wisely retreat from Northern Ireland once their sense of mortality is honed to piercing, so this dark progression was left to be described in the prosaic catch-all, 'the troubles,' as if Job had called his plagues 'the unpleasantries.'" Do you think such poetic writing is appropriate to newswriting? Outside Ireland?

5) "'Why would anyone want to do that?' she asked so simply later." Reporters generally distrust and dislike adverbs. Should we delete "simply" and "later"?

6) This news article captures the mood of a few days in Northern Ireland rather than reporting any news. Who is the audience for such a piece? Do "mood pieces" have freedoms that normal newswriting lacks? Find specific instances in this article.

A portrait of the artist as a young man of letters

MAY 9, 1988

DUBLIN—Mute and spastic, prodigious and twin-kle-eyed, Christy Nolan went straight to the point in the first sentence of his autobiography, typing each letter laboriously with the "unicorn rod" jut-ting strapped from his forehead down toward the typewriter: "Can you credit all of the fuss that was made of a cripple?"

Four years ago he slowly nudged and butted his story on from this question while his mother, Bernadette, steadied his forehead for each letter painstakingly chipped like mosaic bits from the keyboard. And now the grand irony of that open-ing question should only be seen in Christy's smil-ing, wily eyes as he sits in his wheelchair and contemplates his arrival on the best-seller list in the United States with his autobiography, *Under the Eye of the Clock* (St. Martin's Press), and his own visit there a few weeks ago as a ranking author be-ing shepherded about the book-promotion circuit.

'FRESH TINGLES'

"Breasting along gold limousines, tinted glass creating able access to mighty loot," the 22-year old author typed wryly for a visitor as an impres-sion of America. "Certain fresh tingles romping through my heart," he continued, "as crippled I managed to bite into the Big Apple."

He punctuates this with a clear and certain sound of exclamation, a sudden crackle of joy, as, with the sentences pecked into being on paper, a reader en-joys them. Christy is leaning in his wheelchair, ema-nating a certain contagious spirit of relaxation in his own wayward posture. His power to listen is palpable, his ear a funnel to the universe in the way his father, Joe, first dandled him as a baby and gave him endless stories, poems, jokes, songs, and monologues that fixed Christy onto spoken words that are the heart of storytelling.

In the living room of a humble attached home in a Dublin outskirt, no words seem to be wasted on mere politeness before Christy the artful listener as his mother, Bernadette, his wit's factotum and ferryman, serves as the conversation broker. She is carefully pulling words and concepts not from the air but from his eye signals to myriad common reference points in the living room and beyond.

A TOUCH OF GOADING

"What can you come up with next, Christy?" his mother echoes a question with a loving tinge of goading, a question already being asked by critics who have hailed Christy's original literary style. "You can't rest on your laurels, you know."

Christy Nolan eyes the question and needles his mother that she would probably rather snack lazily somewhere than continue her own prodigious art in opening the world to her son at the keyboard, clasping his heaving forehead in the timeless gesture of a mother's concern.

What next for him? "I'll go on the drink," Mrs. Nolan translates with a whoop of laughter at Christy's eyeful wit. But he has already typed out an answer: "I'd like to try my head at writing fiction. In fact the next book is already borning itself, characters are nodding to me, and the compunction to mould my characters into literary form is making life insecure for me."

He has not pecked a word of it onto paper since starting the first chapter in November and then finding life disrupted by his winning the major English literary prize, the Whitbread book of the year. But he confidently indicates that the novel is under silent construction in his head as the writer is trundled beyond the fun and ego trauma of international acclaim for his life story.

It was only 11 years ago that, through a limited breakthrough with rehabilitation therapy and a muscle drug, he first hesitantly zeroed in on a typing keyboard and found epiphany.

The 11-year-old, broken of body, was no longer

mute and had a poem ready, "I Learn to Bow," in which he vowed to open the eyes of readers to see that "Polarized, I was paralyzed, Plausibility palated." Others followed day by day, celebrating all manner of storehoused experience, from the delicious "apron oligarchy" of the family kitchen at Christmas to his grandparents ("Aged sentinels, sampling Death's eclat") to a Joycean description of his own birth as a "gelatinous, moaning, dankerous baby boy." He thus made clear what his family long knew to be true, that his body, rendered paralyzed and spastic at birth, masked a gleaming intelligence and fascination with life and its language.

CRUCIAL TANTRUM

His sister, Yvonne, two years older, knew this well and treated him as an equal competitor, famous in the family for asking as a toddler, "What are you agitating for now?"

And Mrs. Nolan knew this most bitingly, for when Christy was 3, with an IQ estimated at the level of a child twice his age, he suddenly confronted her with a terrible tantrum of accusation, self-pity, and tears, refusing to be soothed as he eye-gestured over his own useless body. "The days of fobbing Christy off were over," she recalls. "He really put it up to me that day. He made me feel I was dealing with an adult."

In his biography, Christy recalled that she put him down in his chair and bluntly said: "I never prayed for you to be born crippled. I wanted you to be full of life, able to run and jump and talk." And she told him: "But you are you." And: "You can see, you can hear, you can think, you can understand everything you hear." And: "We love you just as you are."

"Then I let him get on with the crying," Mrs. Nolan recalls, marking that day as the end of the tears and the beginning of Christy's creative life. "He was teaching me at 3 how to accept that he had his wits about him and he had sized up life and that he didn't like what he saw but, OK, he's decided to live with it."

The mother carefully adds, "None of us will let him run away with himself." And Yvonne chimes in, saying his knack for poetry can fade to "a tendency to shoot the bull." Christy exclaims his pleasure at this needle, rollicking in his chair.

The Nolan family remembers well how Christy spent the first 11 years of his life praying, asking God for a means of expressing what was going on in his brain. Now that he has triumphed across the second 11 years, Mrs. Nolan said she had to ask him, "How do you feel now with what's happening?"

With another crackle of joy, Christy, jolting in his wheelchair, affirmed that he had replied: "I had to tell God he's mad."

Observations and questions

1) Clines keeps returning to the device Christy uses to type. What would happen if we pulled all those references into one early paragraph of explanation, describing the whole apparatus and procedure only once?

2) This profile of a mute man confined to a wheelchair brims with motion and speech. Work your way through all the images and watch how Clines animates what could have been a static piece.

3) When Francis X. Clines, the wordsmith, profiles Christy Nolan, the wordsmith, the reader expects literary fireworks. Is Clines more poetic here than in his straight news pieces?

4) This piece has many potential endings inside it. Identify them and test each for effect. Remember that if you move a passage, you have to move what it replaces somewhere else, and you have to patch the hole it leaves.

5) This portrait of a hopelessly crippled writer could easily turn into a real "weeper." How does Clines prevent such sentimentality? What does he leave out?

6) Clines closes with Christy saying, "I had to tell God he's mad." How many meanings of that sentence can you think of, especially in that position?

Communion, tenpence,
and terror along the wall

MAY 27, 1988

BELFAST, Northern Ireland, May 22—The specter of the Shankill Butchers, an infamous sectarian murder gang that ravaged Roman Catholic ghettos a decade ago, is rising again on the pitiless streets of North Belfast, where fear and grief are running heavy from fresh homicide raids.

"I have 14 widows to see to," said Brian Feeney, the city councilman for the most embattled Catholic minority areas, speaking of a two-year toll of homicide by hit-and-run raiders from surrounding Protestant neighborhoods.

Four of the widows were created in the last 10 days, their husbands innocent of involvement in rival Catholic nationalist violence but shot down with the sudden, shocking randomness well-remembered as the special mark of the Shankill Butchers 10 years ago.

Twenty-six Catholics were killed in a four-year reign of terror before that North Belfast murder gang, named after its Shankill Road base, was brought to ground, pursued by both the police and the rival gunmen of the Irish Republican Army who say they are the Catholics' only reliable hope of defense.

A SUDDEN DRIVE OVER

As in the past, the new wave of killers suddenly drive over from neighboring Protestant ghettos to shoot a pedestrian or a casual Sunday pub drinker, then easily dart back behind 15-foot-high security walls that run through the yards and back alleys of abutting sectarian enclaves. The humble row houses and wary streets of North Belfast are a deadly turf, having suffered 500 killing victims in less than two decades.

The fear of the reincarnation of the Shankill Butchers is palpable here in precincts with the "for

sale" signs of a new generation of fleeing Catholics
and with the debris of nightly rock-and-bottle hurl-
ing contests across the city's ever-rising, ever-ex-
tending "environmental interfaces"—miles of high,
eerie security walls.

These walls range from corrugated metal sheets
that blow in the wind to high-tech bullet- and fire-
resistant ramparts that lend an Orwellian silhouette.

Councilman Feeney concedes violent groups in
both communities are the main beneficiaries as
these new barriers arise as the main visible change
during the last two years of the British-Irish agreement. This is the political pact directed at limiting
violence and encouraging moderation, a pact that
Protestant politicians have adamantly boycotted
while Protestant paramilitary groups have been reported stocking fresh arms. The IRA sees it as an
extension of the British presence in Ireland.

On Saturday afternoon, a marching band of
Protestant loyalists from the Tiger Bay ghetto
strode up to one of the walls of the Cliftonville
Catholic ghetto and played what are well-known as
"Thump the Pope" tunes in a provocative, drum-
beating tattoo directed at the new widows.

Outlawed Protestant paramilitary gangs have
been taking responsibility for some of the latest
Catholic killings in press announcements florid
with self-justification, insisting the raids are limited to IRA-related targets. But this is denied by the
police, who are under increasing pressure to either
track the killers or face fresh waves of vigilantism.

The stakes are high, with the Protestant-domi-
nated police force, the Royal Ulster Constabulary,
insisting anti-Catholic bias in the ranks is a thing of
the past. But the embattled Catholics are increasingly fearful in their own homes and streets.

"I'm not a fighting man, not a bit tough, but I'm
not leaving," said Bernard Murphy, a man in his
70s who is a legendary figure as the lone holdout
against a terror drive that reduced Roe Street to a
lunarscape of despair. Protestant gangs prevented
Catholics from ever occupying five refurbished

homes there. The street is bricked up but for No. 28, where the Murphy family has lived for 32 years including happier times when they had Protestant neighbors.

What rent control is to a Manhattan politician, a new wall is to Councilman Feeney. "Sure, I deliver," he says ambivalently of the barriers, checking the Murphys' lone fortress of a house where three fire bombs recently landed against the back windows, a hefty lob across the wall. The Murphys say they want no part of IRA defenders and so they pepper the police and council with alarms.

DEMONSTRATION OF THE MAJORITY

Protestant paramilitary gunmen style themselves as their community's defenders, akin to IRA claims of being strictly guerrilla fighters. Statistical studies show the IRA is more likely to target British soldiers and Northern Irish police, both on duty and at home, while the Protestant "paras" are likely to kill Catholic civilians randomly. Mr. Feeney notes there are retaliation killings of innocent Protestants, too, in a further muddying of the moralistic rhetoric.

Three of the latest Catholic victims were shot down in a pub, the Avenue Bar, when a Protestant coolly walked in and sprayed the place with a machine gun a week ago. The foray recalled the notorious era of the mid-1970s, when a score of Catholic pubs and a dozen Protestant pubs were attacked in a storm of vendetta.

Mr. Feeney is a 40-year-old Belfast-born schoolteacher who gets about $130 a month as a councilman and faults the nearby Irish middle class in particular for ignoring the ghetto problems. He admits he is in a difficult position, counseling fellow Catholics to hold out for moderation and shun violence even as the Protestant paras step up the killings of innocent citizens. The IRA has promised vengeance, but Mr. Feeney stresses how counterviolence made things worse during past terror.

"It only ups the ante," he said, finding respite in his widow-visiting this weekend by greeting neighborhood children in their pure white First Communion outfits and making each smile with the gift of a tenpence coin.

"It's the widows I never get used to," he said. "I've had so many. You visit them and you mouth the traditional things. 'Sorry for your troubles,' you do say that," he said, gazing along a quarter-mile of new wall that cuts this place clean as a cleaver.

Observations and questions

1) Clines leads like this: "The specter of the Shankill Butchers, an infamous sectarian murder gang that ravaged Roman Catholic ghettos a decade ago, is rising again on the pitiless streets of North Belfast, where fear and grief are running heavy from fresh homicide raids." What expectations would such a poetic lead raise in readers? If you write a first sentence that poetic, what will you do for a second sentence?

2) Examine each of Clines's verbs. Graphic power comes from action as well as from nouns and adjectives.

3) The author unifies this piece with walls and widows. Study how he weaves these two images around his meaning. What images might appropriately unify a city council or a school beat story?

4) "These walls range from corrugated metal sheets that blow in the wind to high-tech bullet- and fire-resistant ramparts that lend an Orwellian silhouette." What's "an Orwellian silhouette"? Does Clines expect his readers to have read George Orwell?

5) "Mr. Feeney notes there are retaliation killings of innocent Protestants, too, *in a further muddying of the moralistic rhetoric.*" Here Clines does not lean toward editorializing; he simply editorializes. He would call those phrases merely telling the facts. What do you think?

6) I expected this piece to end with a return to the Shankill Butchers. Cover up Clines's last paragraph and write a new one invoking Shankill. Which works better? Why?

A conversation with
Francis X. Clines

DON FRY: Who taught you how to tell stories?

FRANK CLINES: I don't think I learned it anywhere. It's just a certain way my mind works, just
my inclination to write that way. I read a lot when I
was a very young kid, things that were forbidden,
like Mickey Spillane. Those stories heightened
things. There was reality, and then there was a story about the reality. I've always liked that.

Who taught you how to report?

Oh, some of the *creme de* reporters and editors.
You know how valuable a good editor is, much
more valuable than a good reporter. I've had several good ones over the years. You deal with them,
and you learn implicitly how to behave in the story.
An editor has just retired that no one outside the
Times knew of, a man named Sheldon Binn. He
was on the city desk for all my years in the city,
and he was just a very smart, very gentle, very curious man. You would report to him at the end of
the day, and that really focused what we were doing every day. You had to tell him a story.

**Did you talk to Binn before you wrote the story,
or afterwards? And what kind of things did he
ask you?**

Before, and the most basic questions, nothing arcane. He would say to you, "And then Rockefeller
did what?" [Laughter] He would always stay on
the level that I like. And he'd laugh or not, and say,
"You know, that guy's unbelievable," just like in
the street. By the time you wrote the story, you
were reinforced in what was amusing or important.
He was always human.

Did he praise you when you did well?

Very little, but his praise was in his reaction. If you talked him the story and set it up right, then you heard him roar with laughter, and you knew you had him. Once in a while, a few times over 10, 15 years...

"A few times" he praised you over 15 years?

We just understood each other. It was shorthand, and it was a brotherly, father/son type of thing. Yeah, he praised me, but with him, you didn't need it. What you needed was his honest reaction to a story, and if you had Shelly, then you knew you were rolling.

Were any reporters models for you?

Not so I hounded them. Every day you have to read the paper, so there's this enormous tradition you can't avoid, and you read it on any number of levels. All that reading seeps in, and you learn an awful lot.

Did you imitate anyone?

Nowadays newspapers feature feature writing. But 20, 25 years ago, a lot of general assignment reporters were very fine feature writers, so you'd learn a bit from each of them. But the best, pound for pound on a given story, would be Homer Bigart....

The legendary Homer Bigart...

Talk about stories, he really believed in stories. He believed that what he was writing was in entity a story, and not an open-ended thing where you're just packing information in. You could feel the beginning and the end and everything else in the story, and he was very original in his vocabulary. I like reporters who as much as possible try to tell you what they saw, and Bigart had that gift.

All the war stories about Bigart turn on one thing: he wasn't afraid to ask stupid questions.

That's right. A lot of different guys I met in different places interested me and motivated me. For example, on the *Buffalo Evening News,* there was a political reporter named Jerry Allen, who covered the legislature. He was a wonderful reporter, who wrote always close to the edge, very dry, wonderful vocabulary, and loved to get things in the paper, as we say, to go beyond the paper's own style and taboos and sneak things in. And he was the best at it, and he was good company, and his curiosity was of the finest, and he also would ask anything at a press conference.

You're off to Moscow in three weeks. Was that your idea?

Yeah. One of the nice things and one of the necessities of our business is that you have to reinvent yourself every so often...

What do you mean by that?

You know, just get a fresh deck of cards. It's easy to just nail something down so it's a formula that works, and people are pleased enough, and then you just keep repeating it. So the trick is to try to keep moving, and when you sense yourself much too stagnant, push out a bit. I had done a lot of the stuff in New York that I might have wanted to do, so I just took it on the road, and they let me. The same urge came after I'd been in Washington awhile, and you'd be crazy not to go on the foreign staff if you can, and the time seemed right.

Did you originate your own stories in London?

Yeah, pretty much. There were so few breaking stories that you pretty much have to invent your own. I was the second guy in London. We had two, three guys in London.

In a bureau like that, do you divide it up by function or by regions?

Nah, it's very informal. I would have my little curiosities and just mention that I was working on them, if there was nothing more urgent from any of the other sections. All those sections are always demanding copy, so it's not like you're looking for work. You want to do mostly what you want to do, within what they need done. Also, you've got to have some balance.

Did you get edited by the bureau, or in New York?

I get edited in New York.

Isn't that hard, because you can't talk to the editors?

Nah, it's working out great, because the desk I work for now is very, very fine, and I had no trouble with copy editing through the foreign desk.

Did you get edited much at all?

Nah. I honestly can say I didn't get edited much at all, and I had a very happy relationship. Honestly.... You know, you're inviting me to bitch, but I don't have any open wound that I want to show you.

Actually, I'm not inviting you to bitch. I just want to make sure that the effects we talk about are yours and not the desk's.

Oh, yeah. Once in a while, something would get mauled, but that's...very minor. I never had what I would call a critical problem. They were always professionals. And usually if I liked the story, they would like the story.

Is Northern Ireland dangerous?

It's not as dangerous as it sounds. I didn't know

what to expect about danger, but I never found it at all dangerous. The police aren't that jumpy, but the soldiers are, because they get shot at from time to time. If they just wander the streets, they'll get picked off. Sometimes you turn down a block in your car in the midst of an evening of sporadic troubles, and you might just turn right into a patrol, and the guy lowers a rifle at you, and you make sure you don't do anything herky-jerky or anything, and you just show them your hands. But that's very rare, and I never felt the danger. I covered the '60s riots at the universities, the anti-war stuff. It was guys throwing rocks, cops rushing them with tear gas, that kind of thing, while you were off to one side watching. There's a lot of that in Belfast, and you just have to know where to stand.

Great stories....

It's a very readable story. That's a terrible thing to say. After you do it awhile, you get to dislike what a good story and what a compelling story it is, because you realize that people are living up to a very, very tragic stereotype. And there's no way most readers can avoid that story, even if they're sick of it. And, as a reporter, you realize it's predictable, it's cyclical, and terrible.

The Irish have grown up in a storytelling tradition that tells them what to do, and tragically makes them do it.

Yeah. And the people there are so open. They just let you into their lives, and they believe in words. Quotations you'll get from people in those situations are unbelievable, so I got to like the story on that level. I greatly admired the people. And it was good for me to realize how absolutely real and different they are from all the stereotypes in our country about the Irish, and how important that is, not just for them, but for all reporting.

Did your being Irish help?

It's one thing to be Irish; it's another thing to be Irish-American. It helps in small talk when they find out that you have some relatives from County Mayo, but that's minor. I'd heard a lot about Ireland, in very oblique and very erroneous ways over the years, but the reality is much different from what I expected.

What had you expected?

Well, I didn't know what to expect. All I knew was the centuries of trouble, to the point where, in some people's minds, it's almost traditional. But that isn't the case at all. All of the acts of violence are fresh, new, individual troubles that strike down real, new people. Attempting to view it just through a prism of tradition and stereotype and history is a problem in itself, and trying to apply pure history in a journalistic setting is very difficult. That's one of the things you have to learn while you're writing that story: you always have to have some context. You have to know how to handle history so that it doesn't dominate the story.

Indeed.

You also discover all the sorts of readers out there with various biases on this subject. You wind up having to rely on yourself, and taking their complaints with the compliments that will come from others. It is one of those situations where you're not so upset if you displease various types of people who have various views about it.

Let's talk about your first story. Were you in the graveyard?

Oh, sure. The funeral for these three IRA heroes, which is part of the ritual there, was an obvious funeral to cover. Right there at graveside, this guy shows up from the other side (there's more than one violent pathology there) and starts throwing grenades...

How far away?

I was right at the graveside, and his arm didn't quite reach graveside with the grenade, so maybe 75 feet...

To him, or to the grenade?

To the grenade.

Yike! What did you do?

Well, first of all, there's one small point here. One issue in all these IRA funerals is whether there'll be paramilitary flauntings, where the IRA puts on their berets. It's all melodramatic, and they shoot rifles into the air as volleys. So at first, I said, "Oh, someone has just taken out a rifle or two for the ceremony." [Laughter] And then I saw little blots of smoke in the air, and by then the third or fourth grenade was going off, and I said, "Uh-oh." And then some people were jumping behind tomb-stones, and then I saw a woman whose face was just bloody. So I knew there was some nitwit in the crowd.

Were you standing up all this time?

Oh, yeah. I was kinda watching from behind a tombstone. And I took some notes, and it was just a wild scene. Reporters always want to witness what they write, and when you do witness, then you know there's no way the story won't be inter-esting. I was wondering whether they had buried bombs and whether the graveside would be nasty. Then I saw the crowd was chasing this guy who did all this, and by standing on top of a tombstone, I could watch as he ran down the hill. He wheeled on them, shot a few of them dead, and they finally caught him out on this expressway, and the cops arrested him. Even then, after that, the funeral of the three IRA people resumed.

That's very striking in the story.

Oh, there's no way to make this stuff up. And the locus of funeral and death and requiem is endless there, and somehow there's always a new twist. You don't need to take many notes because you're seeing it, and it's rather easy. You just want to sit down and start writing. That's all you have to do.

How long did you stay there?

I stayed until practically everyone had left, and by then it had gone off into predictable fashion where some of the political types are denouncing and describing everything as a pure conspiracy. You can imagine how the people felt. They were paranoid by this point. "You can't even bury the dead," that kind of thing. Then I went over to one of the social clubs where that community can safely gather behind locked doors, and hung out there and had a beer or two, and talked to some people. There was a news conference of sorts, where the issue got even more heightened as to who did what and why, and who this guy was. The other side was trying to say, "He's just a pure nut job," which is almost amusing. When you have a history of that kind of pathology, to denounce the particularly superaberrant individual is really ingratitude, it seemed to me. I used up all of the day that I could, and finally went to a place where I stayed.

Frank, why didn't you rush out to file?

Let's see. What time would it be? I have a five-hour lead-time between here and New York, which is a wonderful thing overseas. It can work against you in other parts of the world, but in this case that was a luxury. So by 7:00 or 8:00 p.m. Belfast time, it's only 3:00 in the afternoon in New York, so I just had to get a summary in at a reasonable hour, and then I was free to keep reporting. And I wanted to find out how much there might be to the pedigree of this guy, who he was working for, and what the cops' explanation was for letting him get in.

So then you went back to your room to write. How did you put this piece together?

Everything grows out of the lead, and the only problem in this case was that so much happened. You want everything to be rooted there, and you want to leave yourself options to pop all over the place, just the way the story did. So naturally you have to get the number of people who were killed, but quickly get beyond that to this notion of people in a graveyard. Not a "cemetery"; I wanted "graveyard." You start picking words right away: "coming in" and "throwing grenades" and "people panicking." A lot happened here. And that's quite a circuit of emotion, I thought. So I got all that in the lead. And then once you have the lead to where you're satisfied, then it's making sure you hit enough of the different keys quickly enough.

Do you plan the parts out ahead, or do you just write them?

I just write them. I know, as I'm going along reporting, that this particular piece that I just saw will keep the story going.

So you picture the piece as you're reporting?

I picture the energy of it, because if something's difficult and you can't get at what you're going to write about, then you know there's a problem with energy in the story. If you witness it, there's no problem with energy. You just say, "I'm going to tell you what I saw." After all the stories you have to do, you're so grateful to have seen what you have to write about, and have something loaded with information, that narrative takes over. It's the difference between talking with someone who heard about something and someone who saw it. The guy who saw it is going to give you the pure stuff. You're not going to start rearranging his narrative, because he's the best witness.

How many people would you say you talked to?

First of all, I have the authority of being a witness, so actually you might talk less with people, because you've seen what you need to know.

Sure.

I talked with three or four people about what happened when they caught the guy down the hill. At the cemetery, I talked with maybe a dozen, someone who might have been wounded, someone who was next to someone who was killed, people like that. And you remind yourself, "Just pay attention and witness what's happening here." Every once in a while there's an original event on the theme of life and death, and my God, here was one.

Anyway, I would see bits and pieces of the story as I went along. I would put a quick note down and circle it or star it, knowing that's a sure thing. And when you have several of those, you have all of these renewed stories, so the energy never runs out.

Let's talk about the lead: "Three people were killed and dozens wounded today as an assailant threw grenades into a screaming crowd at a funeral and then fled across the graveyard from enraged mourners." Hard-news lead. Did you consider any other kind of lead?

No, not for my paper. I like my paper because they want something for the record, and they want more. In this case, it was all self-contained. When you have that kind of information, you would naturally point on to the next graph. I mean, grenades in a graveyard has a certain ring to me...

Yes, it does. [Laughter]

...and the idea that mourners screamed and then went into a rage, that's enough. You'd be a fool to try to get literary with a thing like that.

I like the bare literariness of your lead.

Yeah. You have to do less writing when you have all that information.

Look at the 19th paragraph, beginning: "Today, until the intruder appeared..." At that point, you retell the story from the beginning of the action.

That's right. I've done enough over the years to know that this happens naturally, but it's also a great device. Someone ought to teach it, I suppose.

We teach it. We call it the "champagne glass." You write an inverted pyramid on top, and then right in the middle, you retell the story from the beginning.

Sure, it's perfectly natural. If you talk again with the real people who were at a scene, they begin all over again, and they have to keep telling it. It's that compelling. The strategic reason is because you have more information to get in, and there is enough energy left in the story to retell it on a different level. So I just did that naturally. And it's a long story, longer than we're usually writing, so that naturally invites a retelling with other things in it, with more detail and more color.

Six paragraphs from the end, you say: "The gunman ran out from under his tweed cap as he fled out onto the motorway." How did you get that detail? Did you see it?

Yeah, oh sure. I don't know why I chose that construction, but you want to say what you saw. Every paragraph should have something like that in it, because you're in this invaluable situation where you're describing what you have seen.

You actually don't tell us very much: a gunman and a cap and two verbs and a place.

I love small sentences with just bing, bing, like

that. It's hard to premeditate them. But you're grateful when they come along.

"...when they come along"? They just happen, huh?

Yeah, sure.

I don't believe it. [Laughter]

Well, when you have a bag full of stuff to write about, you're naturally very tight in your writing, and it's fun. The sentences are coiled more, and simpler. And you're into good old Anglo-Saxon almost.

Listen to your ending, about the kids with Down's syndrome: "'Gentle prophets in a violent world,' Father Toner said, pointing to the youngsters. 'They testify to the infinite value of every human life,' he told the people shortly before they arose, walked outside, and headed with the three coffins toward Milltown Cemetery." Why did you pick that scene for the kicker?

I had gone to the funeral Masses, and the most interesting thing was the sight of these sweet kids with Down's syndrome. Of all the people you saw that day, they were the most unimpeachable. Everyone else has anger and misery and trouble, and it's just hard to deal with everyone. And you're sick of being the vulture reporter. I saw the Down's syndrome kids, and I thought, "Well, there's an honest news story here." So I had a different story, before the guy threw the grenades. I knew I would end that piece back at the funeral Mass, because that's when the more thoughtful things had been said. Then it struck me, then I remembered the Down's syndrome children, and I realized I must end with them.

During the reporting, had you thought of that as a possible ending?

No. I thought of that as a possible lead on the non-violent story, and then all the grenades started going off.

This ending gives an upbeat tone to a dreadful event.

Instead of ending with various leaders vowing this or demanding that, it's a decent, honorable way of withdrawing from the event, and not leaving the reader in typical politics. I was grateful when I recalled that as an ending. I knew that was the right ending as soon as it occurred to me. I went back through my pad and found that quote about "gentle prophets in a violent world."

Beautiful quote.

Oh, yeah. Boy.

The American reader might have trouble keeping all these characters and forces and names of organizations apart. Did you consider that?

You must keep the reader in mind, because all the reader knows is: "The Irish. The Irish. They're at it again." There are separate factions that you have to quickly identify in passing without stopping the story. There is a certain amount of history you have to just touch on as you go along, and a certain amount of honest grievance in various places. There's a certain position the minority there is in, that you have to allude to honestly.

Look at this example in the middle of the piece: "Protestant politicians also quickly pointed out after the cemetery attack that the IRA had exploded a bomb at the graveyard entrance to a Protestant funeral on March 13 last year. But Sinn Fein leaders insisted there was a qualitative difference because only police officers and no civilians were injured." The word "But" makes it work for the reader.

Yeah, that's right. I didn't realize that, thank you.

You're welcome. There's a kind of queer logic in there, but I guess it's a country full of queer logic.

You got it, and that's the value of that graph, to show the sort of pathology that's involved. It's not only real vendetta; it's rhetorical vendetta all the time. And you can ruin your story if you let those guys move in, the guys who are history tellers. But you have to let them in once in a while.

How do you keep from taking sides?

I don't think it's difficult at all. I mean...

That guy threw a grenade at you.

He didn't throw it at *me*. I was there. He threw a grenade. Most or all violent people are creatures unto themselves, and so there's no way I could take it personally. I might get afraid and duck, but I would never take it personally to the point where I wanted to get even with that guy. I looked at him as an aberrational human being, and I was, in a perverse way, pleased to be able to see that. And I view him as someone of value, because I finally could see what we're always writing about, violent individuals. So I'm not out to condemn him. All you have to do is describe the circumstances, and the reader will follow.

Reporter instinct, maybe.

Well, if you try to grind axes, you screw up good stories.

Were you tempted to put yourself in this story?

Nah. That's one thing I like about my paper: they frown on that, and so do I.

Let's go on to "In Belfast, death, too, is diminished by death." Great headline, by the way.

How did you find Kathleen Quinn?

I was just wandering around, looking at things, and waiting outside the church, and there was this cute little kid who chatted me up, Kathleen Quinn. And it reminded me of all sorts of things. She was very healthy about the event in a strange way, I thought. She was...you know...childlike. So I enjoyed talking with her, and I took some notes. You're always looking to see what else there is besides the event.

So she could have become the lead to the funeral story if the grenades hadn't been thrown.

Well, outside chance. No, I knew she wasn't. I knew the Down's syndrome kids would be the first lead. But you're always putting stuff away.

The next day, the Sunday "Week in Review" wanted a piece. I thought I'd begin with her because of her attitude, and because, frankly, I was sick of the whole requiem of everything. And she was a counterfigure in an innocent way, so I thought I'd just begin with her and see where it went.

I found this story much more poetic than the previous one.

Yes, and that's my point. I had a lot of disparate information, and it would take more writing to put it together as a single piece. So that's why the writing shows more.

This piece has a long lead: "Beyond the coffin, out in the churchyard, red-haired Kathleen Quinn was full of fun and flirting shamelessly for all her eight years of life. 'Mister, I'm to be on the TV tonight,' she told a stranger..." I assume that's you?

Right.

"...squinting up happy and prim. Kathleen had taken her brother's bike and skinned her knee bloody, all while people were praying goodbye

inside the church to another rebel body in another coffin.

"Soon the cameras were watching the coffin being carried out from the windowless fortress of a church, down the curl of the street in the simple hamlet, and on to the ever-filling graveyard patch devoted to republican rebels.

"As it turned out, the television ignored Kathleen and missed a classic Irish truth, a sight for sore eyes. She climbed back on the bike and headed off in a blur, oblivious of a piece of nearby graffiti that seemed about all of life's withering dangers: 'I wonder each night what the monster will do to me tomorrow.'"

Her skinning her knee and bleeding and the coffin, maybe those are different leads.

You're telling the reader that this is going to be a leisurely telling.

Oh, yeah. I wanted to try to give it a little bit of the flavor of the funeral beyond the usual, and cite her as an outlet for the natural anger you have at all the wasted life and all the terrible events.

A little later, you say: "The best hometown poets wisely retreat from Northern Ireland once their sense of mortality is honed to piercing, so this dark progression was left to be described in the prosaic catchall 'the troubles,' as if Job had called his plagues 'the unpleasantries.'" What a wonderful sentence, but very un-newspapery.

I'd done a magazine piece on a poet in Ireland named Seamus Heaney, who left the north and went south, and I thought of him. I am always annoyed at that phrase "the troubles," and I thought, "Here's my chance to puncture that stupid, overly poetic phrase a bit." I hate that...I hate...I've grown to hate, having worked there, the attempt to make something lyrical out of something terrible. I am very wary of a kind of schmoozy look at Ireland that some people have. This is real, fresh, warm blood in the streets each time it happens. It's not some "noble thing" or some "terrible beauty," as they say. So, in a thing like that, you've got to work over all of the usual references and not accept them.

Three paragraphs later, you say: "There is at least as much fighting over words and symbols as over flesh and earth. Most metaphysically absurd was the attempt..." Who's the reader for such a passage?

I'm pitching the American reader, who cannot fully understand Ireland. He gets a lot of rhetoric and propaganda launched at him about Ireland. And so I wanted to take that bit of undeniable fact, that situation, and push beyond it a little bit. In a way, I'm the reader, but I'm a reader who knows maybe a little bit more, and I just wanted to bring the other readers along to what I think I know, you know?

I know. I also know that your paper is a high-style paper, but this is very high-style writing, and that presupposes a high-style reader, doesn't it?

Yeah. The reader is what saves the paper. No one knows who the reader really is, but you dare not write down to the reader.

You tend to signal the reader when you're about to deliver something complicated, and then you explain it. A little further on, you say: "One point of rare agreement among nationalists, loyalists, and the British authorities is that atrocity tends to be layered like slag here, not woven linearly. So the latest sensational deaths at a funeral instantly diminish the importance of the preceding outrage." You give us the poetry, and then you explain it.

Well, that's very important, particularly to the Irish story. That's part of the syndrome, that one event tops another. I say: "...among nationalists, loyalists, and the British authorities..." There's three different pieces to this thing, dear reader, and keep that in mind. But then I get on to the point that I wanted to make: "You think this is terrible? Hang around."

This is a wonderful piece, a heart-rending piece.

Thank you. And it was perfectly natural to get back to Kathleen at the end.

We were all waiting for her.

So was I. It's only a question of how.

And then came "British soldiers killed at IRA rites."

The press hung around after the grenade thing for a day or two, and then we all went back to London. Early Saturday morning, I had just finished the Kathleen Quinn piece when the first bulletin came over on this story. So I grabbed a Tandy and all the agency copy off the wire. I raced out in a cab and got on the shuttle to Northern Ireland. I got into town very quickly, and there was still plenty of the story left to report. I was grateful to get over there to report it and to put an honest dateline on it, because the Sunday deadline in my paper is early, and I had no time to fool around.

I let the desk know it was coming, and I wrote a very brief summary on the way over, then filed that from a pay phone at the airport. I ran out to the scene, and did the reporting. I figured how much time I had to set aside for writing, an hour or so, and finally left the scene. I called the Royal Ulster Constabulary. It's quite like being a police reporter back home, and you ask the desk guy, "What else is new?" In this case, there was great controversy initially over who these two British soldiers were. They were in civilian clothes, and there was immediate suspicion that they were provocateurs. I don't think they were. I think they bungled into this thing, and behaved terribly. On the other hand, in England, this is an atrocity story. The British press wrote it as "Two of our own were dragged and stripped and executed by these Irish animals," that kind of thing. The IRA guys, who pulled them aside and took them down behind a fence and beat them, had time to consider. They treated it as a military action by the IRA, saying they were invaders. So there's a lot to get in that story in the way of sensitivities, of different perspectives.

That's what I like about it. I can sympathize with everybody in their logic and terminology.

Yeah, in events like this, you can. Indeed, this is an embattled minority and a historically mistreated minority. There's no denying that. And you just say it. You don't have to say, "There are those who think...," that kind of nonsense.

Let's look at the lead: "There was more macabre violence at an Irish Republican Army funeral today as two armed British soldiers in civilian clothes drove their car into a crowd of panicked mourners and were seized, beaten, and finally shot to death." Traditional hard lead.

Yeah, and word for word the way I wrote it. I was very worried about that. I wanted to use the words "macabre" and "finally." That word "finally" was important to me, to imply that the people who shot them had time to think about it. And I was surprised that you could coil all that into a sentence now and not look too foolish.

Well, it worked. Let's talk about "macabre." Why did you want to get that word in there?

It was just the requiem nature of things. This was what people were discussing: death upon death, death in death, that sort of thing, macabre. And you come to this second event and a new twist on that same situation, and it cried out for "macabre." How many ways can requiem include innovation?

"Macabre," of course, skates towards editorializing.

Yep, yep, yep.

Did you think about that?

Not at all. [Laughter] I'm not commenting. Am I blaming someone? Nonsense. Here are two funereal situations where the events had actually darkened, which is a hard thing to do there. And even if it is a comment on a certain way things occur in this place, it's undeniable. So anyone who wants to quarrel with that would truly be quarreling with reality.

It ain't opinion; it's just fact, right?

Well, no, it's both. It's easier to defend your opinion when it also happens to be a fact. It needed an adjective that commented on the week. That's why I did it.

One of the things that interested me about this piece is that, although a lot of people were involved in the action, there aren't a lot of people in the story. You select your characters rigorously.

Absolutely, and it's a simple matter of space. If you're not careful, you can let too many people into the story, who will more or less make the same point, and eat up the story, so that you haven't told the story. It is, after all, a story first, and not a catalog of comments. I have to rerun that every time: don't let a crowd into the story. I always feel guilty when I interview a lot of people and then don't use many of them. But you're interviewing them for your telling of the story and not for their telling of the story, unless they were in some unique position.

"It is, after all, a story first, and not a catalog of comments." We ought to print that on the cover of every reporter's notebook. Well, for a change of pace, let's look at "A portrait of the artist as a young man of letters."

That's precisely what I did. Almost two years earlier, I had put aside a note on him, and I regretted that I didn't get to him earlier. When you cover Ireland, you're absolutely obliged to tell more than "the troubles."

How much time did you spend with him?

Whatever he could afford, a couple of hours. I had read a lot of his stuff beforehand, and I'd talked to his mother and his sister, and I knew that just going there and seeing him was the story. So that's what I did.

Well, you let me see him. Listen to this: "He punctuates this with a clear and certain sound of exclamation, a sudden crackle of joy, as, with the sentences pecked into being on paper, a reader enjoys them. Christy is leaning in his wheelchair, emanating a certain contagious spirit of relaxation in his own wayward posture. His power to listen is palpable, his ear a funnel to the universe in the way his father, Joe, first dandled him as a baby and gave him endless stories, poems, jokes, songs, and monologues that fixed Christy onto spoken words that are the heart of storytelling." Beautiful paragraph.

Somebody did a story on him once and described, in foolishly realistic terms, the way he looks. His mother told me how Christy was hurt by that, that the reporter couldn't see what else is there. I thought it would be good when he read my story to see that graph, as a payback, that the press doesn't always have to be an annoyance. So it was a pleasure to take care of that.

You don't tell us very much, and yet I can see him very graphically. Look at this paragraph about his mother: "In his biography, Christy recalled that she put him down in his chair and bluntly said: 'I never prayed for you to be born crippled. I wanted you to be full of life, able to run and jump and talk.' And she told him: 'But you are you.' And: 'You can see, you can hear, you can think, you can understand everything you hear.' And: 'We love you just as you are.'" A lot of journalists worry about writing a paragraph like that, because they fear being thought sentimental.

Yeah, well, that's always a risk. But here, there's no denying the reality of his predicament and the incredible nature of his recovery with the help of this woman. So I'd be at fault if I didn't deal with them the way they deal with themselves. This guy was entitled to live in self-pity, and that would have been a moral enough life under the circumstances. But he happened to have his mother, who wouldn't accept it. She's a very interesting woman, because she does know how responsibility and love work together. So it's very naked, the way they talk about it, but because of the situation, you have to just quote them.

Right, and just let cynics think what they please. Finally, Frank, a general question. You keep telling me that you write "naturally." What does "naturally" mean?

You read, and you know what you like when you read, and that rubs off. It's give and take, and you're always self-adjusting. It's a learning process, but it's self-taught. I don't think someone can take you aside and teach you things. He can show you an awful lot of your errors, or how to keep stories tighter, but...

I can, because I'm an analytical type. Let me try a different tack. Do you revise much?

Yeah. I do a lot of revising. I cut a lot of words, and I tighten phrases, a lot of small stuff that's important to me, that takes out sprawling writing. But I do it quickly as I go along. I don't write once and then go back over it and over it again and again. I just know that there's something in a graph I don't like, and I'll get back to it in a minute. I'll look at it and say, "Yeah, well, I shouldn't have done all of that." I can take out this and that, and still save the one word that makes it okay. I do it quickly though.

My version of your notion of writing "naturally" happens when I'm revising. I sometimes say, "This doesn't sound like me." I revise it until it sounds like me, but I'm not sure I could tell you what "sounds like me" means.

Yeah, and you're always imagining whether you're getting in the way of the reader or not. So you picture yourself staying out of the reader's way, but also conveying what you thought was the most interesting thing, particularly the most interesting feeling. You know when you have an honest reaction. That's important to get into the story, so the trick is to find an oblique way of doing it. That, to me, is as important as some guy's name. And that's the fun of it. That's the human part of it. That's the thing that makes it a story. It's one human being saying, "Look at this." And that way you're talking as an individual to another individual.

Good.

Good.

David Jay Remnick
Deadline Writing

DAVID JAY REMNICK grew up in Hillsdale,
New Jersey, and graduated from Princeton University in 1981 with a major in comparative literature.
He had the great fortune there to study with John
McPhee. He taught English at Sofia University in
Tokyo for half a year. In the summer of 1982, he
interned in the Style section of *The Washington
Post,* which he considers "the greatest job in
journalism." He moved through night cops and
sports and the magazine before becoming a Moscow correspondent.

In Spitak, survivors comb ruins of devastated town

DECEMBER 15, 1988

SPITAK, U.S.S.R., Dec. 14—In Spitak, the living are searching for the dead.

One young man in his 20s walked up and down the rows of coffins today, opening their lids, looking for his brother. Finally, he found what he did not want to see, and at the sight of his brother, he climbed into the coffin with him, ready to join the dead.

Nothing prepares you for Spitak. Nothing prepares you for a small town stadium filled with coffins and bodies left out in the cold. A town of 20,000, surrounded by the Armenian Caucasus Mountains, Spitak was a beautiful place to live a week ago, people here say. But then the earth moved beneath it, and in minutes Spitak was destroyed. At least half its people are dead. Eight kindergartens, eight schools, factories for soap, sugar, and elevators—all of them are rubble.

On every street, the curbs are lined with coffins and the detritus of ordinary life: a stack of Armenian novels, a pile of cabbages, a boot, a half-eaten loaf of bread, a torn reproduction of a portrait. And everywhere the smell is of smoke and snow and the dead, rotting in their makeshift coffins of rough pine.

"In this town, it used to be that when one person died, we all cried," said Artavad Kogosyan, a sugar worker who was still looking for his daughter today. "But now only a few can cry. We have no more tears left."

Those who survived and spend their days turning over slabs of concrete in hopes of a miracle are slowly giving up. A woman named Annichka Karapityan stood high on a heap of rubble, her home, and flipped through pictures of her family, close-ups of her daughter, a family outing in the mountains.

"It all happened in an instant," she said. "A noise,

a terrible swaying, and then there was no one."

All she salvaged from the debris were her pictures and, strangely, a pair of high-heeled shoes, a kind of memorial of long-past family events. "I have to leave this place," she said. "There is no life here anymore."

The Soviet army troops that are organizing the relief effort in Spitak have ordered foreign rescue workers and the townspeople to begin leaving. Starting Thursday, the army will commence exploding mines under the countless ruined buildings, the hulks that lean at grotesque angles.

"We are being asked politely to stop working and leave," said Norman Roundell, a British fire inspector. "I must say I think it's premature. The woman that was found alive today will live. It's only one, but still I'd like to stay. Of course, we are not giving the orders."

Other rescue workers, from Italy and the Netherlands, agreed that it was too soon to leave and destroy the town, but they also said that after a week, it is a "miracle" to find anyone alive under the rubble.

"The organization here is just total chaos," said Paul Newton, a British welder who volunteered to help in the rescue mission. "There are lots of bulldozers, but no one knows what to do with them. You know, I've been working here for six months on a British project and I've found one thing: that these are the most lovable people that you could find anywhere. They would give you their last ruble if you asked them. But there's no order here, and I think that is killing them. It has gotten till it is almost too late to do any good."

On Tuesday, rescue workers discovered 10 people still alive in the debris, including an 8-month-old baby who was found in a pocket of the ruins sucking on her pacifier. One rescue worker, a nursing mother, immediately put the child to her breast. The baby is expected to live.

But generally the Armenian earthquake—which struck Dec. 7, killing at least 55,000 people and ruining much larger cities—was unforgiving and surgically quick in Spitak. Everyone in Spitak describes the same feeling, a tremendous shock "like a bomb," the eerie feel of rocking, and then collapse. One woman said she thought fast enough to grab her child by the hair and yank her through a doorway and into the street. But few could think so clearly or act so quickly.

Today a young woman named Larissa Margachyan and her father sat around a log fire on children's stools near the ruins of a kindergarten. Larissa had lost her 7-year-old daughter somewhere under the concrete just 10 feet away. For days, she has not left that spot, sitting and sleeping in a long vigil in the snow and the fog.

She had been working her day shift at the elevator factory when the earth began to shake. Somehow she managed to run out the door and into the street, heading for her daughter's school.

"I was too late and what am I supposed to think now?" she said, weeping and directing her question to the sky. "I must go, I must leave Spitak. There is no town here anymore. Everything is gone. My whole life. The school is nothing more than a grave. For nights, we have just slept by this fire, out in the open air, but we are leaving soon. I am afraid just to stand here on this ground. At any minute, I expect the earth to start shaking again."

Nothing prepares you for Spitak. Nothing prepares you for a playing field turned into a morgue, the dead stacked on row after row of bleacher seats.

"This was the center of everything good and enjoyable for us," said one boy who survived only because he was running an errand outside for his mother when the quake came.

Outside a Red Cross tent, 30 bodies—crushed and bloated and growing purple and black—lay on stretchers. They must wait for hours here. Someone from the town's Communist Party committee must register them, give the bodies names before they are put in coffins and prepared for burial in a field behind the stadium.

No one covers their faces. And the dead stare

into a bleak winter light.

Two soldiers from Krasnodar sit near the bodies at a fire, warming their feet and drinking mineral water from blue bottles. There is something painfully slow about the way the work is progressing here. Dozens of army officers give orders. Many more soldiers sit by their fires "keeping order." It seems only a few people are really working with much purpose anymore.

On the heaps of rubble and in the half-toppled apartment houses, men and women search numbly for all they can find of their old material lives. One boy who lost his parents in the quake gathered his father's collection of history books. "He had 3,000 books, he was like a scholar."

An old woman, wrapped in an army blanket, looks for shoes. Others just stand in the stones, as if they were guarding their family graves.

"This is what the end of the world must look like," said one factory worker. The gathering places of Spitak—the post office, the schools, even the local party committee—are all turned to nothing by a single moment of geology.

The front wall of the sugar factory still stands, but its long red-and-white propaganda sign—"Our great *perestroika* is the new beginning"—is shattered and slowly falling off the facade in hunks.

Of all the places leveled by the quake, there is something unique about Spitak, about the completeness of the damage and the loss here. "So few are left," one old woman said, "and a lot of us who made it now cannot stand to be alive."

All of Armenia is mourning this town and those like it. Along the three-hour drive from Yerevan to Spitak, hundreds of people have hung red-and-blue Armenian flags from their apartment balconies, careful to tie strips of black crepe to the poles.

Despite all the coverage on Soviet television and newspapers, the horror of Spitak is unimaginable until the town itself comes into view. Even on a gloomy day, when relief helicopters cannot fly for fear of crashing into the mountains, the road is a wonder, running through a spectacular mountain pass with sharp switchbacks down into the valley. There is hardly any sign of Spitak's tragedy on the road, no preparation. Just a few miles before Spitak, shepherds are herding their goats through small towns that seemed safe, quiet, and fine.

But then the signals of disaster begin. First an ambulance marked "for pregnant woman and birthing mothers," then a series of cranes used to hoist the debris, then a few concrete garages collapsed like abandoned accordions. And finally sirens and heavy traffic, and in the distance a smell, an awful yellow burning in the lungs—Spitak.

The wreckage here makes everything else in this country—all the "unprecedented" party conferences and "monumental" Supreme Soviet sessions—seem small. Mikhail Gorbachev is a superstar around the world and in most parts of the Soviet Union, yet when he came here the other day to survey the damage and console the people, the townspeople just stared at him, like family members turning in their pews trying to figure out this curious guest at the funeral.

"I saw Mikhail Sergeievich [Gorbachev] in our streets, but in Spitak he is just another man," said Oshot Avakimanyan.

In Spitak, Gorbachev promised that the town would be rebuilt in two years. It is almost impossible to believe. When the ancient capital of Armenia was destroyed by an earthquake more than 1,000 years ago, Armenians let it rest as a kind of grave and moved on, eventually, to Yerevan.

But there are some here who vow they will come back.

Siromark Grigoryan, a worker in the local soap factory, stood on a high hump of concrete and ripped mattresses. Her face, so grim and clenched, was more determined than grieved. "Somewhere under these rocks is my son, my 10-year-old boy," she said. "How can I just leave him here? We will build this place again, and my family will live here forever."

Observations and questions

1) Remnick leads with this anecdote: "In Spitak, the living are searching for the dead.

"One young man in his 20s walked up and down the rows of coffins today, opening their lids, looking for his brother. Finally, he found what he did not want to see, and at the sight of his brother, he climbed into the coffin with him, ready to join the dead." Look at each anecdote in this piece and assess its potential as a lead.

2) The third and 18th paragraphs begin, "Nothing prepares you for Spitak." Notice how this statement draws readers into the description, puts them there at the scene. What would Remnick gain and lose by presenting this material in the first person?

3) The author had to deal with a certain amount of gory description, such as: "Outside a Red Cross tent, 30 bodies—crushed and bloated and growing purple and black—lay on stretchers." How can we judge how much gore our readers can take? How can we suggest gore without getting too graphic?

4) The author uses similes (comparisons introduced by "like") to describe the scene, for example, "a few concrete garages collapsed like abandoned accordions." Are similes decorative, or a way to describe the indescribable? How can we use them in daily news without seeming arty?

5) Remnick keeps repeating the name "Spitak" until it almost becomes a refrain. How could he avoid that repetition? What effects does he achieve with it?

6) This piece has half a dozen potential endings, not counting what Remnick left in the notebook. Consider each as a possible kicker. If you chose any one of them, where would you move Remnick's ending, Siromark Grigoryan's wonderful quotation?

Residents, relief workers abandoning Armenian city

DECEMBER 16, 1988

LENINAKAN, U.S.S.R., Dec. 15—The exodus has begun. Every day 7,000 or 8,000 people leave Leninakan by truck, bus, or on foot. In the center of town, cars with loudspeakers mounted on them call out all night for women and children to evacuate the city.

As the people swarm out of their ruined city in the aftermath of one of the century's worst earthquakes, foreign and Soviet workers are still searching through the wreckage of Leninakan, a city in the Armenian Caucasus that a week ago had a population of 290,000. Tens of thousands are believed dead here, and many have not been found.

While the town of Spitak is one endless pile of rubble, the much larger city of Leninakan is haunting in its own way. On the outskirts, buildings still stand, seemingly undamaged, and on some—a school and a local party Presidium—just one wall has collapsed to reveal the blackboard and official desks of an earlier life. The local statue of Lenin survived unscathed.

The human desperation here is beyond exaggeration. Today, a 46-year-old man who lost his entire family in the quake got up from his hospital bed, grabbed a knife, and stabbed himself to death.

The streets are slurries of mud and slime from an exploded sewerage system. People stand in long lines for a supper of soup and rice, Armenian bread, and, if they are lucky, a shred of beef. Some cannot bear to leave their homes, and risk their lives sleeping in the unstable hulks of their highrises. Others sleep next to fires built from scrap wood or old tires. Some have even thrown wet mattresses on the floor of the KGB building, making that their home. For the first time, local residents are discovering that KGB headquarters featured a grand piano in the hall.

No one knows the precise death toll in Lenin-akan or in Armenia as a whole from the quake that struck eight days ago. Moscow officials, such as Health Minister Yevgeny Chazov, have put the count at between 50,000 and 70,000, but some for-eign rescue workers here say it is much higher.

French rescue specialist Pierre Schaffer said he thought more than 100,000 could be dead in Leninakan alone and tens of thousands elsewhere. Soviet officials said that 32 villages have "com-pletely disappeared." Other small towns are badly damaged and are getting even less help than the people in Leninakan and other cities. The other night the news program *Vremya* showed a woman in one town telling Prime Minister Nikolai Ryzh-kov that "every child, everyone has been killed."

Karen Vanyan, a senior official of the Armenian Construction Ministry, said that in addition to the people leaving Leninakan on their own, nearly 13,000 have temporarily been evacuated by the government to rest homes and hospitals in other re-publics. "We have months of work ahead of us," she said. "We must knock down the whole center of town."

There are teams here sifting through the rubble from France, Austria, Israel, Britain, and many ar-eas of the United States, including Fairfax County.

The Americans are using an office in the local KGB headquarters as a command post. "Check out that alarm system," one worker from Pennsylvania said. "That's what tipped us off that it was KGB."

Today a team from Juneau, Alaska, known as the Sea Dogs, showed up with a golden retriever named Taco and a German shepherd named Cap-tain. They are specially trained sniffer dogs that dig furiously at the first scent of a body under the de-bris. Last week, workers with such dogs were get-ting calls from around the city for help.

"Usually we got reports of voices from one of the locals. The first few times we jumped right out there. But then it turns out it is not a moan but the building shifting," said Bruce Barton, a relief work-er for the Agency for International Development's

Office of U.S. Foreign Disaster Assistance.

After eight days, the dogs are finding only corpses and, more often, nothing at all. "Our dogs are totally out of it," Barton said. "They are physically exhausted and the smells are getting worse."

Slowly, the foreign rescue teams are giving up on Leninakan. So much time has gone by that they have gone from being rescue workers to undertakers. The bodies have been under the rubble for so long that they often only come out in parts. "It breaks your heart in half," said Pat Stenton, a self-described "tunnel rat" from England.

[In Moscow, the AID office's director, Julia V. Taft, told reporters that most of its 45 rescue workers would return to the United States on Friday, Reuters reported.]

This afternoon, Stenton and rescue workers from Vienna, Seattle, and Juneau stood atop a mass of concrete and beams that had once been a five-story apartment building on Leninakan's Gorki Street. Television camera crews hoped desperately for a "live find."

"I can't sell rubble on the air anymore," one TV correspondent said. Dozens of reporters and 200 residents stood in a circle around the rescue workers as they chipped away at the building.

"These buildings are terrible," said Dennis Andrews, a rescue worker from Kent, England. "The makeup of the concrete is extremely weak. On some buildings like this one, you can pick up the concrete and it just crumbles in your hand."

In warmer climates, rescue workers say they "think in terms of 14 days," but there was not much hope that more survivors would be found on Gorki Street, where temperatures have been well below zero at night.

"There have been reports that there was a child alive under here," Stenton said. "Sometimes the reports are real, but by now most of them are just imagination playing tricks."

The workers thought that the hollows in some parts of the wreckage indicated that the first-floor walls had held up and that there still might be someone down inside. After tearing away at some of the concrete and the rusty wiring, the Juneau Sea Dogs let loose Captain and Taco.

"Come on, Taco, search!" one worker said as the Armenians looked on with expressions of hope. Everyone was waiting for the dogs to begin digging after a scent.

But there was nothing. This time the workers dug into a hollow that turned out to be a kitchen. They handed up huge unbroken jars of plums and pickles. A few of the Armenians began to leave. One man, however, stood on the rubble, his gaze fixed on a small snapshot of his 24-year-old daughter. "She lived in this building," he said. "I don't know where she is."

A crane drove up and started lifting concrete, sometimes revealing a stack of books or a frying pan. Another hollow was discovered and again the dogs sniffed out the debris, and found nothing.

Suddenly, across the street, a Soviet team using shovels, picks, and crowbars found the corpse of a woman in a local administration building where residents used to pay their gas and electric bills. One man explained that the woman's mother and daughter had been crushed in a car as they waited outside. There was something about it all, the plainness of the scene transformed by a shift of the earth to tragedy, that made Leninakan seem like a new Pompeii.

The crew gently placed the woman into one of the hundreds of coffins that line the streets. They covered her with a pale yellow shroud and loaded her onto a dump truck.

"I think everyone has just about had it," Barton said. "We are getting out of here tomorrow. I don't care if it is Aeroflot or Air France, so long as it is a plane."

Observations and questions

1) Remnick leads with people leaving Leninakan: "The exodus has begun." But the piece mostly describes rescue efforts. Rewrite the lead to make it fit better. Now reconsider whether Remnick's original images might work better. Why?

2) Journalism depends on the specific. Yet officials knew very little for certain in this disaster, forcing the author to use vague numbers like this: *"Tens of thousands* are believed dead here, and *many* have not been found."* Study the piece to see how Remnick plays the known against guesswork.

3) Remnick plays with the readers' emotions by listing everyday objects found: a blackboard, desks, pickles, etc. Why do such homely objects affect readers so powerfully?

4) Journalistic wisdom says, "Get the brand of the beer, the color of the car, and the name of the dog." So Remnick tells us: "Today a team from Juneau, Alaska, known as the Sea Dogs, showed up with a golden retriever named Taco and a German shepherd named Captain." Why should we name dogs? Why not just say "two dogs"? Or "a golden retriever and a German shepherd"?

5) "This afternoon, Stenton and rescue workers from Vienna, Seattle, and Juneau stood atop a mass of concrete and beams that had once been a five-story apartment building on Leninakan's Gorky Street. Television camera crews hoped desperately for a 'live find.' 'I can't sell rubble on the air anymore,' one TV correspondent said." Is this ironic passage appropriate in a tragic story?

Soviet pain exposed in 'landscape of nightmares'

NALBAND, U.S.S.R.—Amayak Ogosyan was in the fields tending his sheep and cows when he felt the earth slide under his feet. In a matter of three minutes, the roof of his house caved in, killing his wife. The local school collapsed, killing his son and daughter.

And suddenly, Nalband, a village of a few thousand livestock farmers, was a ruin, a grave.

In the cold mountain night, Ogosyan stands near the demolished school and says that of the more than 500 children and teachers there, "only 20 or 25, no more, survived. I think they were all in the eighth grade."

In the dark, the wreckage here is haunted, the jagged, shadowy landscape of nightmares. The only light is from a scrap of moon and the campfires of the homeless.

Government officials, foreign rescue workers, and Armenians themselves have expressed anger and dismay at the Soviet response to the earthquake. In the city of Leninakan and the town of Spitak, foreign relief teams appear to be the only people working with any organization, and now many are leaving. In villages such as Nalband, there was almost no aid at all.

"We did get a few tents," Ogosyan said. "But they are thin. We are freezing here." In the village of Dzhadzu, townspeople had to beg government officials for bread and coffins.

In the face of these scenes of misery in Armenia —soldiers forcing generations of Armenians to leave their ruined homes, coffins stacked up on bleacher seats, people stunned with grief sifting through the rubble for a pair of shoes, a carpet, a photograph of the dead—it is almost disrespectful to think in political terms. And yet the tragedy is likely to be one of the signal events of President

Mikhail Gorbachev's historic attempt to transform the Soviet Union.

The earthquake here on Dec. 7—which may have killed as many as 100,000 people and left at least 500,000 homeless—and the nation's relief effort present visitors with a horrifying example of many of the Soviet Union's profound economic and political problems—disorganization, nationalist tensions, an infrastructure so decrepit it can hardly respond to everyday needs, much less catastrophe.

Almost nothing about the quake has been hidden from view. Compared to Chernobyl, a nuclear plant disaster two years ago that was nearly sealed off from the Soviet and foreign press, the authorities have opened themselves up to unprecedented scrutiny and criticism. Perhaps more than any other event here since the siege of Leningrad during World War II, the Armenian earthquake has shown the world the Soviet Union at its most vulnerable and painful moment.

In a country that has long been known for its xenophobia, it is stunning to read Soviet commentators praising foreign building construction, relief teams, and seismographers, and then criticizing their Soviet equivalents.

"Everyone knows that if an earthquake like this had happened in San Francisco, there might be 10,000 dead, at the most, not 100,000," a doctor in Yerevan, the Armenian capital, said.

On Soviet television a few days ago, Prime Minister Nikolai Ryzhkov, who is heading the Politburo commission on the earthquake, berated a Foreign Ministry representative for failing to provide the foreign rescue workers with translators. Mixed with their unguarded sadness, Soviet leaders seem profoundly embarrassed about their helplessness amid the chaos.

"Why do you sit back there in Moscow? Instead of holding briefings there, you should have come here!" Ryzhkov said, as he railed at the ministry official. "Some of the foreign groups are leaving now with heavy hearts, and not because of what they have seen, but because of the treatment they got here."

RESCUE

In four days of touring the disaster sites in northwestern Armenia as well as a hospital and refugee center in Yerevan, it is clear that Soviet workers could do precious little to organize the relief effort or supply adequate machinery and competent manpower. The spectacle did little to confirm U.S. intelligence reports that the Soviet Union is prepared to handle serious civil emergencies.

In Spitak and Leninakan, the streets are lined with tanks and soldiers holding machine guns, as if the army is here to ward off a foreign attacker. Ill-equipped and shattered by what has happened, the best that most local residents can do is lift one stone after another with their bare hands.

From the start, the Soviet government knew that physical circumstances—the magnitude of the quake and its distance from major cities, like Moscow or Leningrad—combined with the country's lack of expertise and technology demanded foreign aid.

This is the first time in decades that the Soviet Union has even permitted many Western countries, including the United States, to provide disaster relief. Deputy Foreign Minister Valentin Nikiforov said that Moscow has received more than $100 million in emergency aid. To get the aid it needed, the government appeared to understand the value of foreign press coverage. There would be no secrets this time.

The Soviet press coverage has been so open, so unforgiving, that it has even reported on the savage side of such a tragedy, including articles on widespread looting in Leninakan and a thief stealing jewelry off the wrists and fingers of corpses. Another article said that some Soviet crane operators in the city refused to hoist rubble before extorting money from people whose relatives were dead or trapped inside the building.

Last night on the evening television news, a

police officer stood by his desk and described how the young, bearded man sitting beside him had tried to steal a sack filled with cash from a local bank. Then the camera cut to Armenians on the streets of Yerevan berating the thieves.

"They are worse than enemies," one man said. "They should get no trial. They should be shot."

At first, Moscow-based foreign correspondents relied on television reports, press briefings in Moscow, and articles in the Soviet press for information. Then the government simply turned a blind eye, letting reporters buy tickets to Yerevan at Moscow's Vnukovo airport and move freely around Armenia, hiring cars or hitching rides from trucks.

Asked last Tuesday if reporters could just "show up" in Armenia, Foreign Ministry spokesman Gennadi Gerasimov said simply: "I am closing my eyes." This has not happened in this country in decades. Ordinarily, even simple trips to Leningrad take at least two days to arrange, and no deviations from the schedule are permitted.

What reporters are discovering here is both an almost indescribable human tragedy and the sad spectacle of an earnest but clogged relief effort. The publicity abroad may help finance work by the Red Cross and dozens of other groups, but the portrait of the Soviet organization has been devastating.

There is bravery and honest work being done here, to be sure, but there is also a feeling of futility caused by traffic jams, inexplicable delays, and even the specter of a bureaucrat unwilling to deliver bread to a village because there was no official there alive or healthy enough to sign for it.

In Leninakan, a British fire worker who spent four days battling both the disaster and Soviet bureaucracy described—more out of sympathy than anger—how valuable time was diverted from real rescue work to negotiate with officials and fill out forms for visas, transport, and diesel fuel.

"We had to negotiate just to get our satellite communications equipment in here," said Pete

Wilson of Kent, England. For a few days, they hid
their satellite dish, which they used to communicate with England, behind a stack of cardboard
boxes.

"We were worried they might find out and call
us spies," he said. "That's when I decided we needed to negotiate out in the open."

"'It is not possible, it is not possible.' That's
what [the Soviets] were always telling us," said another member of the British team, Jeff Rook, as he
described his crew's Byzantine attempts to buy a
few cases of mineral water. "It's pathetic."

In Spitak, the local military and Communist Party
officials were ready to give up on the rescue attempts last Tuesday when British and Italian workers convinced them to hold off from spreading lime
over the ruins and bulldozing them for at least another week.

A number of survivors were found a few days
later, and officials said yesterday—10 days after
the earthquake—that a 62-year-old woman had
been pulled alive from a collapsed building in
Leninakan by Czechoslovak rescuers. Still, many
foreign rescue teams are pulling out, convinced
that time and cold have probably killed almost everyone who survived the quake.

"We still get 'live' reports from locals, but, of
course, there's no one there," Wilson said. "By
now, it's mainly just a cry for help." Pierre Schaffer, who headed a French rescue team in Leninakan, said before pulling his workers out of the
city, "They're all dead now and rotting. Now if
you pull them out, it's in parts—an arm, a head...."

Rescue workers are mentally fatigued by a week
of round-the-clock, sickening work. The air is a
thick mist of concrete dust, sweat, and the smell of
tens of thousands of corpses waiting for burial.

"I nearly cracked up," said Terry Wiffen, a
British welder, who left a job near Yerevan to volunteer in Spitak. "I've never seen so many coffins
in my life."

Although thousands of people are pouring out of
the devastated areas every day, the Soviet troops in

Spitak and Leninakan who appear to spend most of their time checking documents and "keeping order" are gearing up to fend off attempts by local residents to stay. Stunned by grief, many seem determined not to move to hospitals, rest homes, or refugee centers in Yerevan and in other republics. Ryzhkov said that some of the work in Spitak is going slowly because some survivors were sitting in front of bulldozers, refusing to move before their relatives were found in the wreckage.

Sitting on a slab of concrete that had been his kitchen wall in Spitak, a factory worker named Suren Mikoyan said: "We won't go anywhere. We'll find food. We'll kill livestock. We won't leave our home."

"Where should we go?" asked Mikoyan's father, Karlen, his eyes filling with tears. "I have no money, no food. I'm just going to live here, in this broken-down bus."

All around the Mikoyans were mountains of concrete, and underneath, the rest of the family—children, wives, aunts, uncles. Foreign rescue workers estimate that as few as 6 percent of Spitak's 20,000 residents survived. Officials said they will bulldoze Spitak this week.

POLITICS

The earthquake has also focused attention on what is perhaps Mikhail Gorbachev's most troubled national relationship, one that is likely to plague him for a long time to come.

Immediately after he was told in New York about the magnitude of the earthquake 11 days ago, Gorbachev cut short his U.S. visit and flew via Moscow to Yerevan, Leninakan, and Spitak, where Soviet television broadcast his solemn condolences, his praise of "heroic" rescue workers, and his vow to rebuild northwestern Armenia within two years.

But then, the interview took a strange turn that still stings here in Armenia. Suddenly, the interviewer brought up the ethnic battles between Armenians and Azerbaijanis that have been raging since last February. The feud centers around Armenian claims to Nagorno-Karabakh, the predominantly Armenian conclave within the neighboring republic of Azerbaijan.

To many Armenians here, the question was a setup, a chance for Gorbachev to use the emotion of the tragedy to isolate and denounce the Karabakh Committee, which has been organizing demonstrations in Yerevan for months.

In a tirade, Gorbachev said "the grass roots" in Armenia supported his decision to send some aid to Nagorno-Karabakh but to keep it under Azerbaijani rule. He called those who continued to wage a political fight "adventurists" and "demagogues."

"Political gamblers must be stigmatized and the public should know this," Gorbachev said. Yesterday, the republic's Communist Party chief, Suren Arutunyan, and the Armenian newspaper *Kommunist* echoed Gorbachev with a more direct attack on the Karabakh Committee, accusing them of a "vain struggle for power." Five members of the Karabakh Committee have been in prison for more than a week.

"From a snug headquarters, the committee contacts hospitals with incompetent information, disseminates wild rumors, and sends spurious data to the republic's Health Ministry," the newspaper *Kommunist* said. Activists in Yerevan have said the charges are not true.

Even during this crisis, sympathy here for Gorbachev is not much greater than it was in July, when he berated an Armenian university president on national television for his stand on Nagorno-Karabakh. Many in Armenia—and not only hardline nationalists—remain cynical about the Kremlin leader.

"Gorbachev is a two-faced man," said a doctor at a Yerevan hospital. "He spoke here sympathetically only because you have to express those feelings as president. But inside himself, well, very few people here feel he means what he says."

The official media, too, have tried to use the event to smooth relations between the two republics.

After showing the Armenian party chief's denunciation of the Karabakh Committee, the evening news cut to an Azerbaijani factory worker talking about the Armenian situation in the most sympathetic terms imaginable.

Now more than ever, the ethnic disputes here and in Azerbaijan are fueled by emotion, history, and rumor. By contrast, the Baltic republics' arguments with Moscow are restrained. At the Ostrovsky Pedagogical Institute in Yerevan, where hundreds of refugees from Azerbaijan and the quake area are sleeping in classrooms, rumors—many of them wild—of anti-Armenian scandals are on everyone's lips.

Institute director Tsogik Mamadzhanyan went so far as to blame the two crashes last week of Soviet and Yugoslav transport planes on "Moslem sabotage." Armenians, who lost 1.5 million people to a massacre by Turks in 1915, generally do not trust Turks or Azerbaijanis, and Mamadzhanyan claimed that "because of the fact" that one plane refueled in Turkey and the other in the Azerbaijani capital of Baku, they were sabotaged. The planes did not stop in Turkey or Azerbaijan.

Perhaps because he recognizes that he himself is an emotional issue in Armenia, Gorbachev has retreated somewhat since his appearance on television last week, letting Ryzhkov assume center stage in the republic.

Considered a moderate supporter of reform, Ryzhkov has tried to emulate Gorbachev's hands-on style, traveling to devastated areas, listening to complaints, and making pointed remarks about failures in the relief effort. Although Ryzhkov lacks Gorbachev's ease and presence, he seems more welcome by many Armenians.

Ethnic politics is an emotional issue here, but, for the moment, a secondary one. Even though Gorbachev and some nationalists have clashed since the earthquake ripped through Armenia, almost all attention, here and around the country, has been on the loss of life and the attempts, no matter how chaotic, to treat the wounded.

Dozens of foreign relief workers interviewed throughout the republic mixed their criticism with a sense of sympathy for the people of Armenia. "This is totally outside my experience," said British rescue worker Pete Wilson. "How can you imagine anything of this nature? It gives you a good idea of what the Second World War must have been like."

In Stepanavan, Lt. Col. Anatoli Khludnyev interrupted a long-delayed nap the other day to talk about what the earthquake may mean for the Soviet Union.

"With Chernobyl, we formed commissions and spent a lot of time trying to figure out why it happened," he said. But the earthquake has been a "sharp contrast."

"Now everyone in the press and the public realizes that people must understand that the pain of your neighbor is your own pain. It's the 'new political thinking.' We had such slogans in the past, but now it takes on a new, real form."

Observations and questions

1) In the third paragraph, the lead shifts into the present tense: "In the cold mountain night, Ogosyan *stands* near the demolished school and *says* that of the more than 500 children and teachers there, 'only 20 or 25, no more, survived.'" When do we shift from our traditional past-tense storytelling into the present? What effects does the shift cause?

2) It may be "almost disrespectful to think in political terms," but journalists tend to think that way about everything. Do our political fixations limit our vision of the human? Do they determine what we see when we report?

3) Remnick uses phrases like "it is stunning to read..." and "it is clear that..." Why shouldn't journalists just put themselves in the story rather than using such awkward wording?

4) The author faced the problem of describing the Soviet's inability to deal with the crisis, their disorganization, shoddy building practices, etc., while at the same time keeping the readers' sympathies with the victims. How does he manage this feat? Can you distinguish between describing negatives and criticizing people?

5) The second part of this piece deals with the ethnic minorities, the Armenians and the Azerbaijanis. Would this piece improve by splitting it into two articles? How would you lead the second one?

6) This article seems disjointed compared to Remnick's others. Play the role of friendly copy editor and rearrange it to make it read more smoothly. Start by redefining the sections.

Centuries of suffering tear at the souls of Armenians

DECEMBER 19, 1988

SPITAK, U.S.S.R.—A young woman, wrapped in a torn, dank blanket, wandered the streets of this ruined town the other day, by shattered factories and schools, past the coffins of her friends and families. "We Armenians," she said, "we have always lived under a black cross."

To visit Armenia now is to meet with a people who are often on the brink of despair. "Sometimes we feel as though even the heavens are against us," said Larissa Margachyan, a woman whose children were killed when a nursery school in Spitak collapsed.

The Armenian sense of suffering is centuries old, coming long before an earthquake here last week killed up to 100,000 people in Spitak, Leninakan, Kirovakan, and villages throughout the republic's mountainous northwest. The emotional life of any close-knit region—so hard to capture and simplify—plays a crucial role in its political and social life, and that is likely to be the case in the coming months in Armenia.

During a trip several months ago to Yerevan and other towns, then in the midst of ethnic tensions with neighboring Azerbaijan, a visitor's conversations with a hotel clerk, a cab driver, a novelist—anyone—immediately shifted to the tragedy of Armenia, its gradual loss of territory over the centuries, and, especially, to the disputed Turkish massacre of 1.5 million Armenians 73 years ago.

Small talk would abruptly turn to the inevitable: "Surely, you know about 1915?" The next question: "Have you been to see the memorial in Yerevan for the massacre?"

"Armenians all know that they are not the only people in the world to have suffered, but they continue to suffer from the fact that the world refuses to acknowledge what has happened to them," said

Armenian novelist Harand Materasjan.

For nearly a year now, the foreign press has been reporting on what must seem at times like only another of the world's endless number of territorial and ethnic conflicts. The mass Armenian movement to wrest control of the tiny region of Nagorno-Karabakh from Azerbaijan somehow seems—compared to the more wide-ranging demands of nationalists in Estonia, for example— outsized and single-minded.

But the emotions surrounding the Nagorno-Karabakh issue stem from what Armenians see as a worldwide ignorance and indifference to their history. Many countries, not wishing to offend Turkey, avoid official mention of the 1915 massacre.

When the U.S. Congress, for example, considered a resolution in 1985 to commemorate "all victims of genocide, especially the 1.5 million people of Armenian ancestry who were victims of the genocide perpetrated in Turkey between 1915 and 1923," the administration strongly opposed it.

The U.S. ambassador said it would be seen by Turks as a "gratuitous insult" and could "only harm our otherwise excellent relations with a strategic ally and loyal friend."

Caspar W. Weinberger, then defense secretary, warned that the resolution would "embarrass the United States and strain relations with this critical ally."

Secretary of State George P. Shultz said that while the State Department "greatly regrets and does not dismiss the tragic events early in this century when...widespread massacres struck at Armenians and members of other ethnic groups in an area encompassing what is now eastern Turkey," adoption of the resolution could "diminish sharply" his department's "ability to maintain the smooth and effective relationship" with Turkey and would be seen by present-day Armenian terrorists "as an encouragement and justification for their acts."

The Ottoman Empire ruled millions of Armenians early in this century. Although thousands of

Armenian soldiers fought for the empire during World War I, the Turkish leadership soon turned against what they saw as an unreliable element sympathetic to the Allies.

Throughout Turkish Armenia and Asia Minor, Armenian men were herded out of their towns and shot, according to Armenian accounts disputed by Turkish sources. Soldiers forced women and children to walk south on a "death march" to the deserts of northern Syria. Few survived. Some were thrown overboard from ships and drowned in the Black Sea, according to these Armenian accounts. Others died in concentration camps.

In the end, 1.5 million were dead and more than 500,000 became refugees, beginning a diaspora that is concentrated in Marseilles, New York, Beirut, and Los Angeles.

Because so many countries feared offending the Turks, the Armenian massacre was, for years, overlooked or explained away as a two-sided battle in which there were many Armenian reprisals against the Turks.

Shultz, in his 1985 letter to Congress, said "over 60 of our most distinguished scholars of Turkish and Middle East studies have questioned the historical assumptions" of the resolution on the "genocide."

Even in an age of *glasnost*, or openness, the Soviet leadership does not allow much mention of the massacres, for fear of disturbing its relations with Turkey.

Armenians feel that few people know about, or have made sense of, 1915. Their persistence in trying to win recognition of the tragedy also has broader meaning. As historian David Marshall Land suggested, "An unpunished genocide undertaken by one set of dictators is likely to breed genocidal views in another dictator, leading by an apparently natural progression to a holocaust such as that suffered by European Jewry."

Adolf Hitler, in order to justify his brutal tactics, is said by some accounts to have told his commanders in 1939, "I have sent to the east my

'Death's Head' units, with the order to kill without pity or mercy all men, women, and children of the Polish race. Who still talks nowadays of the extermination of the Armenians?"

The earthquake in Armenia is a natural disaster, but it is likely to compound the sense of desperation that many Armenians in the Soviet Union feel so intensely—and that could have political consequences. Soviet President Mikhail Gorbachev and other members of the leadership have tried to capture the moment of the earthquake and use it to denounce and trivialize the persistent demands of Armenians as the attempt of just a few "demagogues" and "dishonest people" to "hold power."

What Gorbachev ignored in his televised interview during his visit to the region last week is that his opponents here are many, not just an "immoral" few. In a republic of just over 3 million people, demonstrations of 500,000 cannot be considered a splinter movement.

Few Armenians believe the official media's attempts to emphasize Azerbaijan's sympathy and relief role. Resentment of the "Turks"—the all-embracing word Armenians use for Moslem people—is too intense. Many Armenians are willing to believe only the worst about Azerbaijanis, and hold the "Turks" responsible for nearly every injustice.

The emotional life of Armenia is likely to keep the republic at the center of the Kremlin's attention. How Armenians and Gorbachev respond to one another in the wake of the earthquake promises to be one of the most volatile issues in the coming months.

Observations and questions

1) This piece, labeled "News Analysis" when it ran in *The Washingaton Post,* starts with two devastating quotations from a suffering Armenian woman, but the rest reads like a historical treatise. Remnick could avoid that problem by deleting Larissa Margachyan, and starting with the third paragraph. Should he? Should we use "people" leads on analytic pieces?

2) Remnick says that "the emotional life of any close-knit region [is] so hard to capture and simplify." Yet he does just that for the Armenians. When you attempt something difficult, signal the reader ahead of time.

3) The author describes the 1915 massacre as if it really happened, distancing himself with attribution: "according to Armenian accounts disputed by Turkish sources." Reporters tend to curse attribution as clumsy and limiting, but sometimes it gives us latitude to write with assurance.

4) "Adolf Hitler, in order to justify his brutal tactics, *is said by some accounts...*" Again, notice how vague attribution serves as shorthand for complex controversies. Estimate how many paragraphs you would need to explain the intricacies of validation in "some accounts." We call academic writers "stuffy" because they explain such matters at length. Perhaps they lack our lack of space.

5) The "visitor" in the fourth paragraph is Remnick himself, trying to keep himself out of the story. Would it be appropriate to use the first-person pronoun in news analysis?

6) Study the word "massacre" in this piece. Merely using the word gives tacit validity to the Armenians' claim. What other words could Remnick use? Would they cause the same problems? Few words are neutral, and any word choice tilts meaning.

A conversation with
David Jay Remnick

DON FRY: Who taught you to write?

DAVID REMNICK: By far the most influential teacher I've ever had was John McPhee, who taught a course in non-fiction writing at Princeton. He's the best journalist I can think of.

I think so, too. How did he teach writing?

It was a semester-long course with 15 students. He gave these extraordinary essay exercises designed around learning things like structure and the role of detail. He would take his own pieces and describe how they were structured. He would spend three hours on word choice or syntax or developing a character. These are all revelations when you're 18, 19, 20 years old. You would do a piece of writing every week, and then have private conferences every week in which he would spend one hour just talking one-on-one with you about your piece. I can't imagine a better preparation of any kind than to sit in a class three hours a week just listening to John McPhee talk about writing.

Indeed.

I was also very interested in poetry, and probably spent the majority of my academic time on it. You learn things from poetry like scansion and meter, and it's enormously valuable for learning the value of sentences and the order of things. The sound of words may not be applicable every day in journalistic work, but it certainly is somewhere in your foundation, running through the back of your mind.

That sound gets into your bones and creates your voice. How did you get to *The Washington Post?*

In the summer of 1982, I interned in the Style section, which is the greatest job in journalism. It's just a feast. *The Washington Star* had folded, and there were very few jobs at the *Post,* and especially not in the Style section for somebody two-and-a-half seconds out of school. I went into the office of Howard Simons, the managing editor at the time, and said, "I'm broke. I love it here. Please give me a job." He said, "The *Post* owns a newspaper in Everett, Washington, and..." I said, "Howard, there are no Jews in Everett, Washington." And he said, "You are absolutely right. You're on night police starting next week." So I was on night police for any number of months, doing the usual things to get off night police, which was to come in during the day and do other stuff.

I think night cops is the best training ground for reporters, don't you?

Well, at *The Washington Post* at that time, it was mostly police briefs, and I was terrible at it. [Laughter] The *Post* wasn't that interested in what goes on at night. At the time, it seemed that the Metro section was much more oriented toward features, which I didn't mind, because that's what I did.

How long were you on night cops?

It seemed like 12 years, but it must have been four or five months. Then the sports editor said, "I like your writing and style, and I know you don't have a real permanent slot, so do you want to write sports?" I said, "I guess so, but it's not like I have any experience at it." He said, "Do you know anything about sports?" I said, "I watch it on the weekends, don't take it very seriously, and certainly don't want to do it forever." [Laughter] He said, "What do you really want to do?" I said, "I really want to go to Style and write profiles." He said, "OK, let's make a deal. Give me two years, and I'll get you there." Everybody else agreed to it, and that was that.

What did you cover?

I started out with the world's worst beat, covering the first season of the U.S. Football League. The Washington Federals went 2-16. [Laughter] I would be the only reporter in the press box who was working. While the Redskins had overflow crowds (Washington lives by the Redskins), no one gave a flying damm about the other team. Every Sunday it poured rain, and every Sunday their three best players would get injured. On and on they chugged. Once that was over, I did NBA basketball and boxing, which I loved despite how awful it was, because the people were interesting to be around.

I traveled around the country, and that was an education. In one year, I got to go to the Super Bowl and Wimbledon and championship fights and the World Series. I covered the Orioles, but I probably didn't appreciate it. I went to all these great events and had a great old time, and felt that this was real life in journalism, which it is not. Earthquakes are, I guess.

So did George Solomon keep his promise?

He damn well did. I then went to the Style section for what you could roughly call "the Brain Beat." [Laughter] I told them I wanted to do a 4,000-word profile of Harold Bloom, the literary critic at Yale. They said, "Sure, go ahead and do it." Once you have somebody's confidence in a section like that, which draws on writers doing what excites them, for better or for worse, they'll say "yes" until you screw up. I think I worked in more sections than anybody there. Then I did a year at the magazine, its first, very troubled year.

What did you do at the magazine?

My favorite story there was a piece about an 18-year-old Chilean kid who lived in Washington, and whose mother had been tortured after the over-

throw of Allende. This kid grew up with the burning desire to see his homeland, so he went there as
a photographer. At a demonstration, he somehow
crossed the line between being a photographer and
being a participant. He was driving with a girl, and
was pulled over to the side of the road. They
poured gasoline all over them and put a match to
them. He was burnt to death, but she survived. The
editor sent me down to San Diego, and I did a very,
very long piece on this kid's life and death. I got
the bug from that.

How did you land the Moscow assignment?

One day, a note on the bulletin board said we were
picking our next Moscow correspondent, which is
a sure sign at newspapers that it has already been
picked. So I went in to the foreign editor, Michael
Getler, and said, "Look, I know this is kind of
crazy, and I'm a feature writer, and I don't know
how much of my stuff you have even read, but the
Soviet Union is a deep place for me. I studied
some Russian in college, and I'm intensely interested in it. In Style, I wrote all the time about various immigrant authors and Russian subjects. But,
of course, I know this is already taken by Michael
Dobbs." And he said, "Actually, Michael has the
job that comes right after it, which is the bureau
chief. This job is actually open." And I went.

**You have a real knack for directness at the right
moment! What's your beat in Moscow?**

Basically everything. We don't split it up by subject. There are only two of us, and so for large
hunks of time, one is alone in Moscow because of
vacations or because the other guy is on the road.
We really don't specialize. Dobbs does slightly
more on international affairs and more diplomacy.
I've done more of the cultural end of things.

Can you interview in Russian?

Yes. But Russian is the kind of language where you never get to the end. It's a very, very difficult language. I worked pretty hard at it, and I hope by the time I'm ready to go home, it will be very good. As every foreign reporter knows, you learn tricks to make sure you're being accurate. You just ask the same dumb question over and over. That was McPhee's method of interviewing: to be a complete moron so that the interviewee takes an almost maternal attitude toward you.

Dumb questions work just as well in America as in Russia. Do you originate most of your own story ideas?

Yes. In baseball terms it's a very, very fast pitch, because so much is going on in Moscow these days. If you are interested or obsessed with a topic (and almost every reporter I know there is on the border of crazed obsession), it's not a matter of finding ideas so much as sorting them out and putting the priority on one over another. When you are living in Moscow, there's not much else to do other than work. When you have Russians over to dinner, everything has to do with what's going on. Conversation goes on for hours about it, so you're always working.

This question might sound odd to a guy who is "always working," but how do you know when to stop reporting? How do you know when you have enough?

Look, in every single one of my jobs after sports, you felt you "had enough" almost to an excess. You always had an extra day, you always had an extra week in Style or the magazine. You may have not used it intelligently or the best you could, because you're a little bit spoiled. But, in Moscow, you have to make choices on when enough is enough. There are some subjects that require speed because it's in the air, and you have to get it out. When you're starting to hear the same things again and again, and you're pretty sure of what you want to say, even though there's a certain dimension you're not going to get, then it's time to write it.

Saul Pett says that when he hears the same anecdote three times, he has enough. [Laughter]

He's right on the money. That's frustrating in Moscow simply because you want to look back over the year and not have just six perfect stories. You want to have hundreds of them. There is a real addiction. When I came back for the first time after a year, the editors said, "Maybe you should lay off a little bit." I got a very funny letter from an editor once that was kind of a pat on the back, but the final sentence said, "Don't burn out, but don't tail off either. Best Regards...," which tells you that your editor wants you to live, but maybe only three years. [Laughter]

After you finish reporting, how do you organize your materials?

Obviously, it depends on the speed. On the fly, you read through your notes, and you do it in your brain. When speed is involved, it's very helpful for me to get something on the screen, even if it never makes it in, just to fool myself that I've started. Maybe it's that absurd thing we call "the so-what paragraph," just to make sure that you're not going to start writing in shorthand, a thing you're in danger of falling into when you're abroad...

Or at home...

...or anywhere. Remember you're talking to somebody who has been abroad for one year. Frank Clines, who is the greatest thing since sliced bread, has so much experience that to listen to me on anything like this is ridiculous.

I interviewed him earlier, and, in fact, you're very much alike in your answers. He considers himself a "natural" writer.

Natural or unnatural, he's terrific. I've always liked his stuff a lot. He has extraordinary range, and he's hilarious. I hope when he flies to Moscow, his plane goes to China or someplace like that [Laughter], because the last thing we need is more competition in Moscow. Frank is a master of the column-length feature, just incredibly compact and Japanese about it. I've gotten used to all this room, and probably it's bad for my health after a while.

Once you get that first stuff on the screen, what do you do?

If I know I'm writing for the Style section, I can take a much more leisurely (and for me, a more comfortable) path toward a story. For example, one night I was writing a long piece about Boris Yeltsin, who was running for this new legislature, and it was up in the air whether they wanted it for the front section or Style. I just said to myself, "I'm just going to write it the way I want to do it, and no great compunction to get on the front page." The first 500 words have him getting out of his limousine and walking to the hall, where he proceeded to act like the Soviet Huey Long, not exactly the speediest lead in the world. And lo and behold, it went in the Style section, and it was the sort of lead that comes out of the gospel according to Wolfe and Talese, and all the rest of those people who broke all that ground a long, long time ago. For writers my age, that's mother's milk, just what we were raised on.

If you have the leisure to write a story slowly, do you plan it ahead, or do you just write it?

Because I had all this sports stuff, which was deadline writing by the minute and rewriting, I got to be pretty quick, and it really did help. It was about nonsense, of course, about the Bullets against the Warriors or something, but you got to where you know how to order a story upside down, and you could file it backward. It helps. Everything helps.

Roger Simon says he likes to write fast so he can report longer. [Laughter] When you file a story, do you get edited very much?

With whining, or without whining? [Laughter] No, not very much. When I do get edited, I'm usually pleased. Unless it's on deadline and unless it can't be done, I want to know about changes. If they want something cut for space, I'd rather do it myself. You know, I'm a typical pain-in-the-ass reporter.

Where were you when you heard about the earthquake?

Dobbs went to New York, and I was alone in Moscow. Gorbachev gave a speech at the U.N. that was written up around the country as the most important piece of political oratory in decades. So that day I did the usual reaction story. And there was this funny little earthquake, which was reported by the usual suspects, Tass and *Vremya,* the evening news. I wrote it up, and then a little bit more information came in. I remember telling the desk, "Look, they're saying, 'many deaths,' and anytime the Soviet Union reporting on disaster says 'many deaths,' you better watch out."

Very early in the morning, having gone to bed at the usual time, which is about 2:00 or 3:00 in the morning, I got a phone call from the foreign desk, saying that Gorbachev is going home. The phrase "a thousand dead" was used, and nobody in the States believed that Gorbachev would go home for an earthquake. They thought there was something wrong in the defense ministries, because there had been reports, probably true, that people in the military had objected to the idea of unilateral troop cuts. And in classic 1970s style, the person who was calling me from the desk was relaying a message from someone who said, "Take a swing by the defense ministry to see if anything is up" [Laughter], which is classic 1970s "Are the lights on in the Kremlin?" kind of thing. So, just absolutely beat, I threw on sweat pants, got in my car, and drove past the defense ministries. And lo and behold, a great big shock at 9:00 in the morning, there were lights on. So, I made a phone call, and for the last edition, with my name on it, it says on the front page, "David Remnick reported from Moscow that there was no unusual activity at the defense ministry." [Laughter] Just classic horseshit.

Then more stuff came out about the earthquake during the day. Luckily I had people I could call in Armenia, because I had been there that summer. It was obvious this was a major disaster, and the Soviets responded in unprecedented fashion. They told just about as much as they knew almost as quickly as they knew it. It was an incredible change from Chernobyl.

So how did you get to Armenia?

It was impossible to travel right away to Armenia, especially if you were in Moscow. People from the West got in sooner than the people from Moscow. Tom Brokaw was there before I was! [Laughter]

Why was it hard to travel from Moscow?

We weren't allowed. So I was locked in Moscow. *Vremya* was just extraordinary, showing all kinds of film, sparing nothing, twisted bodies and collapsed buildings. Obviously they emphasized the fraternal brotherhood of republics pitching in, but there was a radical departure from anything that had happened before. And so for several nights, the way to report on this was through phoning your finger off to Armenia, though there were no phones left in any of the afflicted areas.

That must have been frustrating.

The big missing piece was how many died, and to this day we still don't know. The Soviets say they have extracted nearly 30,000 bodies, which is a fairly meaningless figure, considering God knows

how many more are underneath there, and how
many refugees there were. We were hearing anything from 50,000 to 100,000. And hundreds of
thousands of people homeless. Dobbs eventually
made it back, which was enormously helpful.
Dobbs couldn't get down there.

So how *did* you get down there?

I got lucky. Finally the foreign ministries said,
"We'll take a planeload," and I went on that plane
load. However, the same day a lot of reporters also
got lucky. That day, the Foreign Ministry press
spokesman, Gennadi Gerasimov, was asked, "Do
we really need to do the usual thing for traveling?"
In the Soviet Union, that requires a letter, two days
of waiting, acceptance of your proposed itinerary,
and it can go on for days. They can find any number of excuses to say "no," and when the system is
overloaded with requests, you can be sure they can
find a reason to say "no." And Gerasimov said,
"I'm closing my eyes." That was the phrase he
used, which meant: "If you want to just hop on a
plane and go, don't worry about it. We won't throw
you out of the country. Just go." So any number of
reporters also showed up the same day.

How long did it take you to get down there?

About three-and-a-half hours. We left in the afternoon, and I wanted to get a story that first night
even though I knew we wouldn't go to the earthquake site until the next day.

Where did you go?

We flew to Yerevan, which is the capital of Armenia. I noticed half the flight was press, and half the
flight was soldiers. These soldiers were on leave
from posts all over the country to go back to see if
their families had died. We interviewed all these
soldiers on the plane, asking them about themselves. Imagine you're 18 years old, and you're

flying back to discover whether or not your family is still alive.

Once I got into Yerevan, I had a couple of hours to drive around town. I went to a hospital to talk to people who were hurt. So I got a sense of the place without actually being there. I screamed all that crap into a telephone to Dobbs, who then filed it from Moscow. You were in big trouble if you didn't have somebody in Moscow. To get a phone line was a bitch to begin with, but to get it to New York or Washington was impossible.

Where did you stay?

At a hotel in Yerevan I had stayed in before. I knew half of the people who worked there, which helped a lot.

Why did you choose Spitak to go to first?

Spitak was where we could get the bus to go on the first day. We were going to fly by helicopter, but there was terrible fog. We had this moment of journalistic panic that we would get nowhere that day, so we said, "Let's take the bus and go to Spitak," and they said, "Fine." We had three hours to just run around like hell. Remember my background. I haven't spent years running around Beirut and the Congo and Vietnam and all the rest.

What was it like?

It's very, very painful to think about. This was a town of 30,000, with a couple of factories, absolutely leveled, every structure, kindergartens, homes, factories, Communist Party headquarters, everything, just complete rubble. You're driving in the foothills, and all of a sudden out of nowhere is this town, just one big smoking ruin. Five days had gone by, but still I never smelled anything like this, and I hope I never will.

In the story you say: "And everywhere the smell

**is of smoke and snow and the dead, rotting in
their makeshift coffins of rough pine."**

The most chilling part of the town was a small soc-
cer stadium, with some bleacher seats. They were
using this stadium as the boneyard and the hospital
and the collection area for the coffins. Imagine
your high school football stadium covered from
the 50-yard line down through the end zone in
coffins. All the bleacher seats stacked with coffins.
Most of them filled, lots of them filled and just
opened. And people, the few survivors, going from
one coffin to the next, opening the lids looking for
their families. Uh...I don't know what to say....

**Uh...how did you deal with that? You had noth-
ing...nothing to prepare you for that.**

Nothing. You're working though, and you're
working hard, and you know you have three hours
in absolute overdrive. And you're shaken here and
there by these things, but something very...cold
and...professional takes over for a brief period of
time. I just hope I never do get to that cynical
point, but you begin to understand why veteran
foreign correspondents are like that, because they
see this all the time.

**David, did you have to trick that attitude up, or
did it just happen?**

It just happened, but I don't want to tell you that I
walked around there unaffected. It was just awful,
and your clothes stank of it. I remember there were
a lot of little campfires all over, and people would
sit there numbly, not doing anything. I went to this
one campfire, and I was sitting there talking to this
woman whose children were underneath the rubble
of the kindergarten. And...you know, it's everything you can do to not just completely lose it. Yet
you do it in conveyer-belt style for 20 minutes, and
then something in the back of your mind says
you've got to go on to the *next* scene and talk to

the *next* person, because you know you only have a certain number of hours. You've got to get the bus back so you can write something and scream it into a telephone for two hours.

David, I think I could deal with all those bodies, but not with all that grief.

To be very blunt about it, there was less grief than in other places because almost everybody was dead. Almost everybody alive in Spitak was not *from* Spitak. But believe me, there was plenty of grief to go around. Now, what did "to deal with it" mean? "Deal with it" means you...you...you get to the next moment, and you thank God that it's...not you and everybody you love. You just do it, and then after it's all done, at night you don't sleep, as simple as that. Two weeks later, when it's all over, and you've washed your clothes or burned them, you sleep even worse, or you're in a faintly bad mood, and you don't know why.

Well, here you are four months later. Can you sleep now?

Yeah, but I think about it all the time. It changes you, not in some tricky, banal sort of way, but you can feel something slip beneath your feet a little bit.

So how did you write the story in such conditions?

It was a long bus ride, and you think about it a little bit. I gave myself about an hour and forty-five minutes, because filing was a bit of a bitch. The phone lines are very bad, you couldn't be heard at the other end, and it switched off every eight minutes. There are big lineups for the phones, tensions are pretty high, and everybody has laryngitis because you're screaming into the phones. It was a pain in the neck, but everybody got through it.

What could you assume your readers knew?

Five days had gone by, and wire reporters had been there, one little pool from outside. So the readers knew the essential facts, and maybe even a decent bit about the feel of the place. Without getting too purple about it, I was after the emotional aspect, especially five days later. It's different when this many people die. We think of the great earthquake of San Francisco, but there only several hundred people died. Several hundred people matter, of course, but it was startling how enormous the destruction was.

Your stories focus on people, not on things. The San Francisco earthquake seems less horrible to us because we see pictures of buildings, but very little of people, and certainly not stadiums full of coffins.

I think that's true.

How long did it take you to dictate?

Longer than it took to write it. In those conditions, that's what you do.

And the next day, you went to Leninakan.

Yes, Leninakan, in the next day's story, is a sizable city, 120,000, 130,000. It was not completely leveled, which was grotesque in its way. A whole wall of a school building would be stripped down, and, in an almost voyeuristic way, you could see classrooms. That city was just filled with horrible grief, because a lot of people did survive.

You capture that in a simple sentence: "The human desperation here is beyond exaggeration." And you give us vignettes.

Leninakan had all sorts of bizarre things about it. I remember feeling how tragedy destroys the absurdities of government and authoritarianism, so much so that the KGB headquarters became the area where the foreign rescue workers had their headquarters. They were sitting there joking about bugs in the walls. I remember spending hours standing on a collapsed building where these foreign rescue workers with dogs tried to dig someone out who wasn't there. You could see the disorganization, part of it manmade, part of it created by the situation itself. If anything were going to explode the myth of the Soviets' much-vaunted civil defense system, it was their ability to react to an earthquake.

Let me ask you about gore. You say: "Slowly, the foreign rescue teams are giving up on Leninakan. So much time has gone by that they have gone from being rescue workers to undertakers. The bodies have been under the rubble for so long that they often only come out in parts. 'It breaks your heart in half,' says Pat Stenton, a self-described 'tunnel rat' from England." David, this is all beyond description, but you're writing for a newspaper, and you have to describe it enough to make it real. How do you judge that?

I don't want to condescend to the reader, and I don't want to soften the blow. And I...how to put this best...in this situation, it had to be specificity, specificity, specificity, details, details, details. And details in this situation are not pretty. They were awful, and the awfulness was behind why everybody reacted why they did. Let's face it, standard-issue newspaper language is designed to give information of a certain kind, but not to deal with emotional or descriptive information of another kind. I don't see why that should be, nor do I think most people see why that should be.

Did you see anything that was so terrible you couldn't put it in your stories?

You know, the things that are so terrible are personally associative. You'll see some mangled body that looks like somebody you know, that's what makes you really upset. That's what made me really upset. There were bodies that were ready to explode and purple. You try to have a sense of the overall scheme of your story, and one grotesque image will go a very long way. This is not art, nor is it a horror movie, nor am I trying to scare anybody, but it's not a litany of grotesqueries either. It's assumed that one detail is meant to be emblematic. You don't need to bombard the reader.

They'll stop reading you. How long did you spend in Leninakan?

It's hard for me to remember. Longer, five hours, six hours, I'd say.

So that night, you went back and wrote and filed again? And the next day...

The next day, I went all over, and decided not to file on deadline. I wanted to be out there longer. Because of the filing situation and because Sunday was coming up, I thought that I'd get stuff for at least one or two stories.

Nalband is the size of your back yard, in the middle of absolutely nowhere. I wanted to write a big Sunday piece, and I wanted it to start in the village, because we hadn't heard from the village yet. There were areas which didn't get help, such as it was, nearly as quickly or halfway decent. People were completely wiped out, not knowing what was going on. I also wanted to put this event in perspective in terms of the press and *glasnost,* and in the political context, that all these so-called earth-shattering events are not so earth-shattering.

How did you get all the historical background when you were out in the field? Did you just have it in your head?

No, I flew back to Moscow late Friday or early Saturday to write the Sunday piece. I wrote the

Sunday piece, and then on Sunday wrote a piece for Monday, and then early Monday morning flew back down.

So in the office you had access to all the historical stuff and your clips.

And the ability to call people. I knew the area pretty well, as well as you are going to know a non-Moscow area. And the clips were all right, because Armenia was such an important story in '88.

Yes, and you had been covering the dissension down there. The Monday story was labeled "News Analysis." Did the desk ask you to do a step-back piece?

No. The desk figures you know what's going on. The responsibility is startling for somebody who has not been a correspondent, the extraordinary freedom and responsibility both.

I like this lead: "A young woman, wrapped in a torn, dank blanket, wandered the streets of this ruined town the other day, by shattered factories and schools, past the coffins of her friends and families. 'We Armenians,' she said, 'we have always lived under a black cross.'"

I remember that distinctly. Armenian history is not exactly the first thing on an American's mind. When I left for Russia, I had only a vague knowledge, that there may or may not have been a lot of them killed at some point in time. Then you go to Armenia, and you're there for five minutes, and everybody you meet says, "Well, of course, you remember 1915." As a Jew, it was very striking for me to get a sense of the holocaust they lived with. It enters into everything they do and feel. It enters into their sense of self and their sense of grief. When the earthquake came, they had a real sense of persecution by nature.

So even in these worst of circumstances, they fall back on their terrible history. In the story "Soviet pain exposed in 'landscape of nightmares,'" I'm struck by this British rescue worker, Pete Wilson, who is trying to make sense of it, too. He says, "How can you imagine anything of this nature? It gives you a good idea of what the Second World War must have been like."

World War II is his touchstone, his reference point.

I was 9 when the war ended. But this earthquake was worse than World War II because Spitak was just flat, and everybody was dead.

I imagine in World War II there must have been some places like that. But the Soviet Union is in a revolution where nobody is shooting anybody. It's a great story, extremely exciting, the most interesting thing I can imagine. Yet no one is getting shot or killed. Then, the next thing you know, thousands and thousands of people are dead. It's just a freakish thing.

Student journalists often worry about their ability to face real horror. They want to, but they're afraid they won't have what it takes, when they get there. What would you say to them?

That they won't know until they get there. You want to believe things about yourself as a human being, and you have an impulse to say, "I could never do it, I would collapse." And that makes you a better person, a more sensitive person. You are not Mother Teresa, but if you can make it through to the other end, you are relaying a piece of experience to people thousands of miles away who can't experience everything through television, thank God.

And you just do it, don't you?

I just did it, but I don't know what will happen the

next time. I hope there's not a next time, because these things mean a lot of people get killed, but I am not that stupid to think there definitely won't be.

Yes, alas. Thank you, David.

Michael Skube
Commentary

The News and Observer

MICHAEL SKUBE grew up in Springfield, Illinois, and majored in political science at Louisiana State University, graduating in 1966. He continued graduate study there, but somehow couldn't write the first sentence of his thesis, entitled "On the Concept of Freedom in Marx and Mill." He taught arithmetic in a black grade school outside Baton Rouge for two years before joining the U.S. Customs Service for almost eight years. In 1978, he became the capital bureau chief for the *Winston-Salem Journal*. In 1982, the Raleigh *News and Observer* hired him to write editorials. After four years, he became book page editor. Skube also won the Pulitzer Prize this year for criticism.

Peter Gay's biography puts Freud's life into context

MAY 1, 1988

Late in his life Karl Marx took stock of his disciples and declared sourly, "I am no Marxist." Sigmund Freud, the other 19th-century Victorian who established the terms of discourse for the 20th, was no more fortunate in his followers. One hundred and three years after opening his consulting room at 19 Berggasse in Vienna, what Freud envisioned as a liberating science of the mind is a babel of competing voices—Freudians and neo-Freudians, Jungians and Adlerians and Laingians, behaviorists, family counselors, clinical psychologists, and just plain quacks.

Psychoanalysis—the rigidly determined "science" that owes its existence to Sigmund Freud—is fractured into as many sects as Marxism, and into as many schools of interpretation. In the wake of Freud, we lose sleep over our dreams, watch for slips of the tongue, and plumb the dark pool of our unconscious for the submerged springs of our actions. And we think about sex an awful lot. We are Freudians, like it or not.

Time, even so, has not been kind to Freud, and with the advent of feminism he has more to answer for. His most basic concepts—the unconscious, the death wish, the function of dreams, and the nature of sexuality—are as unscientific as Marx's labor theory of value. But they are common coin all the same.

Peter Gay's elegant new biography puts Freud's life into the context of his time while attempting to explain him for readers who cannot escape his shadow. In Gay's hands, the Olympian figure is almost within mortal reach. He is still a remote man, cold, convinced of the rightness of his own logic, distrustful of others, dependent on male comradeship, fascinated by the mystery of woman. His virtues are the ones of fortitude—an iron will and courage in the face of death from cancer—and his failings are the ones of a man unaccepting of the failings of others.

It was good, in a sense, that Freud died before the era of complete disclosure. He did not suffer intruders into his conscience, and he did not change his mind easily. He spent 30 years studying "the feminine soul," and concluded that woman was "a dark continent." His famous question— "What does woman want?"—was merely, Gay argues, an age-old cliche in modern dress: "Men for centuries had defended themselves against their obscure fear of woman's hidden power by describing the whole sex as unfathomable. But it is also a helpless shrug, a measure of his discontent with the gaps in his theory." When Freud was certain of something, Gay writes, he said so. "But with woman he was not quite sure."

GIVING FREUD JUSTICE

Gay, a distinguished cultural historian at Yale and a writer of great style and sophistication, is himself a trained psychoanalyst. He is deeply respectful of Freud and at pains to explain the man, who would never have explained himself. He gives Freud, I think, more justice than he is due, but he is not an apologist. He acknowledges that Freud, a product of a century in the thrall of science, created an intellectual edifice so rigid and closed that only Freud himself had clearance to enter.

But the validity and usefulness of psychoanalytic inquiry—implicit in the very book he is writing—Gay takes to be demonstrable and conclusive. Given the mixed results psychoanalysis has to show, his position suggests the championing of phrenology, the 19th-century fad of reading character and intelligence into the shape of the skull. Suffice it to say that the person who takes either of them completely on its own terms ought to have his head examined.

This isn't a personal prejudice, but an argument based on the logic of science. The peculiar attribute of psychoanalysis—for which Freud must take responsibility—is that it establishes a framework and then assembles facts to fit it. Which, of course, is precisely the opposite of the way science proceeds. The late Peter Medawar, the Nobel Prize-winning biologist, has written:

"The lack of good evidence of the specific therapeutic effectiveness of psychoanalysis is one of the reasons why it has not been received into the general body of medical practice. A layman might be inclined to say that we should give it time, for doctors are conservative people and ideas so new take ages to sink in. But it is only on a literary time-scale that Freudian ideas are new. By the standards of current medical practice they have almost an antiquarian flavor."

And yet Freud, like Marx, thought of himself as a scientist first and last, and fought all his life to defend the "scientific" purity of psychoanalysis. He most of all feared that the American medical establishment would attempt to take over the brain child to which he had given his life. His fears were unfounded; what he had most to fear was his own fractious followers who would force him to say, today, that he is no Freudian after all.

Observations and questions

1) Skube sweeps aside a whole profession: "What Freud envisioned as a liberating science of the mind is a babel of competing voices—Freudians and neo-Freudians, Jungians and Adlerians and Laingians, behaviorists, family counselors, clinical psychologists, and just plain quacks." No reporter could get away with such a mean generalization. Do reviewers have a license to kill?

2) Rearrange the list in the previous question so that "just plain quacks" comes first. Why does putting "quacks" last make the sentence punchier?

3) The second paragraph ("Psychoanalysis...like it or not.") would make a good lead. What would you gain or lose by starting the review there? Where else could the first paragraph go?

4) Skube says: "Time, even so, has not been kind to Freud, and with the advent of feminism he has more to answer for." Skube does not develop the feminists' attack on Freud, but assumes readers know about it. How can we gauge how much to assume about readers?

5) Skube takes a swipe at Peter Gay's assumptions: "Given the mixed results psychoanalysis has to show, [Gay's] position suggests the championing of phrenology, the 19th-century fad of reading character and intelligence into the shape of the skull." Study the whole paragraph to see if this comparison with phrenology seems fair.

6) This review begins with Karl Marx declaring, "I am no Marxist," and ends with Freud forced "to say, today, that he is no Freudian after all." How does this echoing of lead and kicker help the reader?

7) Freud asked: "What does woman want?" Well... what do men want?

Western lit from Milton to Zane Grey (and others)

JUNE 12, 1988

Jane Tompkins of the Duke University English department is evidently an expert on Westerns and a professor besides, so I should be sheepish about betraying my naivete. But I have read some Zane Grey in my brief time—not just as a fifth-grader but one frivolous night last month—and I missed the deep stuff altogether. Mostly there were horses and cowboys, a sheriff or two, and enough desert dust to do a Ph.D. dissertation proud. But not a lot of Significance, unless I mistook it for sagebrush.

One should never be surprised to hear what's in style in the English departments, but when I read last week that Zane Grey was *au courant* (Louis L'Amour, too!), I thought I was back in the sixties. In fact, I was, although the foment for social change back then overlooked the writers of the purple sage. It pretty much contented itself with the "people" and the pigs, and let it go at that.

That's why James Atlas's fawning article in *The New York Times Magazine*—an excerpt of which was carried in the *News and Observer*—peeled the scales from my eyes. In the furor over what is afoot in the humanities these days, it had escaped me what was at issue: not just the racist-sexist West but the Wild West with it, and anything else a professor can stake his tenure to. Overspecialization has drained the great wells of Western literature dry. The humanities, a skeptical Walter Jackson Bate of Harvard told Atlas, are in "their worst state of crisis since the modern university was formed a century ago." Bate, distinguished biographer of Keats and Samuel Johnson, said of the new enthusiasms, "They're looking for things to write. You can't write the 40th book on the structure of *Paradise Lost*."

So the English departments—long a burial ground for anyone wishing to become a writer—

now become excavation sites. Hidden meanings are found where none had been suspected; forgotten masterpieces are exhumed; neglected writers are canonized, literally and figuratively.

All this is well and good. There ought to be more to literature than the short row of marble busts extending from Homer to T.S. Eliot—dead white men, as the insurgents are wont to say. But as usual in academia, proportion is lost, and what is peripheral to literature's enduring concerns becomes someone's career. Professor Tompkins teaches a course titled "Home on the Range" (and, as Professor Tompkins is a feminist, you may be sure the range is not the one in the kitchen); she also teaches courses on the novels of 19th-century American writers who would be flattered to be called even minor.

Why, though, do courses need to be taught on these writers? Walter Jackson Bate's answer—that young professors are scavenging around looking for something, anything, to write about—only gets at part of the truth. More to the point, as Atlas reports, the curriculum has come to be seen as an instrument for social and political change. And the change is to the left. As Marjorie Garber, director of English graduate studies at Harvard, instructs us: "It wasn't only women we'd neglected. It was the whole Third World."

A SONGFEST AT STANFORD

Whatever is eventually unearthed from those lost libraries of Khartoum, I wonder whether it is worth it to torch everything else. We see, at any rate, what the songfest was about at Stanford last year, when the Rev. Jesse Jackson played pied piper and the little girls and boys tagged along chanting, "Hey, hey, ho, ho, Western culture's got to go." Those were English majors, I will wager—why, they may have been English *professors*. They call to mind Bazarov in Turgenev's *Fathers and Sons*, the perfect embodiment of 19th-century nihilism, who would destroy for the sake of destroying.

Well, let's not call them nihilists. They're simply students and professors going about with cliches and jargon pasted to their foreheads like bumper stickers. Western literature is Eurocentric, it's phallocentric, it's logocentric. One would like to think it was once heliocentric as well, young minds turning like buttercups toward the light of reason.

But let's don't haul out the platitudes. Perhaps it was all a sham. Perhaps there's more to literature than what is universal in human experience. In the canon-busting that's going on at Duke, Stanford, and elsewhere, there is also a large measure of campy politics, and it is the politics more than the literature that counts. "Gynocriticism"—the study of women in literature, for you simpletons who didn't know—is everywhere. At Harvard, Marjorie Garber is doing something to Sherlock Holmes called "cross-dressing" that doesn't sound good, and at Duke, Professor Frank Lentricchia is hard at work feminizing Wallace Stevens's image. I don't know what will become of the Jane Austens and the Brontes and the Willa Cathers who have long been a part of the literary tradition of the English-speaking world, but the professors are shuffling the rankings. Even in the provinces, from N.C. State to Quaker State, the humanities are in ferment.

I suppose I am out of touch on this as on much else, but *Paradise Lost* I always took to be the story of man's fall from grace. I never stopped to think that Milton was male and white, only that *Paradise Lost* was not, as they say, a fast read ("No one ever wished it longer," Dr. Johnson rued). Neither did I, one night last month, interrupt *The Thundering Herd* to ponder the deeper meaning of it all. I took Zane Grey at face value, just as I did when I was a kid, and let him put me safely to sleep. Naive me.

Observations and questions

1) The author makes himself a character in this essay. Describe that character only from what you read here. Do you find the character believable or just a pose? How can you tell?

2) Skube says: "Mostly there were horses and cowboys, a sheriff or two, and enough desert dust to do a Ph.D. dissertation proud." Study how the simple words and phrasing in the beginning crash into "Ph.D. dissertation" and the archaic phrase "do...proud." This sentence says a lot of mean things without saying them.

3) The next sentence says: "But not a lot of Significance, unless I mistook it for sagebrush." Decapitalize "Significance" and study the effect. Why is the capitalized version meaner?

4) List all the images of death, burial, and dryness in this essay. What does all that gloomy stuff have to do with ferment in the humanities?

5) Is this essay fair to English professors? Is it balanced and complete? Is it accurate? How can you tell? Do personal essays in a newspaper have to meet these four standards? Should they?

6) Skube says, "They call to mind Bazarov in Turgenev's *Fathers and Sons*, the perfect embodiment of 19th-century nihilism, who would destroy for the sake of destroying." Is he showing off his own literary background, or beating the professors at their own game?

7) This essay begins and ends with Skube calling himself naive. Think about the advantages of the naive observer position when describing the shenanigans of intellectuals. How could you use that pose on government beats?

Intimates and strangers, and fathers and sons

JUNE 19, 1988

Robert Penn Warren has not quite been around forever, but in his 84th year he has acquired the gnarled nobility of things rooted in the long ago. So it is at once touching and arresting to find perhaps the grandest man of American letters recalling a prior time and reconstructing from it a picture of the father who died writing a letter that got no further than "Dear Son—."

To say that he does so with any chronological coherence is as irrelevant as it is wide of the mark; his intent in *Portrait of a Father* (University of Kentucky Press, $12) is not biography or even portraiture. Rather it is a searching of the kind that men seem not so much inclined to undertake as fated to.

For this, you might say, we can blame our fathers who art in heaven and on earth. Untouchable under the armament of authority, the father bequeaths to the son obligations that cannot be satisfied in the father's lifetime. Doesn't Freud somewhere say the death of the father is the emancipation of the son? But it is the life of the father, and particularly the father as boy and as young man, that holds peculiar mystery for sons.

"My father was not secretive," Warren writes, "but somehow he had sealed off the past, his own past. In a strange way he was depersonalized. I cannot remember that he ever in his life said, 'I feel bad,' or 'I feel good.' Never in any fashion did he remark on a purely personal feeling. Not even in an extremity of grief."

Intimates and strangers at the same time, father and son often find themselves seeking out one another when time is running short. Or the son does so after the father has gone to the grave, in profoundly personal reminiscences like Warren's and those of a number of other male writers. Four

come immediately to mind: William Humphrey's
Farther off from Heaven; Frederick Exley's *A
Fan's Notes*; Geoffrey Wolff's *The Duke of De-
ception*; and Lance Morrow's *The Chief*. None of
these is anything like a filial elegy to a lost father,
though in each of them there is much tenderness,
remorse, and deep-felt love. There is the memory
of love unrequited as well—or love at a distance—
and it is the image of this that bores into a reader's
memory.

LAYING A PARENT TO REST

There most certainly are like-minded mem-
oirs—though that really is not the word—of women
who must write about one or another of their parents before they can lay them to rest. But the effect
of father on son, if literature is any testimony, has
no counterpart.

Which is not to say that it is always painful or
paralyzing, only that fully unraveling the tie of father to son is seldom attempted. I don't know of a
more affecting book than *Farther off from Heaven*,
now 11 years old, and its author, novelist William
Humphrey, well into his 60s. When I read it new, I
imagined him a middle-aged man (as a 56-year-old
man has every right to expect), but a man within
reach still of his boyhood. William Humphrey's father was a mechanic, and young Billy was envied
by friends who wanted nothing more than to "soak
up the talk of magnetos and carburetors and cut-
outs, and be asked, joy of joys, by the black-faced
man lying on his dolly underneath a car to hand
him a certain wrench." And yet in time, as the boy
approached adolescence and came to recognize the
lines of social class, there would grow an ambivalence toward his father's place in the town:

"He never talked shop with me. Whenever I
asked my father what kind of car was the one that
had just passed, a question which absorbed every
boy, when we collected car-sightings as avidly as
bird-watchers collect birds and gained stature with
our friends when we could claim having seen an
Auburn or a Marmon or some other exotic marque,

172

he sometimes pretended not to have been looking. Finally some of his sense of inferiority about being a 'grease monkey' wore off on me, to the extent that whenever I was with a friend on the square and a car came through with my father lying on the hood of it listening to the beat of the engine to diagnose what ailed it, I did not know whether not to notice him or to swell with pride."

William Humphrey's father and Robert Penn Warren's father both grew up in Clarksvilles— Clarence Humphrey in Texas, Robert Franklin Warren in Tennessee. With his mother, young William would leave before he was barely into his teens, and not return until he was a grown man. His leaving was the result of trauma: his father, a tough and hard-driving runt of a man, was killed in an auto accident in the early morning hours of the Fourth of July in 1937. *Farther off from Heaven* is, on one level, the story of the 13-year-old boy awakened from the security of sleep at 3 a.m. by his frightened mother and told to dress quickly. In his middle age, having lived in France and established himself as a writer, William Humphrey returned to Clarksville to recover the father he lost when he was a boy—and then to let him go at last.

A MAN OF MYSTERY

Robert Penn Warren's boyhood saw nothing so traumatic, yet only something deep-seated moves a man in his 80s to write: "My father, as the years since his death pass, becomes to me more and more a man of mystery." He means, of course, not the man whose physical features he remembers vividly—"two bony big toes curling up from the cold floor"—but the man who did not let himself be revealed. Once, father and son were out driving the country roads, with the 15-year-old son at the wheel. They approached, off in the distance, a large house set back from the road:

"My father told me to slow down, and scrutinized the place. He then said: 'Your grandmother was born there. A long time ago.' I may have asked him if he meant his mother—as it was bound to have been. That girl who had lived in that yellow house and who had married a young man coming back from four years of war suddenly became for me a single totally isolated mystery in the big mystery of my father's life."

Robert Penn Warren's inquiry into his father's life is a search for whence he came. But it is something more, too. In its modest way it attests to a man's need to know the long-dead father who was himself once a boy, who knew his own uncertainties, who courted his mother, who made his way in the world. Are boys left to wonder about this more than girls are? I suppose not. But the slender shelf of literature written by sons about fathers suggests to me something very human. If a boy yearns most of all for a father's sponsorship in the world, to borrow Lance Morrow's lovely phrase, he will yearn in his maturity to know who that man was that sponsored him—or did not.

Observations and questions

1) Study the sentences in the first two paragraphs of this piece. Is such structural complexity appropriate for newspapers? Can a reader in a hurry understand them? Can we and should we write different types of sentences in different sections of the paper?

2) The first paragraph ends with "a picture of the father who died writing a letter that got no further than 'Dear Son—.'" Study all the ways Skube reflects this image as he discusses fathers and sons and their intimate estrangement.

3) In a piece ostensibly about Warren, Skube digresses at length about William Humphrey. Do we have room in newspapers for digressing? Is this middle section really a digression? How can you tell?

4) Is this piece a review of Warren? Or is it an essay on fathers and sons? Or both? We have to answer those three questions to judge the success of this piece, because the standards for each would differ.

5) In the middle, Skube gets trickier, with sons wondering about fathers wondering about their own fathers. Study how he keeps all these layers straight in a short piece, without explaining them to death.

6) Twice Mr. Michael Skube implies that men wonder about and write about parents more than women do. If you are a woman, dear reader, does that idea offend you? Does it seem true? If you are a man, equally dear reader, does it offend you yet seem true? Our perspectives may limit what we can see and feel.

7) The last phrase of the last sentence turns the essay in a new direction: "he will yearn in his maturity to know who that man was that sponsored him—or did not." What does Skube mean here? Does he end abruptly, or does he send the reader off to think?

North to Alaska with James Michener

JULY 3, 1988

James Michener's new cinderblock of a book, *Alaska*, is 868 pages long, and I think I began reading it sometime toward the end of the last Ice Age. I have been chipping away at it, in any case, for what seems an awfully long time. *Alaska* (Random House, $22.50) is not a book to be read so much as got through. Events move along at glacial speed, an inch at a time, until the dinosaurs are gone and the oceans have receded and the landmasses have emerged and at last something we might recognize as Alaska comes dimly into view. When you've not read one in a while, you forget just how long a book James Michener can write.

Everyone knows, of course, about Michener. He writes woodenly, he appeals to people who move their lips when they read, and his books sell by the truckload, like so many boxes of bran flakes. It is all true and it is also shooting fish in a barrel to assert it every two years when Michener sits atop the best-seller list. Maybe a little snobbish, too. This is a plump and tough old tuna, and he has taken many a shell from his more literary detractors.

There's little point, then, in a critic's making a pre-emptive strike when the trucks dock outside the bookstores, freighted with spanking new Micheners. They will sell anyway. *Alaska*, which arrived in the stores less than two weeks ago, has made its first appearance on *The New York Times* best-seller list and is immediately No. 1. It will remain at the top or near it for a long while, in hardback and then in paperback. Michener's readers don't care what any reviewer thinks, and who knows that they are not the wiser for it?

More to the point, the reviewer doesn't set himself up to sell or not sell books. He offers unsolicited opinions about them, among other things. In Michener's case, the temptation is always strong to fire a few well-aimed BBs at the barn door and knock off for the day. I wondered, though, what it is that readers find in novels heavier than the dictionary and shapeless as a sack of potatoes. I kept thinking of what two writer-friends—both of them people I respect—happened to say recently. One was talking about Michener's energy: "Say what you want about his style, his writing, all of that. Here's a man 81 years old doing a hell of a lot of research and writing books that people want to read."

The other friend confessed to having read Michener's *Covenant*, his South Africa saga: "All I knew about South Africa from papers and TV was that its crazy government wouldn't let black people have the vote, so violence and strikes persist. Because the book started with events that happened something like 300 years ago, I understand better how South Africa got that way."

HISTORY AS FICTION

So it's "history," is it? Or at least the feeling of history. With Michener, fact and fiction are never far apart; indeed, one wonders if he does not write something we should call "faction." Regardless, his appeal is for many readers the feeling of real events, of history done up in fictional dress and on the march. "At least when I read Michener," I've heard people say, "I feel like I'm learning something." You might grit your teeth, as I did mine, but it's worth considering why intelligent people know so emphatically what they like.

Equally, it's worth considering that the line between fiction and non-fiction is not so inviolate as we sometimes think. Since the appearance more than 20 years ago of Truman Capote's *In Cold Blood*, fiction and non-fiction have borrowed from one another with scant regard for veracity or authenticity. E.L. Doctorow, in *Ragtime, World's Fair*, and other novels, places historical figures in situations that could not have existed. Robert Coover, in *The Public Burning*, has a narrator named Richard M. Nixon (he makes an appearance in Kurt Vonnegut's *Jailbird*, too). Joseph Heller's *Good as Gold* has a character who could only be Henry Kissinger. Gore Vidal not only puts his own words into Lincoln's mouth but gives him, in a manner of speaking, syphilis.

The reverse of this occurs at least as frequently —applying the storytelling techniques of fiction to journalism or history. Bob Woodward and Scott Armstrong's book about the Supreme Court, *The Brethren*, rests heavily on conversations the authors could not have overheard. Likewise Norman Mailer's "true-life novel" about the convicted murderer Gary Gilmore, *The Executioner's Song*.

"For many novelists," says the critic Michael Wood, "there comes a point when you think, 'I don't want to write another book about me and my divorce. My next work should be *significant*.' And so you go out hunting for historical material."

He was not speaking of James Michener. Historical matter is Michener's meat and he serves it up like hamburger. In *Alaska* (once we've made it out of the Bronze Age), we follow the Dutch navigator Vitus Bering, on commission from Peter the Great, tracking the vast emptiness east of Siberia. There are more Cossacks than Mikhail Sholokhov could ever have imagined, Aleuts and Eskimo chiefs, whale and walrus and an old wise woman called the Ancient One, the Gold Rush, and, if you make it that far, the Alcan Highway. And all this in a novel. There are people who say things like, "Son, if you take that route, you and me is gonna cross swords," and thoughts for the day like, "A man's character reveals itself on an ice pack or a mountain slope." There's a sex scene—I guess that's what it was—that made me think of two sawhorses.

Not to put too fine a point on it, this is not minimalist fiction. It is not a wan story about wan little people in which nothing happens. And that is precisely why Random House manufactured 750,000 copies of *Alaska* for first printing, and has already gone into second printing. Its octogenarian author, a publicist at Random House tells me, is on location in Miami researching a new docudrama—

Caribbean. Don't hold me to it, but I predict he will take us from roughly 1 million years ago to the Age of Fidel and Jimmy Buffett. And he will weigh in at just under 1,000 pages. When this man turns on the faucet, he lets it run.

Observations and questions

1) This review turns on Skube's exasperation with having to review dopey best sellers: "Michener's readers don't care what any reviewer thinks, and who knows that they are not the wiser for it?" Do we disbelieve a reviewer who belittles himself? Why?

2) Skube uses a composite quotation: "'At least when I read Michener,' I've heard people say, 'I feel like I'm learning something.'" Our profession's wisdom says that readers distrust unattributed quotations. Apply that standard to unattributed composites. How could the writer overcome this problem?

3) Skube quips: "There's a sex scene—I guess that's what it was—that made me think of two sawhorses." Study the understatement in this gag. Notice the lack of a verb after "sawhorses."

4) This sentence describes Michener's slow pace: "Events move along at glacial speed, an inch at a time, until the dinosaurs are gone and the oceans have receded and the landmasses have emerged and at last something we might recognize as Alaska comes dimly into view." Does that sentence read slow or fast? What creates the pace? How could we speed up or slow down the reader, and say the same thing?

5) Notice the images of heaviness: "cinderblock of a book," "a plump and tough old tuna," "in novels heavier than the dictionary and shapeless as a sack of potatoes," and "weigh in at just under 1,000 pages." Skube makes the reader feel Michener's clunkiness.

6) Skube snipes: "Everyone knows, of course, about Michener. He writes woodenly, he appeals to people who move their lips when they read, and his books sell by the truckload, like so many boxes of bran flakes." Reviews of pop fiction skate a fine line between judgment and offense to readers who simply like good stories.

T. S. Eliot's solitary search for salvation

NOVEMBER 6, 1988

"Nothing but a brilliant future behind me," T.S. Eliot said in 1934. He was 45 years old, the most revered figure in modern poetry, a man who with a single poem—"The Waste Land"—had given voice to an age. His triumphs were public and historic, his failures were private and hellish. It is these latter—the long shadows in T.S. Eliot's solitary existence as a man—that Lyndall Gordon explores in this second volume of her masterly biography. With its predecessor, *Eliot's Early Years*, it penetrates better than any previous biography to the skull beneath the skin (to borrow Eliot's famous words), and it does so in a manner that is as sympathetic as it is judiciously critical.

It has not always been easy to accord T.S. Eliot a measure of human sympathy. He was not a man whose feeling for others exactly bubbled over. His look was cold, severe, wrathful. The poet and essayist Donald Hall, in his fine book *Remembering Poets*, recalls first meeting him when Mr. Hall was editor of the *Harvard Advocate*, the campus poetry magazine: "His face was pale as baker's bread. He stooped as he sat at his desk, and when he stood he slouched like the witch in the gingerbread house. His head shook forward slightly, from time to time, almost as if he nodded toward sleep. He smoked, and between inhalations he hacked a dry, deathly, smoker's hack. His speech—while precise, exact, perfect—was slow to move, as if he stood behind the boulder of each word, pushing it into view. Eliot was *cadaverous* in 1951."

T.S. Eliot died in 1965, about the time his star went into full eclipse. We're apt to overlook in 1988, on the centenary of his birth, how supremely Eliot shone in the firmament only half a century ago. *The Cambridge History of English Literature* assigns to three writers alone the custody of entire periods of poetry and prose. In the *Cambridge History*, there is no Age of Milton, no Age of Dickens, not even an Age of Shakespeare. But there is an Age of Dryden and an Age of Johnson. And there is an Age of Eliot.

THE PRIVATE ELIOT

Lyndall Gordon—a lecturer in American and English literature at Oxford—doesn't waste her time or ours arguing Eliot's place in literature, although her incidental judgments strike me as sharp and discerning. Her real subject is Eliot as ambitious poet, unhappy husband, searcher for spiritual salvation, monk manque. The outward facts of his life are well-known. He grew up in St. Louis, went to Harvard, then to England after graduating. His interests were originally in philosophy—he finished a doctoral dissertation on F.H. Bradley—but he had written verse in his Harvard years. In Europe, he was befriended by Ezra Pound, who suggested he cut here and recast there a poem Eliot showed him. The poem, published in 1915, was "The Love Song of J. Alfred Prufrock."

In June of the same year, Eliot married a woman he had known less than three months, Vivienne Haigh-Wood. The marriage was a disaster, for both ("The awful daring of a moment's surrender/which an age of prudence can never retract"). It is one of Ms. Gordon's central points that "The Waste Land" was a reflection not only of the cultural disintegration of the postwar years, but also of Eliot's precarious sanity. The Eliots separated in 1933, Vivienne half sane and half not, her husband saved only by his conversion to the Anglican Church.

Eliot embraced the faith in 1927. The same year he renewed his friendship with Emily Hale, a woman he had been in love with before he sailed for Europe 12 years earlier. Emily Hale, in Lyndall Gordon's telling of the story, was the woman Eliot should have married and did not. She was the woman Eliot could have married once he and his wife separated, and still did not. "Emily Hale," Ms. Gordon writes, "never claimed, like Vivienne, to

have been Eliot's muse. She was concerned more
with the man than the poet.... Of the latent monk,
and the heights of a destiny that would exclude any
close human contact until it was fulfilled, she saw
perhaps not enough."

AN ETHEREAL LOVE

To a deeply unhappy T.S. Eliot, Emily Hale represented an idealization of love—she was pure
and, for Eliot, inviolable. Eliot, whose bloodline
was New England Puritan, had never been entirely
comfortable with the sordid rushes of the flesh, and
he never forgot his wife's adultery with Bertrand
Russell, his one-time benefactor. In Emily Hale,
Eliot saw "the material of religious poetry," Ms.
Gordon writes. "And when his poetic searching of
the soul came to an end, so too did his interest in
her."

The notion is magnificently Eliotic, and maybe
a little idiotic as well. In any event, "what Eliot
needed was not love in the usual sense, passion or
care, but love's transforming power, the idea of a
momentous drama, partly on the model of Dante
and Beatrice, partly a Jamesian drama of buried
sensibilities." Eliot was not the first to ask more of
love than love can give. By the time of his religious
conversion, the pre-eminent poet of modernism
was prepared to renounce love for salvation. Miraculously, he would find both. In 1957, eight years
before he died, he married his 30-year-old secretary, Valerie Fletcher.

"Marriage," Ms. Gordon writes, "brought out a
sense of fun that was always there, in the child on a
St. Louis street corner, smiling mischievously with
his nurse, Annie Dunne; in the middle-aged Eliot
who had entertained Janet Adam Smith's children
with readings from *Uncle Remus*." He had won the
Nobel nine years earlier; now the impulse to write
poetry was fading. Now he exchanged fan letters
with Groucho Marx (hanging his picture on his
mantelpiece alongside Yeats). He permitted himself domesticity, discussing cake shops and green-
grocers: "He liked to play the humorous pet, like

one of his cats who represent, in caricature, some aspects of Eliot himself. Macavity, the monster of depravity, vanished in this period, but Gus the theatre cat remained, and Jennyanydots, the domestic purrer."

The peace of which T.S. Eliot wrote in the years of his celebrity—the "still point in a turning world" —he found where he had never before looked. It is not the least of Lyndall Gordon's gifts as a biographer that she somehow portrays this most saintly and rarefied man as a man after all.

Observations and questions

1) This lead begins with a quotation: "Nothing but a brilliant future behind me." Think about the effects of beginning with the quote as opposed to the attribution. How does this quotation set a tone for all that follows?

2) Skube structures his review with an estimate of Eliot's changing stature, followed by a chronological retelling of the poet's life. What other structures might prove effective here?

3) Study the structure of the third paragraph: "T.S. Eliot died in 1965...And there is an Age of Eliot." How does Skube use repetition for rhythm and pacing? Could you shorten this paragraph without hurting it?

4) What is a "monk *manque?*" Would the average newspaper reader understand this reference? The average reader of a book page? The reader of a review of Eliot's biography? How can you tell?

5) Notice the variety of ways Skube cites names: T.S. Eliot, Eliot, Lyndall Gordon, Ms. Gordon, Vivienne, Emily Hale, Jennyanydots, etc. Would the piece gain clarity by consistent citation form, or would it lose variety? Now try to apply your opinion to an education beat story.

6) Skube has the privilege of writing his own head-lines, in this case: "T.S. Eliot's solitary search for salvation." The headline has a nice sound with all those esses. Does it capture the essence of what the review says?

7) The review ends: "...she somehow portrays this most saintly and rarefied man as a man after all." Skube gives us a sense of Eliot the man and of Gordon's book about him, all in a short space. Study how rigorous selection produces this sense of brief plenty.

A conversation with
Michael Skube

DON FRY: What was your first newspaper job?

The *Winston-Salem Journal* hired me to be its
Raleigh correspondent, that is, the capital bureau
chief...

**You mean you went from no journalism job at all
to being a bureau chief?**

That's right. [Laughter]

**That's what I call landing on your feet. What
does the Raleigh correspondent do?**

I covered state politics, the government, the capital, mainly the legislature. I think I was probably a
pretty good reporter because I have a taste for gossip [Laughter], and there's no getting around it, a
reporter has to have a taste for gossip.

How did you learn how to write news stories?

Well, they just threw me into the water. I walked
into the state legislature, and I knew that the House
was on the left and the Senate was on the right. I
instinctively knew that you have to say what happens first.

Did you get edited a lot in the beginning?

My news stories didn't, but my column did, and
that really irritated me, because I was very naive.
The column was a non-opinion column, and I was
not accustomed to writing that way...

A non-opinion column?

Well, it's a column in which you comment on

things without the slightest trace of opinion.

How do you do that?

I don't know. I couldn't do it. I couldn't say, "Water runs downhill." I'd have to say, "Water, most hydrologists think, runs downhill." I found it very confining. But I enjoyed reporting. I did not want to do it all my life, certainly, but I somehow took to it.

And you stayed in Raleigh, my hometown, by the way.

Yes. *The News and Observer* hired me in August 1982 to write editorials. I made that change because I wanted to be a book editor at some point, and I knew this would put me closer to doing that. *The News and Observer* had a book page, and the book editor was close to 60. And in January 1986, the editor, Claude Sitton, made me book editor. This is my dream job. I love this job.

Who taught you to write book reviews?

Really nobody. This evolves back 15 years. I opened up *The Miami Herald* one Sunday and saw the book page and thought, "Well, I could probably do this." I read a lot of Jonathan Yardley's reviews there. The first one I wrote was about 85 percent English and 15 percent Latin. I used one phrase, *ex nihilo*, "from nothing." I was trying to sound learned, which now embarrasses me. But Yardley did not print it, and he said, "Look, this is not a learned journal; this is a newspaper." I learned that lesson very quickly by reading other things.

What "other things"?

Well, *The New York Times, The Washington Post, The New Republic,* magazines in general. I would read something and try to imagine how I might have written it. I would look for ways not to write it, too, such as awkward expressions and indulgences, the things that any writer whose ear is always working will notice.

That's a very powerful way to create voices. I learned to teach by avoiding the things the bad teachers did.

Oh, I believe that. If you're writing all the time in your head, your ear has to be very active, so that when you're listening to anything at all on the radio, or you hear people talk, something registers. This is something largely inborn, and you do it from grade school on.

Are writers born or trained?

I would say both. I think you can teach a person how to write adequately and maybe fairly well, but for a writer who has a distinctive voice, that's probably inborn. Certainly there are writers who are natural writers who could use some tutoring, that is, they have a natural voice, but they don't pay much heed to the mechanics of writing. Conversely, there are writers who handle the mechanics quite well, but are just not interesting.

What do you mean by "natural voice"?

Well, a voice that's theirs almost alone. Someone who naturally will hit upon a phrase, or who hears something and knows that that's one way to say something. Someone who has an ear for a cadence, a rhythm, or a turn of phrase.

Do you think voices can be created?

I don't think so, no, no. Any writer can become a better writer, and I read people now with that largely in mind. I read writers I think are very, very good, and I try to see what they're doing. I have tried to let certain sounds register unconsciously in my head, and later to recall ways of saying things, not words, but rhythms.

Do you edit the free-lancers on your book page?

Yes, I do. I want them to write a book review, that is, a strongly opinionated comment, rather than a book report. And I've been just astonished at the kinds of people who can't write. I would have thought that certain Southern novelists would be good reviewers, but I saw their copy, and it was just unpublishable.

Maybe they had good editors in the publishing houses. Do you ever have writers who don't need editing at all?

Oh, yes, indeed. They're just very good writers. Anne Tyler, the novelist, writes for me, and her prose is just impeccable. But one time, I thought one sentence was uncharacteristically awkward, and I changed that sentence. She wrote me a note and said she did not like her copy being edited. Well, I don't like mine being fiddled with either. I wrote her back and said, "Anne, you've written about 10 reviews for me. That is about 800 sentences. I thought 799 out of 800 was pretty good." That was the only sentence I had ever changed of hers, but I would feel the same way.

You would? Why are writers so possessive about their sentences?

I think it's pride. Oh, I get terribly upset unless someone shows me that it's clearly better, and they have, sometimes. Fred Chappell is very unpossessive, and I admire him for it. He tells me to chop wherever I want to, rewrite as needed. So is Ed Yoder, who reviews for us. I've rewritten them, and I've not heard a peep out of them.

Do you think the rest of us object out of insecurity?

In large measure, yes.

Why are writers insecure?

Well, we're so proud, so vain of our own prose that we don't want to see someone else tampering with it.

How should an editor deal with us when we're proud and vain?

The editor ought to show why the sentence as it is does not work as well as it could. And certainly an editor's first duty is to do no harm...

[Laughter] "Do no harm," that's good.

...and the editor ought to read the piece through and try to get a sense for the piece as a whole, rather than read it and make changes as he or she goes along, and many editors do precisely that, especially newspaper editors. They make major changes because that's the way *they've* been changed.

My colleague, Roy Peter Clark, says you can tell someone's an editor if he reaches for his pen as he reads the first sentence. [Laughter] What makes a good editor good?

It's someone who has a sense for what you're trying to say in a piece, and who, at the same time, has a very good ear for language herself. And I say "herself," because the best editor I've ever had is my present editor, Marian Gregory. She very rarely changes anything in my copy, but she reads very critically, "critically" in the good sense of that word. I've been amazed at the questions she'll ask, and they are always illuminating.

Does she let you do the changes?

Yes, she does. She'll find things that never occur to me, perhaps where meaning did not necessarily follow, where even commas created a sound I never intended to create. She's just very, very astute as a reader. But many editors edit by habit. They've been doing the same thing every day, over and over, until it's the only way they know how to do it. And many of them do not know the language as well as they should. They think a word means one thing, when in fact it means something else. They don't have a sense that a paragraph has its own internal architecture.

I gave a workshop the other day on sentence clarity, and a reporter came up to me and said, "I didn't know that sentences had structure." [Laughter] He just wrote them.

I just cannot believe that.

You'd be surprised how unaware people are sometimes. They can write, but they're just clueless about how.

And some editors are condescending to readers. I recall an editor once who explained who Mickey Mouse was. A news story mentioned Mickey Mouse, and she appended, "..., a cartoon character created by Walt Disney." [Howls of laughter] If she's going to do that, she ought to also explain who Disney was! [Laughter]

OK.

I think that's just terribly insulting to people, and when I see it, I get furious! I've seen places where editors have made a story more clotted and less coherent by trying to explain more than any reader cares to know!

OK.

A story ought to have one or two good editors, but, for God's sake, not six and seven!

OK. OK. Let's talk about your book section. How many books a week do you review, and how much of that do you write?

I have two pages on Sunday. Not counting my column, which is sometimes on a book and sometimes not, roughly six to eight books a week.

How do you decide which books to review?

Well, you have to walk a largely unwalkable line between books that you as editor think deserve to be reviewed, and books that have some public interest. That's not to say that you review every best seller, because you don't. We don't. You try to find books that you think might produce a pretty interesting piece for a book-page reader. We aim for a fairly sophisticated yet general readership.

How do you envision that reader?

I don't. I think it's a mistake to imagine "the reader." I don't know who it is. There are many different kinds of readers. Newspapers talk about "the reader." Well, that's an abstraction. I try to imagine generally sophisticated readers, but not specialists. I want the reviews aimed toward those readers, want them to discuss the book in some larger context.

How do you go about writing a review?

I decide whether I want to write a more or less straight review of the book, as I did with the Peter Gay or the T.S. Eliot book, or whether I want to write a piece that is more a commentary based upon it, as I did with the Robert Penn Warren book. I ask myself which would make the more interesting piece, and...well, really, I guess I ask myself which would interest me more.

And this is while you're reading the book?

Right, yes. It's not something that you're doing actively all the time, but the notion is always there. I find that I often don't want to write just a book review, and yet, out of fairness, I don't want to make someone's book a vehicle for my own ideas. That's just plain unfair.

How do you organize your thoughts?

Well, I'm very disorganized to start with. I may underline here and there in the book. I take notes, far more notes than I can ever use. For a piece with maybe 800 words, I must take 700 words of notes...

We teach that about one note in 20 should get in the story in some form.

Is that so? Well, just last week, I wrote down four pages of notes on a book, and I found out later that I only used a couple of those notes. I thought, "My God, whatever happened to the other things?" But a piece ought to have a shape to it, and it shouldn't be just a grab bag of notes.

Right. That's called "selection." How do you select?

Ahh...I'm afraid that the way I do it would not make for a very good lesson.

[Laughter] That's OK; we're all idiosyncratic.

Well, I am, too. I try to find a point of departure, a lead. I try to make it interesting without knocking someone over the head. I try to have in mind, in a very general way, where the piece is headed, but I certainly don't outline.

How long does it usually take you to write a first draft?

Well, the first draft goes in the paper, I'm afraid. It takes me about three hours.

Three hours, that's pretty good for a book review. That's three hours of fingers on the keys, but you've been writing it since Tuesday, right?

Oh, I've been writing all the time, yes. I delay writing because I'm not sure of what to say, and so then comes Friday afternoon, I have to write something [Laughter], and I do. When you have something to think about, it's easier to think about it than to write it. I try not to overthink a piece, because then it becomes too intellectualized. It becomes too much a piece of interest to you, perhaps, but not necessarily to other people. I will think of the piece forever to change a word here and there, which is a form of writer's narcissism. I'm trying to make sure that things sound just so. I try to plane down sentences to the point where they're smooth.

Let's look at some of your sentences, starting with the review of Peter Gay's biography of Freud. Why did you choose this book to review?

I chose that book because Peter Gay is just a marvelous stylist. I've read him for about 12 years, and I've always envied him as a writer. Also, I've always had an interest in the history of ideas, and so Freud interested me. And I also had a sense that this would be a very important book this year.

Do reviews have leads?

Well, I guess anything has a lead, if you define a lead as the start of the piece, yes.

How about if I define it as a shapely beginning that gives the reader a sense of the piece?

Hmmm. I would say that they should have that, but they don't always.

What's a lead for?

The lead ought to hint at or declare the subject. One of my faults is to write too discursively at the outset. I don't often enough come out immediately and say what's on my mind, and I suppose that

194

writers do that because they're not sure what in fact *is* on their mind. [Laughter]

That's part of the insecurity we were talking about a while ago. It may also be a recollection of magazine form, which has a more discursive opening.
Do you write in sections, or do you conceive a review as one piece straight through?

Oh, as one piece straight through. I know that I'll be writing about 25 inches, 12 inches double-column. I try to keep that in mind as I'm writing, so that I'm not halfway down the track before I've brought my subject to the fore.

Here's a sentence I like: "In Gay's hands, the Olympian figure is almost within mortal reach." Do sentences like that just pop into your head?

Sometimes, yeah. I try to leave myself open to images that seem apt, and I try, if I can, to write in some way that conveys images of things that people can see. I don't recall laboring over that sentence. I find that sentences you labor over usually are the ones that end up sounding labored.

Yes, because they're hard to read. Somebody asked Jane Austen, "How do you come up with such wonderful scenes?" And Jane Austen cried, "Scenes will form."

Oh, that's right, yeah. That's good. That's very good. In that paragraph, I tried to have some variety of sentence structure, but I always try to do that.

Look at the last paragraph of this piece: "And yet Freud, like Marx, thought of himself as a scientist first and last, and fought all his life to defend the 'scientific' purity of psychoanalysis. He most of all feared that the American medical establishment would attempt to take over the brain

child to which he had given his life. His fears were unfounded; what he had most to fear was his own fractious followers who would force him to say, today, that he is no Freudian after all."

That last sentence comes from a lot of debate lately about Freud, which isn't spelled out in this review. What are you presupposing about the reader?

It probably presupposes, and wrongly so, that they're more familiar with the subject than some of them are. The last paragraph tries to tie in with what I said in the opening paragraph, Marx declaring, "I am no Marxist."

Do you try to write endings that reflect your beginnings?

I try to, yes. Often I don't. Although that can be very effective, it can also come off as very predictable and very mechanical. More often than not, it comes off as mechanical. If it's done deftly, it's good.

Good like this one. Do you know how the piece is going to end before you start?

No, I don't.

I always know how a piece of mine is going to end. I shoot for the ending as a target.

Well, that's the way you're supposed to. There have been some pieces in which I've done that, but I'm so disorganized that I let the piece unfold as I write, finding out what I think by writing it. [He laughs; Don doesn't.]

By the way, I know some very organized people who "think by writing it," which is not just the product of messiness. Let's talk about "Western lit from Milton to Zane Grey (and others)," your attack on English professors, my favorite target.

The New York Times Sunday Magazine ran a piece by James Atlas on the English department at Duke [June 5, 1988, 24ff] , which in the past six years or so has become very prominent for literary theory, for which I have very little use. And I thought some of these developments in English departments were just silly, just preposterous. I tried to show the solemnity with which they treat everyday subjects. I was trying to write that not every damn thing in the world needs to be analyzed to death. Many academics take themselves so damned seriously, and it's just fun to prick pompousness sometimes.

Let me file a disclaimer at this point: I'm a graduate of Duke's English department, and I was an English professor for 19 years. I gave up professoring for journalism because of the very things you're talking about here.

Hmmm. It seemed to me that their concerns were so narrow, and they were writing for one another. It also involved the diminution of the academic intellectual in American public life. I like to see people writing vigorously about things of concern to a broad public.

You're a character yourself in this piece, which begins: "Jane Tompkins of the Duke University English department is evidently an expert on Westerns and a professor besides, so I should be sheepish about betraying my naivete" And the piece ends: "Naive me." Talk about the character you're creating here.

Oh, self-mocking, I guess. There's a lot to mock [Laughter], so it's not hard for me to laugh at myself. If you can present yourself in print as just an ordinary Joe, it shows up their pompousness. I don't...

Don't you see the irony of presenting yourself as a kind of naive when you're blasting English professors for suddenly talking about Zane Grey?

Yeah, I do see that. Yes, yes, yes. [Laughter] One of the things that really bothers me is that they trivialize their profession. I absolutely love Zane Grey. I like mysteries. But why do they have to be the subject of so much exegesis? I just enjoy them.

Look at your second paragraph: "One should never be surprised to hear what's in style in the English departments..." Is that a pose, or do you feel that way?

Oh, I feel that way. In the last 10 or 15 years, they've just made laughing stocks of themselves. It bothers the hell out of me that there are many really very fine teachers of composition who are the low people on the totem pole. But people who write these obscure papers are the big names.

Later, you say: "'Gynocriticism'—the study of women in literature, for you simpletons who didn't know—is everywhere." Talk about sarcasm.

The danger is turning away the readers. Satire becomes sarcasm when the bile spills over a little bit. [Laughter] In that sentence, it was their pretentiousness of language and thought that irritated me so, and I wanted to poke them.

As journalists, we spend all of our time writing for the general public, trying to make things clear. So it's difficult for us to deal with people who are trying to do the opposite, make things complicated, even if they're writing about Zane Grey.

Well, they could write about these subjects in a high-toned way, but without resorting to this silly jargon. They try to make what they have to say sound more elevated.

Remember your reporting days, when you had to interview people like doctors...

Oh, yes. They hide behind jargon.

Yes, you want to get it in "people language," but doctors won't think it's real unless it's in their lingo. English department doctors are even worse.
    Let's go on to "Intimates and strangers, and fathers and sons." How did this piece come about?

I was reading Robert Penn Warren's *Portrait of a Father,* a touching little elegy. I had also read a number of other books over the past five or six years on the same subject, two especially, by William Humphrey and Lance Morrow. Warren writes about this subject of fathers and sons being intimates and strangers at the same time. That general notion was how I wanted to frame this piece. I had somewhere recalled a phrase that Lance Morrow once used about the father being the man that sponsored him, the son, in the world, and that struck me as so poignant and so apt that I wanted to share it with the reader. I knew more or less how I wanted to end the piece. I wanted to talk about Warren's book in the context of fathers and sons being intimates and strangers.

If you choose to turn a book review into a commentary, there's probably some reason driving you.

Probably. Here, first, I could talk about what I thought was a more compelling idea than just this one very fine book. Second, I was aware of at least four books that, in some way or other, did very much the same thing. If I had written about just Warren's book, I would have left out of this piece a very rich experience that I knew from other books, and I thought that Warren's book by itself, fine though it is, couldn't stand alone.

Let me ask you about the second paragraph: "To say that he does so with any chronological coher-

ence is irrelevant as it is wide of the mark; his intent in *Portrait of a Father*...is not biography or even portraiture. **Rather it is a searching of the kind that men seem not so much inclined to undertake as fated to."** Is there a difference between news sentences and review sentences? You couldn't write that sentence in a news story.

Oh, no indeed. Well, the difference comes in the columnist's charter to write opinion. A news sentence obviously is more confined, more constrained. It's not as personal. That sentence, although it does not necessarily apply to me, generalizes about men.

It's harder to read than a standard news sentence. You have to work at it.

Yeah, right. It's not a straightforward sentence.

In news stories, we're supposed to drink the sentences. In books, we like to chew them. Yours is a chewy sentence. You said you don't normally deal with best sellers; how about the Michener review?

Not normally, no. I wanted to see if I could really finish a Michener book, and by God, I did. [Laughter] I read one in high school, and I could only get through the first 600 pages. I wanted to ask what it is that makes these things so damned successful, and I wanted to do so without taking pot shots at what seemed to me a straw man. And, of course, I ended up doing just that. I think there is something to be said for someone who's 80-some years old and writing books that people want to read. I admire that. And yet, I wanted to give my honest reaction to what I read. I wrote that piece just looking to have fun.

This piece is a commentary on book reviewing.

Yes, it is, right.

Any reviewer dealing with very popular stuff risks the danger of condescension, saying, "You're fools for reading this stuff."

Yes. Yes. I don't question people's reading Michener. I might question their taste, but it amazes me that they could be so easily absorbed.

Your lead gets that nicely: "James Michener's new cinderblock of a book, *Alaska,* is 868 pages long, and I think I began reading it sometime toward the end of the last Ice Age." Maybe someday Michener will start a book with the Big Bang. [Laughter]

Well, frankly, this was just a piece that I wrote hoping not to sound serious.

I love this sentence almost at the end: "There's a sex scene—I guess that's what it was—that made me think of two sawhorses." How on earth did you come up with that bit?

I was trying to finish the piece. I wanted to mention a sex scene, and I wanted to suggest my own uncertainty about it...well, that sounds pretentious. I just wanted to be wry. I was aware that people had written about this business of fiction and "faction," and that was another subtheme I felt I should mention. Common readers do like these big books that give them a feel of something happening.

Do you dislike "faction"?

Not really. It's not my cup of tea, to coin a cliche. I have a distaste for what I would call the "graduate school novel," because they all sound alike: last year's divorce, things like that.

You skewered them very nicely right after the sawhorse quip: "Not to put too fine a point on it, this is not minimalist fiction. It is not a wan story about wan little people in which nothing happens."

I just don't read those books. I have tried to read them, but they are so self-consciously writerly. I have a real distaste for writers' workshop books. I think that writers' workshops are almost the worst things happening to American fiction. They're creating writers who live insulated in the university, and they write small little stories about small little people. They reduce the universe to the university, and there's no life in those stories. There is a sterility in so much American fiction now that I can hardly bring myself to read it, and that's one reason why I read the Michener, to find out what most people read.

Let's leap to Eliot. Why did you choose this book to review?

I thought this was a book I could write about, not as a specialist, but as a general reader.

People in my generation grew up with Eliot as a model, and many of us went through a phase of imitating him. So he's in our heads as a template we can't escape. Was that true for you, too?

No. I never read Eliot until I was in college. When I read this book, I was interested in the circumstances of Eliot's life much more than in his work. I wanted to find out what made him the man he was, for good and ill. I knew that his star had fallen. I had read his poetry, and I liked it, although it's cold in many ways.

Downright frigid sometimes. I like the way you start off with his wonderful quotation: "Nothing but a brilliant future behind me." It captures the terrible sadness of his life and the wonderful precision of his speech.

Yes, indeed. I wanted to find out about Eliot. A life like his, with all of its sadness, that's what probably attracted me to the book. And I just felt sorry for the man.

Well, he was a terrible person, and he led a terrible life.

Yes, he did. I was probably kinder to him than he may have deserved.

We live in an age of telling all the nastiness of the great figures, like Robert Frost, Sinclair Lewis, and people like that.

Oh, Lewis was a very hateable man. Most writers are, I guess. They're so self-absorbed.

I'm a pretty good fellow unless I'm writing; then my wife can't stand me. [Laughter] Let's talk about the ending: "The peace of which T.S. Eliot wrote in the years of his celebrity—the 'still point in a turning world'—he found where he had never before looked. It is not the least of Lyndall Gordon's gifts as a biographer that she somehow portrays this most saintly and rarefied man as a man after all."
Your reviews all have kickers. Why should we write endings on pieces? Why don't we just stop?

I think a piece, as opposed to a news story, ought to have a shape to it. I try to write "essayistically." I don't like a piece that just ends. It ought to be rounded. Starting a piece, I'm aware that I want it to have a certain form and shapeliness to it. Therefore, I want the beginning to fan out so I can close it. I don't want it to look like a sack of potatoes.

I think news stories need an ending, too. I'm very much opposed to the inverted pyramid. It's destructive of memory.

I bet you probably get a lot of resistance from editors though.

I do, but I go around saying it anyway, because I teach reporters not to write for editors, but for readers.

Reporters know what will get through and what won't, and between you and me, a lot of people learn how not to write by writing news stories. I have found that newspaper writers have a hard time writing pieces for me. I want a piece I can hear a voice in, and most newspaper writers have been trained to still that voice until it becomes dormant. And that's a terrible shame.

Well, I teach writers how to have a voice even in news stories, and the first thing you have to do is abandon the perverted pyramid. Well, Michael, you say you have your ideal job. Are you going to do this for the rest of your life?

I could probably do that, yeah. I like doing this, and I don't think any writer ever writes well enough. Any writer, I hope, wants always to learn to write better. And I see so many pieces of mine that I just know could have been done better.

How can writers learn to write better?

Read good writers and try to see what they're doing. Try to write in concrete terms and avoid abstractions. Try to find models, not just one model, but many models. In some unconscious way, I try to write like writers I admire, Lance Morrow and Joseph Epstein. They are basically essayists, but that's the kind of writing I like. Just learn from them.

And you think it's possible to have your own voice in a newspaper, right?

Yes, indeed, yeah. And that's what readers want to find. A writer should try to affect that reader, either provoke him, amuse him, charm him, irritate him, but don't leave him indifferent.

Absolutely. Thank you, Michael.

Thank you, Don.

Samuel Francis
Editorial Writing

SAMUEL T. FRANCIS, a native of Chatanooga, graduated from Johns Hopkins University, and received his doctorate in history from the University of North Carolina at Chapel Hill in 1979. Until 1981, he worked as a policy analyst at The Heritage Foundation in Washington, D.C., after which he served as a legislative assistant to Senator John East, a Republican from North Carolina. In 1986, Francis joined *The Washington Times* as an editorial writer, eventually becoming deputy editorial page editor.

A brief history of the L-word

OCTOBER 31, 1988

In what may be the most intellectually embarrassing event of the year, a small host of the nation's
literati last week took out a full-page ad in *The
New York Times* to upbraid President Reagan for
his attacks on "liberalism." "We regret," intoned
63 savants, "that the President of the United States
has taken the lead in vilifying one of our oldest and
noblest traditions. He made sport of 'the dreaded
L-word' and continues to make 'liberal' and 'liberalism' terms of opprobrium."

The signers include sociologists Daniel Bell and
Robert K. Merton; historians John Hope Franklin,
C. Vann Woodward, Fritz Stern, and Gordon A.
Craig; critics Irving Howe and Diana Trilling; writ-
ers Ralph Ellison, John Hersey, Eudora Welty, and
Robert Penn Warren; and university presidents
Derek Bok (Harvard), Donald Kennedy (Stanford),
and Steven Muller (Johns Hopkins). The list also
contains the seemingly ubiquitous names of Arthur
Schlesinger and John Kenneth Galbraith, as well as
those of Jimmy Carter's Secretary of State Cyrus
Vance and Robert S. McNamara.

The signers assure the reader that they paid for
the ad themselves and that it "has not been authorized by any candidate" —although you don't need
a Ph.D. to know which candidate most of these
eggheads are supporting. Nor do you need an advanced degree to see through the transparently fallacious argument that an attack on liberalism is an
attack on the principles upon which the American
republic was founded. We thought you weren't
supposed to deal in labels this year, but whatever
name you want to give to the ideas and principles
that informed the American founding, they bear
scant resemblance to what travels the world under
the passport of liberalism these days.

James Madison, Thomas Jefferson, John Adams,

and other founders believed in a free market economy based on private property, divinely given rights and duties, the rule of law, and government by the consent of the governed. For a century and more that creed was known as liberalism, and properly so. The term comes from the Latin word for "free," and it describes the body of ideas that defend and establish liberty—political, economic, and social.

By the early 20th century, however, the meaning of the word changed in subtle but profound ways. The literati of the day endeavored to prove that the Framers were really prisoners of selfish economic interests (Charles Beard), that law is whatever courts say it is (Oliver Wendell Holmes), and that a centralized state could achieve more progress than local, private, and voluntary institutions (John Dewey and John Maynard Keynes, among others). The brainstorms of these and other gentlemen brought us the debacles that many Americans now associate with the L-word, which is why most L-politicians avoid the L-label.

In criticizing contemporary liberalism, Mr. Reagan and other conservatives assail a discredited ideology that has prevailed for 50 years, not the real liberalism on which American government was based. The 63 ad-signers are smart enough to know this. "Words," wrote Thomas Hobbes, another great liberal, "are wise men's counters; they do but reckon with them, but they are the money of fools." America's intellectual weight-lifters ought to pay more attention to the substance of what is going on around them and less to the labels used to disguise it.

Observations and questions

1) The author begins by calling *The New York Times* ad "the most intellectually embarrassing event of the year." He leaves out the answer to the question, "Embarrassing to whom?" Study the unspoken assumptions about audience in this piece.

2) Francis calls the signers "literati" twice, "savants," "eggheads," and "intellectual weight-lifters" in a thoroughly intellectual editorial. He says, "although you don't need a Ph.D. ... nor do you need an advanced degree...," even though Francis has a Ph.D. How does he keep this attack on liberal intellectuals from becoming an anti-intellecual tract?

3) In the second paragraph, Francis lists 19 of the 63 signers. Notice how he groups them and labels the groups. Would a straight list without labels create different effects? How about a bulleted list with each character labeled? How else could he list them?

4) The list has no ideological labels, either on the group as a whole or on the individuals. In our interview, Francis told me that his conservative readers would not necessarily identify all these listed signers as liberal "baddies." Those readers have to do a lot of thinking here.

5) Francis uses a phrase, "what travels the world under the passport of liberalism these days," that will remind many readers of the phrase "fellow travelers," meaning communist sympathizers. Is this kind of sly hinting fair?

6) The author cites the trio of conservative heroes (James Madison, Thomas Jefferson, and John Adams) in his attack on liberals, despite the irony that liberals cite the same trio as their heroes! Think about the different associations these three names will have for different audiences, and how writers might use those associations.

Heroism on trial?

DECEMBER 7, 1988

As the sun of the Reagan administration begins to set, the conservative pack wants Mr. Reagan to issue a pardon for Lt. Col. Oliver North. Columnist Pat Buchanan, the conservative weekly *Human Events*, the editorial page of *The Wall Street Journal*, Sen. Orrin Hatch, and Rep. Henry Hyde all have endorsed the idea on the grounds that Col. North acted as a hero in trying to save the Nicaraguan Resistance from an irresponsible Congress and that a pardon will preserve the rights and power of the presidency from congressional gluttony.

Mr. Reagan firmly rejected this counsel last week in deciding, correctly, that the executive power of clemency ought not to be exercised prior to a trial for the accused in the Iran-Contra matter. It is true that President Ford pardoned ex-President Nixon in 1974, but it is likely he did so out of a sense of the urgent need to awaken the nation from what he called the "long national nightmare" of Watergate rather than from any grasp of the basic purposes of the pardoning power, let alone any belief in Richard Nixon's innocence or heroism. The Iran-Contra scandal, to the immense disappointment of many Democrats, is not comparable to the earthquake of Watergate, nor is a National Security Council aide comparable to a former president. The analogy between a pardon for Mr. Nixon and one for Col. North does not hold water.

The legality of issuing a pardon prior to a trial is not in question. As long ago as *ex parte Garland* (1867), the Supreme Court held that, save for the constitutionally excepted procedure of impeachment, "the pardoning power...extends to every offense known to the law, and may be exercised at any time after its commission, either before legal proceedings are taken, or during their pendency, or after conviction and judgment." What is at issue in whether Mr. Reagan should exercise this power on behalf of Col. North is the wisdom of using it, not its lawfulness.

To say that Mr. Reagan should not issue a pardon for Col. North at this time is not to imply that the defendant is guilty as charged. The dubious constitutionality of the special prosecutor's office, the implications for national security if the trial proceeds, and the vagaries of the Boland Amendment—all five of them—raise serious problems that may make a fair and legal trial impossible. Nevertheless, in the course of implementing what his defenders say was his patriotism, Col. North may have violated several other laws that are less murky than the foreign policy ukases issued by Congress.

Col. North also stands accused of having lied to Congress and to Attorney General Edwin Meese and of having destroyed documents in an effort to obstruct investigation of the Iran-Contra matter. He also faces charges of theft of government property, fraud, conspiracy, and accepting an illegal gratuity in the form of a security system for his home. In denying the motion that charges be dismissed, Judge Gerhard Gesell held that "North did in fact have fair warning that mendacity and obstruction, coupled with destruction of official documents, was illegal. If the allegations in the indictment are factually correct, North breached the high public duty with which he was entrusted."

If Col. North and his lawyers want to challenge Congress's right to conduct foreign policy, and to argue that he violated Congress-made law in order to serve the interests of national security, patriotism, and anti-communism, they are free to do so. But they are not free to argue that our system of law excuses violations of the law by people pursuing laudable public policies.

Nor, for that matter, can a free government, ruled by laws, tolerate the policy vigilantism routinely practiced by Speaker of the House Jim Wright or a small host of other self-appointed private diplomats who undertake to make commitments for the United

States without the slightest authority. If Col. North faces trial and prison for his heroism, such others should also be brought to book.

In the course of a trial on the charges against him, Col. North will have an opportunity to prove his heroism by accepting the legal penalties that a selfless commitment to Nicaraguan freedom involved. He will then be in the position occupied by Henry David Thoreau when, after being imprisoned for refusing to pay what he believed were unjust taxes, he demanded of Ralph Waldo Emerson why he was *not* in jail. If Col. North confirms the selflessness of his conduct, then a presidential pardon may be in order, but to grant clemency now, before a trial has clarified the moral and legal character of the defendant and his claims, would leave the colonel and his professed commitments to freedom and the nation in a limbo from which they would never emerge.

Observations and questions

1) In the first sentence, think about the implications of the phrase "conservative pack" on a conservative editorial page. How will the word "pack" affect the author's authority with his readers?

2) This piece has a number of long but clear sentences. Study how the writer constructs long sentences without losing his readers. Are such weighty but navigable sentences appropriate for newswriting? Are they appropriate in editorials?

3) The second sentence begins with a list: "Columnist Pat Buchanan, the conservative weekly *Human Events*, the editorial page of *The Wall Street Journal*, Sen. Orrin Hatch and Rep. Henry Hyde all have endorsed..." Rearrange this list for different effects. The order of a list has meaning.

4) Francis suggests that former President Ford lacked "any grasp of *the basic purposes* of the pardoning power," but does not explain those purposes himself. Would this editorial improve with such an explanation? How much space would you devote to it, and where would you put it?

5) Francis uses a legal citation to introduce a quotation: "As long ago as *ex parte Garland* (1867)..." Is he being academic, showing off, exercising precision, building his authority, nodding to lawyers, or what? Newswriting lacks footnotes, and any type of citation can look fussy and academic. How else could Francis introduce this quotation?

6) Watch the pronoun "he" in this sentence: *He* will then be in the position occupied by Henry David Thoreau when, after being imprisoned for refusing to pay what *he* believed were unjust taxes, *he* demanded of Ralph Waldo Emerson why *he* was *not* in jail." Pronouns clobber clarity. Rewrite the sentence several ways to make it clearer, while preserving meaning.

Patuxent's animal farm

DECEMBER 14, 1988

The tales coming out of Howard County's Patuxent Institution seem more appropriate for Halloween than for Christmas. The nightmarish stories include that of William Ray Prevatte, who was sentenced to life in prison at age 14 for murder, released on parole by Patuxent in 1977, and who wound up back in the slammer a year later for conspiring to murder again. Sentenced to 40 years, Prevatte was released once more by Patuxent in 1982. Then there's William Howard, sentenced to life for rape but released from Patuxent after serving less than eight years and who proceeded to commit three more rapes after his release.

Defenders of Patuxent's unique rehabilitation program say such failures are not representative, that the program enjoys a recidivism rate of only 18 percent, the lowest in the state. That probably doesn't make the victims of Patuxent's alumni feel much better, let alone reassure Maryland citizens that they are much safer than when the parolees were behind bars. But regardless of the "success rate" of the institution's therapy, the program ought to be shut down because it misses the whole point of criminal justice.

Patuxent's view of crime is drawn from what is usually described as a "progressive" approach but which is really about as stale as last year's bread. The theory is that criminal conduct is only a kind of "disease" for which the crook is not responsible, and that a "cure" rather than "revenge" or "punishment" is needed to control law-breaking. The theory goes back at least as far as the Enlightenment and reflects what criminologists James Q. Wilson and Richard Herrnstein call "the modern belief in the perfectibility of mankind and the responsibility of the state to strive for that perfection."

The problem with the theory is that it denies the moral responsibility of the criminal and in fact opens the door to indefinite incarceration and dehumanizing "treatment." Since the theory essentially denies the moral responsibility of other human beings as well—both law-abiders and law-breakers are motivated by the same uncontrollable forces—it also makes nonsense of the concept of a "just" or "unjust" sentence or law and jeopardizes any restraint of criminals at all. If no one is morally responsible for his actions, then legislatures, police, and courts have no moral authority to pass laws, make arrests, or sit in judgment.

When psychiatry replaces justice, no moral distinction can be drawn between a serial murderer and a shoplifter—both are equally "sick," and the thief's "illness" may in fact take longer to "cure" than that of the killer. Regardless of what sentence duly constituted courts may hand down, the head shrinkers can override what the law authorizes by releasing the convict only when he is "well." That may be soon, as in the case of Patuxent, but it could also be late—or never, if the experts so decide.

By contrast, traditional theories of retributive justice are based on the premise that human beings —even criminals—know what they are doing. That's why most criminals are sneaky about their crimes, taking pains to hide their complicity and avoid capture. If men and women are responsible for their actions, then they merit praise and reward when they do something good and punishment when they do something wrong. The rehabilitation lobby dismisses such elementary notions of justice as "barbaric" and "throwbacks," but as Professors Wilson and Herrnstein remark, "One should be curious, if not suspicious, about a claim that an idea that has endured for thousands of years and through all the cultural changes of those millennia, has suddenly, in our time, fallen into disrepute."

What has fallen into disrepute in our time is the Patuxent Institution's bizarre notion of justice that not only turns hardened and duly convicted criminals loose on the streets but also reduces the humanity of the criminals themselves by denying them the essentially human traits of will and responsibility. That's why Maryland lawmakers should exercise their own moral responsibility and close down a program whose therapeutic view of crime and punishment is more appropriate to veterinarians than to doctors and those sworn to govern by law.

Observations and questions

1) Francis refers to "the 'success rate' of the institution's therapy." Think about the effects of putting "success rate" in quotation marks. Study other uses of quotation marks in this piece. Punctuation is another arrow in the writer's quiver.

2) "The theory is that criminal conduct is only a kind of 'disease' for which the crook is not responsible." Substitute various nouns for "crook" in that sentence for different effects.

3) "That probably doesn't make the victims of Patuxent's alumni feel much better, let alone reassure Maryland citizens that they are much safer than when the parolees were behind bars." Why does Francis use the phrase "Patuxent's alumni"? What does the phrase tell the reader about his opinion of the institution's staff and attitudes?

4) Study the logic of the fourth paragraph: "The problem with the theory...or sit in judgment." What assumptions does the author make? What steps does he leave out of his argument? Editorialists get less space than reporters, but have to say more complicated things.

5) List all the things that make this sentence difficult to follow: "Since the theory essentially denies the moral responsibility of other human beings as well—both law-abiders and law-breakers are motivated by the same uncontrollable forces—it also makes nonsense of the concept of a 'just or unjust' sentence or law and jeopardizes any restraint of criminals at all." Now rewrite it as many ways as you can without changing the meaning.

6) Although editorialists get less space for more turf, they get to use loaded words like "crook" and "headshrinkers." How can reporters use such words without compromising objectivity?

Ché Pell

DECEMBER 15, 1988

If you thought Mikhail and Raisa were a stitch, just wait til you meet Fidel Castro. According to Sen. Claiborne Pell, recently returned from a boondoggle to Cuba and a three-hour chin-wag with the Cuban strongman, Mr. Castro is "a man of great personal vitality and vivacity" and "as an individual he had, I think, a good deal of charisma." From these insights, Mr. Pell concludes that the United States should start "normalizing" relations with Mr. Castro's unreconstructed communist government.

Mr. Pell had an opportunity to observe Mr. Castro's vitality personally when the subject of the projected U.S.-based TV Marti was broached. "He got very excited about this, really leapt around and very upset," says the Rhode Island Democrat, and, perhaps to keep Mr. Castro from jumping his tracks altogether, the senator agreed with him that TV Marti was "a step in the wrong direction." He left Cuba with the belief that Radio Marti, which has been broadcasting to Cuba from a station in the United States, is also a boo-boo that only helps to "continue the bad relationship between our two countries."

Mr. Pell acknowledged to *Times* reporter Pete LaBarbara that Cuba is somewhat remiss in observing human rights. But nobody's perfect, and if Mr. Castro's Cuba looks a bit like the Dark Ages, that's balanced out by the fun-loving personality of El Presidente. "[Mr. Castro] seemed to have a little bit more of a sense of humor than he did 14 years ago, but I guess that's because his regime is more entrenched than it was 14 years ago," says Mr. Pell. Soon after the senator's departure, the jolly caudillo enjoyed himself by rounding up "anti-social elements," including "counterrevolutionaries" and other dissidents, in preparation for the expected visit of Mikhail Gorbachev.

Mr. Pell's reflections, banal as they are, would be unworthy of comment save for the fact that the Rhode Island Democrat happens to be chairman of the Senate Foreign Relations Committee and thus occupies a key position from which to exert influence on the real world. The real world ought to respond to the chairman's latest revelations by ignoring him as much as possible.

Observations and questions

1) In the first two sentences, Francis uses "stitch," "boondoggle," and "chin-wag." What tone does this slang create? What expectations will that tone create for the reader? Does Francis meet those expectations?

2) This editorial uses every type of honorific, from none ("Mikhail and Raisa") to full ("Sen. Claiborne Pell"). Study how Francis uses these departures from the stylebook and consistency to create meaning. Beat reporters seldom have that freedom. How could they gain it, and how could they use it?

3) "Mr. Pell acknowledged to *Times* reporter Pete LaBarbara that Cuba is somewhat remiss in observing human rights." Think about the effect of the word "somewhat" in that sentence. How can we use this technique of understatement to create tone and emphasis?

4) The author calls Castro "the jolly caudillo." Do you know what "caudillo" means? Would your readers? How can we judge which foreign words our readers will know? ("Caudillo" means "chieftain" in Spanish, with connotations of dictatorship.)

5) The author saves until the last paragraph the fact that Pell chairs the Senate Foreign Relations Committee. Why? A reporter would have to glue that title to the first mention of Pell's name. Do editorial writers have less obligation to keep the reader firmly oriented?

6) The editorial ends like this: "The real world ought to respond to the chairman's latest revelations by ignoring him as much as possible." This ending fits the gentle mockery of the rest of the piece, but hits softly. Rewrite this kicker five times, each time making it hit harder, but without violating the tone.

The way we weren't

Once upon a time human beings lived in what was called the "Stone Age," a grim epoch before the Pyramids, the Parthenon, or even the Beatles. Back then, so we were told, everyone looked and talked like Mr. T, lived off nourishing meals of raw flesh, and got married by knocking a woman over the head with the thigh bone of a dinosaur and dragging her off to a cave. Now comes evidence that all this is fantasy. According to last week's *New York Times* Science section, archaeologists are discovering that prehistoric people were what used to be called "civilized."

Students of archaic cultures have long assumed that modern-day primitive societies, such as those of the Kalahari Bushmen in the deserts of southern Africa, are pretty much the same as those of prehistoric man. The problem with that assumption, says the University of Illinois's Olga Soffer, is that "You can't expect fancy things in a desert...people 20,000 years ago weren't all living in deserts. They were living in great places, too."

The places where they lived might not have come up to the standards of Kennebunkport, but the locals seem to have managed. In regions such as central Russia, northern Europe, and the Middle East, prehistoric evidence has accumulated of permanent settlements and buildings, complex social relationships, food banking systems, and external trade. Admittedly, it is difficult to believe that these modern wastelands ever supported civilization, but science often surprises.

One surprisingly developed society was led by people called the "Natufians." Why they are called that is not entirely clear, since they left no written records, and there are no Natufians around today. Nevertheless, the Natufians lived 13,000 to 14,000 years ago in what is now Israel, and according to the

Times, "the Natufians built what are believed to be the first fully sedentary communities: large permanent settlements, with elaborate buildings and extensive storage facilities, semi-subterranean houses— 'everything but mailboxes, practically,' said Dr. [T. Douglas] Price of Wisconsin." There are two possible reasons why they had no mailboxes: (1) there was no one else in the world to send them any mail, or (2) there was lots of mail, but the postal service was too primitive to deliver it—further evidence that the more things change, the more they stay the same.

Then there were the famous cave-painters of Western Europe. Their paintings of animals and hunts 35,000 years ago are now believed to reflect what New York University's Randall White says was "a shared set of social ideas that are very complicated." It would be nice to think that 35,000 years from now some expert might say that about 20th-century art. Not too long after the cave-painters, people on the Russian plain were making and wearing "fancy things no one else gets to wear, made out of exotic materials acquired through long-distance trade, that the ordinary villager could not get," according to Dr. Soffer. Mikhail Gorbachev's tailored Italian suits are an example.

The new interpretation of prehistoric times challenges what the *Times* calls "the view that humans progressed broadly and uniformly through the ages, moving from one clear stage of advancement to another in an almost preordained series of cultural and technological revolutions." In other words, human beings back then were pretty much the same as they are now, with the same needs, hopes, and vanities. The faces that stare back at us from mankind's most distant mirror look remarkably like ourselves, and they whisper to us to be a bit more humble about our own achievements and somewhat prouder of where we came from.

Observations and questions

1) When a piece begins "Once upon a time...," what do readers expect? How does Francis play with those expectations?

2) "Archaeologists are discovering that prehistoric people were what used to be called 'civilized.'" Why does Francis say "used to be"? How does the phrase relate to his conservative stances?

3) Francis lists "central Russia, northern Europe, and the Middle East" as "modern wastelands," and doubts that they "ever supported civilization." Think about the problems potentially caused by sarcasm, which readers might take straight.

4) The author explains why the Natufians lacked mailboxes: "There was lots of mail, but the postal service was too primitive to deliver it—further evidence that the more things change, the more they stay the same." Francis participates in a long satirical tradition of beating up on the present by showing either the superiority of the past, or its similarity. How could we use that tradition in beat writing?

5) Francis cites "Mikhail Gorbachev's tailored Italian suits [as] an example" of how "not too long after the cave-painters, people on the Russian plain were making and wearing 'fancy things no one else gets to wear, made out of exotic materials acquired through long-distance trade, that the ordinary villager could not get.'" This technique, called "anachronism," violates normal time to make a point. How could we use this device in normal reporting?

6) The last sentence takes an unexpected turn, from poking fun at archaeologists' views of the past to taking their conclusions seriously. Does all that precedes this sentence undercut it, or does the sentence undercut all the mockery above it?

A conversation with
Samuel Francis

DON FRY: *The Washington Times* **editorial staff has changed a lot lately, right?**

SAM FRANCIS: Yes. There was a large resignation about six months after I came. The resignation had to do with a matter of editorial policy between the owners and the editorial staff, and I chose to stay, as did another writer. I suddenly found myself the senior writer in the editorial department. [Laughter] I really had no idea how a newspaper operated, or how editorials got from the computer terminal to the printed page.

So six months after you became a journalist, you headed the editorial page?

Well, I was not the acting editor, but I began to function, in some cases, as the acting editor. I started writing editorials on subjects I had not written on before, and editing other writers. And that went on for about two months until the present editor of the page, Tony Snow, was hired in June 1987. I was promoted to deputy editorial page editor in December 1987.

When you walk out of the editorial meeting with an assignment, have you negotiated length, or do you just write to whatever length you please?

I find it very unsatisfying not to know what length I'm going to write for. Because of the space limitations on the page, it's necessary to know, within two to three inches, what the length should be. The advice of just writing until you get through with it and say all you want to, is not good advice.

It certainly doesn't serve the reader...

No. And it doesn't help the writer either. [Laughter] And it's a disservice to the editor, because if eight inches has to be cut out of a piece, there's going to be a serious problem in getting the thing out.

The Washington Times **has a well-deserved reputation as a conservative paper. Do you have a spread of opinions on your editorial staff?**

Yes. We range from...well, one of our writers was a Jesse Jackson supporter last year, and it ranges over to...

Attila the Hun?

I would not quite say that. I would say to the moderate Hun position. There's more diversity in the editorial page at the *Times* than outsiders would be inclined to think.

People have a lot of stereotypes about *The Washington Times.* **How would you describe it?**

Well, it's owned by the Unification Church, the "Moonies," and it was founded in 1982. Its main competitor is *The Washington Post*, of course.

Are you a member of the church?

No.

Is anybody on the staff a member?

Not on the editorial staff. There are members of the church who work for the paper as reporters and editors.

Operationally and intellectually speaking, what does it mean to be owned by the Unification Church?

As far as I can see, it doesn't mean anything. Earlier I spoke about the resignation of the editorial staff in April 1986. This was the issue at the time, that the editor of the page believed that the ownership of the paper had intruded in the editorial policy in dictating an editorial. I just simply disagreed with that interpretation, and I maintain to this day that I was right. I've never observed anything since that time, or, in fact, before that time, that would lead me to think that the church or the owners are dictating editorial content or policy. There have been occasions where both the editor-in-chief and the editor of the page have been out of the building, and I have approved or written or edited and published editorials without checking with anyone, and at no time has any representative of the owners or anyone else ever vetoed or made suggestions or given any orders about an editorial.

How about endorsements? Is that where the ownership gets into the picture?

I've never consulted with the owners about endorsements. I don't know of any editorial writer or editor who ever has.

How would you characterize the political stance of the paper itself, not of the page, but of the paper?

I would say it's generally conservative. There are exceptions, depending on the section of the paper. Some sections, such as the Life section, are generally considered to be to the left of the news and the national and foreign sections. The editorial page itself is centrist-conservative to right-of-center conservative. Jack Kemp would be a symbol of the editorial line of our page. Ronald Reagan would actually be the archetype, I suppose.

Does the paper consider itself a national paper or a local paper?

The paper probably considers itself a national paper, and we do get quite a few letters from readers who are not in the Washington area. I think it's a local paper. It's oriented mainly to a local audience. It has a good deal of coverage of events in the metropolitan area: Northern Virginia, Maryland, and the District.

Who are your readers? I don't mean demographically, but whom do you think of when you're writing?

I personally think of an editorial reader as someone living in the suburbs, a professional or semiprofessional person in the Washington area. I imagine that person has some connection with the government or with public policy-making, either as an adviser, or officeholder, or a decision-maker, or in the private sector, the media perhaps, someone who would be in a position to influence public policy and decisions.

Can you characterize your readers outside the area?

Most of them are probably ideological conservatives who read the paper because it is a conservative paper. They would regard it probably in the same way as they would the editorial page of *The Wall Street Journal,* or *National Review*, or some of the conservative magazines.

Do opinion-makers who are *not* conservatives read you?

We get very angry responses from them on the editorials. And, in fact, sometimes we get similar responses from conservatives. But, simply because the *Times* is a daily paper in the nation's capital, it's required reading for people who want to follow public affairs. The paper has stories that the *Post* and *The New York Times* don't have, and we have opinions that aren't normally represented in those papers. And yet, especially under the Reagan and the Bush administrations, those opinions have a good deal of political power in Washington, so that explanations or defenses or criticisms of those opinions are necessary for policy-makers.

Let's talk about your writing techniques. How do you come up with your own topics?

I look at the newspapers for topics that would interest me, usually cultural themes, or issues or problems in the general political culture. Frankly, I am less interested in the political issue of the day, whether someone will be confirmed or not, or whether a certain bill will pass, than I am in the larger issue: what this represents for the political culture and the political values of American society.

Once you've got your idea and assignment, do you do any reporting?

Yes. Depending on the topic and the nature of the topic, my reporting would generally consist of making phone calls, and occasionally going to a hearing, or meeting with someone, if I had the time to do that.

How do you know when to stop reporting? How do you know when you've got enough?

Well, since this is an editorial, you're writing for a conclusion to support an argument. When you have enough to support the argument, and when you've shown yourself there's nothing that falsifies the argument...

Do you typically do the reporting and then discover the conclusion, or do you usually have the conclusion and go do the reporting to support it?

Again, depending on the topic, often the conclusion is formulated as a hypothesis, at least, this is how it should be formulated. I'm not suggesting you formulate the conclusion definitively and then fill in the blanks. But you should at least formulate a hypothesis, and then the questions and research that you do are oriented to confirming or falsifying the conclusion.

Sounds like the scientific method to me.

Yes, in a sense, although the execution of it is not as scientific as that would make it sound.

How do you organize your material? How do you know what you want to say?

I don't start writing until I know what my conclusion is going to be. And I try to make the lead paragraph point to the conclusion in a variety of ways. I try not only to introduce the subject of the piece, but also to suggest, through the tone and information, where the editorial is going to go. And from the lead, I try to set out the basic facts of the issue, and then have a counterpoint, or a kind of backing away from the lead toward the middle of the editorial, and then rebut the counterpoint, and bring the thing to a conclusion. This is generally the structure I try to use.

Sounds like you've had judicial training somewhere. Maybe that comes from training as a historian.

Well, it may be. I think of it simply as a fair way to present the argument, and what an intelligent reader wants to hear.

Do editorials have to be fair?

Yes. I think they do.

What does "fair" mean?

Well, they have to be truthful, and the truth, by its nature, is going to be fair. You can still be fair if you use hyperbole and irony and all the devices that writers use, but it's a very weak editorial that suppresses something that would contradict the argument, or forces a conclusion that the truth doesn't justify.

It underestimates the reader, doesn't it?

Yes.

OK, you know what you want to say, and you discover what's next by writing it?

Yes. I very seldom write outlines, for example. When I first started writing editorials, I would write outlines. In fact, I was not used to composing at a computer terminal, and I would very often write the whole thing out in longhand. [Laughter] I try to develop a sense of movement in the piece, so that the reader moves from sentence to sentence in a fluid way. Writing outlines tends to inhibit that. I don't necessarily recommend this for everyone who writes editorials, but it works for me.

Are you edited much?

In the past, some of the editorials have been very heavily edited, but these five editorials were not edited significantly.

Is that because you've gotten better, or because you have a different editor?

Well, I think the editor has gotten better. [Laughter] I'm not usually a heavy editor myself. First of all, a writer almost has a right to say what he or she wants to say, and it is not the editor's function to change what the writer wants to say. There are ways that an editor can help a writer say it, but I think that writers should be selected on their ability to say things that the editor is going to be comfortable with, and to say them in ways that the editor will be comfortable with. My editing is usually confined to strengthening editorials. If there are major problems in an editorial, I give it back to the writer.

Good for you. Have you learned anything about writing from editing other people?

Yes. I've learned to express ideas about writing that I had not been able to express before. I can tell people where in a sentence to put things like the time element or place elements, and things like that, that contribute to the emphasis of the sentence, and the sense they're trying to convey.

I find editorial writing a very compressed art form. Editorials have a particular structure in the same way that a sonnet does. The concept of an introduction, development, and conclusion is essential. For younger writers, one of the major problems is the organization and the structure of the editorial. They lack form altogether.

So good editing is a form of teaching, right?

Yes. There's a good deal to be learned about human psychology from learning how to write. You write in order to communicate with people who don't necessarily want to read what you've written, and the idea is to trick them into reading it. I generally write editorials on the assumption that the readers don't want to read them.

So you have to be brighter at the top, right?

Yes. For me the most important part of the editorial is the lead sentence.

What makes a good editorial good?

It's partly the cogency of the argument, but also the vitality of the language. The language has to be written in a way that does not intimidate readers, but will either amuse them or stir their emotions in some way. Occasionally, you may want to lead the reader through his emotions to the conclusion.

Most people think of editorials as analytical and dry. How do you use emotions?

Well, I try to use humor. I try to use a sense of outrage in certain kinds of issues. I tend to use sarcasm. I occasionally will use sentimentality. I'm
not saying that the argument or the conclusion
should depend on that, but they're important to develop, because emotion conveys a sense of the importance of the analysis. The analysis without the
emotion is not going to draw very many readers in.

**Let's talk about some of your editorials, starting
with "A brief history of the L-word." What's the
background on this one?**

During the election campaign in October, there
was an ad in *The New York Times* taken out by this
group of intellectuals objecting to Ronald Reagan's
use of the word "liberalism" in a negative sense. It
came at one of the more frayed moments of the
campaign, when accusations between Bush and
Dukakis were going back and forth over the Pledge
of Allegiance and Willie Horton and Iran-Contra
and whose character was best, and that sort of
thing. So the purpose of the editorial was simply to
clarify some distinctions that had been obscured by
the ad, and by some of the participants in the campaign rhetoric.

**Let's look at the lead: "In what may be the most
intellectually embarrassing event of the year, a
small host of the nation's literati last week took
out a full-page ad in *The New York Times* to upbraid President Reagan for his attacks on 'liberalism.' 'We regret,' intoned 63 savants, 'that the
President of the United States has taken the lead
in vilifying one of our oldest and noblest traditions. He made sport of "the dreaded L-word"
and continues to make "liberal" and "liberalism"
terms of opprobrium.'"
What does that lead accomplish?**

First, it gives you the information necessary to
know what the editorial is going to be about. Second, it establishes the tone, and the direction that

the editorial is going to go. It does that with the word "embarrassing" in the first sentence. The tone is developed a little more with the expression "a small host of the nation's literati." "Literati" is a fun-poking word.

So is "savants."

Yes. "Intoned" is pointing toward a characterization of the people who signed the ad as a collection of pecksniffs. And that's going to be the thrust of the editorial.

I find the tone a little snotty.

It's intended to be snotty. [Laughter] I would assume that one purpose of the ad would be to intimidate people with the prestige of the intellectuals who signed it, because there are some very, very eminent men of letters and scholarship who signed this ad.

Listed in paragraph two.

Yes. And the lead of the editorial punctures, or tries to puncture, that sense of intimidation that the ad is trying to muster.

The second paragraph is essentially a list of signers. Are your readers going to recognize them as, in their terms, mostly "Lefties"?

Probably not, until you get down to Schlesinger and Galbraith and Vance and McNamara. Many of our readers would assume that some of them, or most of them, are liberals, although some of them, in fact, are not so liberal. Daniel Bell is regarded as not so liberal. Robert Penn Warren is today liberal but not always. C. Vann Woodward could go back and forth in some respects. But in general, this is a list of liberal intellectuals. I didn't recognize them as necessarily liberal. If you'd asked me before I'd seen this ad what Robert K. Merton's politics were, or Eudora Welty's, I really wouldn't have been able to tell you. But I do give little nutshell descriptions of the intellectuals by talking about their disciplines: the sociologists, historians, critics, that sort of thing.

Not assuming too much about your readers...

No.

...but giving them credit at the same time.

Yes. I went through the list and picked out the most prestigious. Institutions like Harvard and Stanford and Johns Hopkins connote something. In my editorials, I do generally assume that the reader is a conservative, or shares certain conservative reflexes. Not necessarily an Attila the Hun, but he would see names like Harvard, for example, and his elbow would twitch in some way, if not his knee.

Let's look at the middle of the third paragraph: "Nor do you need an advanced degree to see through the transparently fallacious argument that an attack on liberalism is an attack on the principles upon which the American republic was founded. We thought you weren't supposed to deal in labels this year, but whatever name you want to give to the ideals and principles that inform the American founding, they bear scant resemblance to what travels the world under the passport of liberalism these days."
Is that the heart of this editorial?

This editorial was edited a little, mainly for space. Originally that passage was an entire paragraph. Now it begins in the middle of a paragraph.

It would certainly have more prominence as a separate paragraph.

Yes. Look at the passage above it: "The signers assure the reader that they paid for the ad themselves and that it 'has not been authorized by any candidate'—although you don't need a Ph.D. to know which candidate most of these eggheads are supporting." That passage was a somewhat longer paragraph, and some more quotations from the ad were taken out. The kicker of the paragraph, "although you don't need a Ph.D. to know which candidate most of these eggheads are supporting," was intended to give the lie, as it were, to the idea that this is an apolitical manifesto.

Don't you think "egghead" is kind of a mean word?

Yes. [Laughter] I moved from "literati" to "savants" to "eggheads," and I tried to get a little meaner as I went along. I remember pondering which of these words were nastier. I thought "literati" was least nasty. In the context, "savants" is a little nastier. And "eggheads" is about as nasty as you can get, well, not quite as nasty as you can get, but...

Oh, if you worked at it, Sam, you could get a lot nastier than that.

Yes. I could.

You're being terribly nice. [Laughter] Let's look at paragraph four: "James Madison, Thomas Jefferson, John Adams, and other founders believed in a free market economy based on private property, divinely given rights and duties, the rule of law, and government by the consent of the governed." Could you chisel those words on the front of the *Washington Times* building?

Yes. It's essentially a listing of what most contemporary conservatives would say defines their political thought. But I believe that this is also true of the individuals I mentioned.

Down in paragraph six, you call that "real liberalism."

Yes. I argue that this is what the word originally meant. The idea of the whole editorial is that when Reagan denounces "liberalism," he is clearly talking about contemporary liberalism. He's not talking about liberalism as it would have been discussed 200 years ago.

Let's go on to "Heroism on trial?," about Oliver North. What prompted this one?

The issue of whether Reagan should issue a pardon for North was a controversial topic, at least among conservatives, and Reagan had just stated publicly that he was not going to issue a pardon for North. There was a good deal of discontent about that among conservatives. I myself have never been a great admirer of Oliver North, unlike most conservatives. I have nothing against him, but he's not, in my mind, the kind of hero that a lot of conservatives seem to regard him as. I wanted to clarify conservative thought about Oliver North and the issue of a pardon.

This piece was very much written for conservatives and to conservatives. Look at the listing in the first paragraph about Buchanan and *Human Events* and the *Journal* and Hatch and Henry Hyde. There's virtually unanimous agreement among conservatives that North ought to be given a pardon. And I tried to make the tone as respectful to conservatives as possible.

Now, Sam, come on. You call them a "conservative pack" up there in the second line.

Yes.

Is that respectful? Come on...

Well, originally, it read, "the conservative pack is baying for Mr. Reagan to issue a pardon."

That's even meaner.

Yes. But that's the only nasty thing I said in the piece, and I back away from that. But again, that expression tells you which way the editorial is going to go.

Look at paragraph three: "What is at issue in whether Mr. Reagan should exercise this power on behalf of Col. North is the wisdom of using it, not its lawfulness." To me, that's the heart of this editorial.

Yes.

You have a tendency to stick the hearts about a third of the way down. Why do you put them there?

That tells the reader what it's about at a fairly early stage in the piece, and it creates a kind of turning point in the editorial, after which you would expect the detailed argument for that position. Without that, it can get confusing for the reader. The reader of an editorial is someone who doesn't really want to read the thing, someone who is reading it on a subway in the morning, or over his breakfast while his children are trying to not eat their breakfast. A minority of aides on the Hill and in government and press secretaries sit down and go through editorials with magic markers and analyze them carefully, but I don't think that's the typical reader of an editorial. I've...

But you write for them, too, don't you?

Yes. But if you only write for them, you're going to have a fairly limited audience.

And you won't explain enough.

That's right. This device of putting the tag at the center, or near the center, or in places other than the very end, helps people to organize it as they're reading it.

**I call it "steadying the reader." Readers need to
be reminded what the piece is about, just to assure them that the rest of the journey isn't terribly rocky. I tend to put a guidepost at the one-
third point and at the two-thirds point. I think of
them as road signs on a well-marked freeway.**
  Can we look at the Patuxent piece?

Yes. There is a prison in Maryland known as the
Patuxent Institution, which specializes in a rehabilitation program for hardened criminals, including
murderers, rapists, and armed robbers. Around
Thanksgiving, about a month before this piece was
published, there was an incident there where an individual had been released after having been reha-
bilitated, supposedly, and started committing more
crimes. It was a local issue, all over the *Post* and
The Washington Times. It became as controversial
as it did because of the Willie Horton incident. We
had three or four editorials on Patuxent in November and December. This was the second editorial I
had done on it.

**Although a lot of your readers are out of state, at
the top of this editorial, you don't tell us where
Patuxent is. Would they recognize Howard
County, for instance?**

There had been a good deal of coverage of it in the
news section of the paper, and with all due respect
to our out-of-state readers, it would be a little too
much to say, "coming out of the Patuxent Institution in Howard County, Maryland." You might say
"coming out of Maryland's Patuxent Institution,"
but even that is really a bit too much, given the
publicity. Patuxent had become a household word
by this time.

**Should an editorial writer depend on the read-
ers' reading the news sections?**

You almost have to, but not in detail. In a lot of editorials, I will rehearse the essential facts of a story,

but if the piece is about an event that has been in the news prominently and recently, I tend to assume that the reader is acquainted with the essential facts of the story.

Your lead does summarize Mr. Prevatte's and Mr. Howard's awful careers.

Yes. I thought it was useful to distinguish between these two, because at this point, there had been several people of the same ilk, and there was a tendency to confuse them all. The details (going to prison for murder at 14, then released, and winding up back in jail) really encapsulate the sense of absurdity and terror that I was trying to convey here.

Readers like storytelling. It draws them into the editorial, because they're interested in these dangerous guys. Look at the bottom of paragraph two: "...the program ought to be shut down because it misses the whole point of criminal justice." There's your point at the one-third position again, isn't it? Would you be tempted to use that as the kicker?

No. Because again I'm getting ready to give a rather extended argument there, and the road sign, or whatever you want to call it, is necessary to point directly to the kicker. In this piece, I tried to emphasize getting away from the argument about whether rehabilitation is effective or not. Patuxent's defenders were saying that it was, that they had a low recidivism rate. And I wanted to get to the essentially ethical question, rather than that statistical question about effectiveness. In the second paragraph, I touched on the effectiveness argument, but rather dismissively, justifiably, I think, in terms of what I was trying to do here. But my point is that regardless of the success rate, there's still a larger point to be made about this. That sentence at the end of the second paragraph simply emphasizes that and makes it as crystallized as possible.

I like your final paragraph: "What has fallen into disrepute in our time is the Patuxent Institution's bizarre notion of justice that not only turns hardened and duly convicted criminals loose on the streets but also reduces the humanity of the criminals themselves by denying them the essentially human traits of will and responsibility. That's why Maryland lawmakers should exercise their own moral responsibility and close down a program whose therapeutic view of crime and punishment is more appropriate to veterinarians than to doctors and those sworn to govern by law." Hitting that last word hard, right?

Yes. Here I was trying to develop the idea that this is really a reductionist theory, that it denies the humanity of the criminal, and reduces the law to a meaningless form. It also makes nonsense of the concept of a just or unjust sentence or law. And that points to the idea of treating criminals as sort of subhumans, which points to *Animal Farm* in the title, and the veterinarian in the conclusion there.

How did "Che Pell" come about?

A *Washington Times* reporter told me he had an interview with Claiborne Pell, chairman of the Senate Foreign Relations Committee, and he had done a short story on it for the paper. There was quite a bit in the interview that lent itself to satire that he didn't have a chance to use, and he wondered if I'd be interested in doing an editorial.

Here's your lead, a wonderful, sarcastic lead: "If you thought Mikhail and Raisa were a stitch, just wait til you meet Fidel Castro. According to Sen. Claiborne Pell, recently returned from a boondoggle to Cuba and a three-hour chin-wag with the Cuban strongman, Mr. Castro is 'a man of great personal vitality and vivacity' and 'as an individual he had, I think, a good deal of charisma.' From these insights, Mr. Pell concludes that the United States should start 'normalizing' rela-

tions with Mr. Castro's unreconstructed communist government." What are you up to in that
lead, besides low comedy?

Pell's trip to Cuba was not a highly publicized
event, so there is a good deal of information here
in a compressed way. But, aside from the information, the important thing is to set the tone of the
piece, with "Mikhail and Raisa," and "a stitch,"
this right after Gorbachev and Mrs. Gorbachev had
been in this country.

**I like the language in here. When was the last
time you heard "boondoggle" or "chin-wag"?
Usually we have editorialists writing horrors like
"it ill behooves," so it's delightful to come upon
"boondoggle." [Laughter]**

"Boondoggle" and "chin-wag" and "stitch" tend to
puncture the whole event. Pell's interview conveys
the tone of a man of high seriousness with an almost ponderous view of the world historical importance of his conversation with Castro, and his
recommendations based on it. This was simply intended to puncture that as quickly as possible.

**Well, it certainly succeeds. Wonderful things in
here like "El Presidente" and "jolly caudillo."
Look at the last paragraph: "Mr. Pell's reflections, banal as they are, would be unworthy of
comment save for the fact that the Rhode Island
Democrat happens to be chairman of the Senate
Foreign Relations Committee and thus occupies a
key position from which to exert influence on the
real world. The real world ought to respond to
the chairman's latest revelations by ignoring him
as much as possible." You saved his title, his
chairmanship, until the very end. Why didn't you
tell us at the top? Do you assume we know it?**

No. In the first draft, I put that in the lead. I had
said, "According to Sen. Claiborne Pell, chairman
of the Foreign Relations Committee," or some-

thing. I decided to save that for the climax because the idea here is to portray Claiborne Pell as a bit of a fool. I thought that would be heightened by saving his really very important position for the end.

Oh, by the way, dear reader...

Yes. Many of our readers, probably most of them, would know Claiborne Pell is the chairman of the committee, but even for those who do know that, I think putting it at the climax emphasizes the absurdity of it.

Now, one last general question. How does an editorial writer stay fresh?

Gosh, I'm not entirely sure. There are times when I really don't want to write an editorial. One way is to vary the topics that you write on. I get most burned out with writing when I've been going back and forth on the same topics over and over again. There are some bills that I must have written five or six editorials on, and I just don't have anything more to say on them. What do you think?

I think that as long as the human race stays as silly as it is, you'll never run out of topics.

That's true. But it's generally not a good idea for an editorial writer to specialize, unless he's absolutely devoted to his subject. If an editorial page wants to be a cultural force in its city or in society, it has to comment on things outside narrow political and economic and military events. It has to have pieces on science and religion and art and sports and things that real people really think about and are really involved in. Most editorial writers probably look at them at least as avocations or fillers, but I think they play an important role in making an editorial page interesting.

Yes.

Mark Davis
Government Reporting

MARK DAVIS grew up in Raleigh, North Carolina, and graduated from the University of North Carolina at Chapel Hill in December 1977 with a journalism degree. He began as a photographer for the Jacksonville (N.C.) *Daily News*, which fired him for what he calls "real and alleged malfeasance." He continued to work in North Carolina at the Burlington *Daily Times-News*, the Associated Press in Raleigh, the New Bern *Sun Journal*, and the *Asheville Citizen-Times*. He joined *The Tampa Tribune* in November 1987 as a general assignment bureau reporter.

Anatomy of a road, Part 1: From footpath to freeway

DECEMBER 5, 1988

Earl Davis wasn't surprised. The earth withheld no secrets from him.

He stood on the edge of a gash in the earth at East Bay Drive and U.S. 19 and watched his shadow fall across the young man standing in the hole. The workers laying underground pipes had called him to look at what they'd found six feet under the sandy soil near the Bay Area Outlet Mall.

Oyster shells. The youngster standing below stepped carefully over the sprawling white pile, and Davis mused. The crews might be surprised by all the shells, but he'd learned to expect almost anything in four decades of road work. It took more than some buried shells to take his breath.

Davis, the state Department of Transportation's manager for this project, had seen his share of them along U.S. 19, beginning when he was a lean youngster. He looked down at the hole again. If anything surprised him now, it happened at land-acquisition settlements in courtrooms and real estate offices—not on the job itself.

The money surprised him. Analysts said the state likely would shell out $15 million or more for 50 parcels of land lining both sides of the 1.6-mile bridge and road-widening project and along the intersections where East Bay Drive and Whitney Road crossed U.S. 19, a highway so choked with traffic that locals call it "Useless 19."

And that didn't even include the $17.6 million construction cost.

A road-building veteran who helped hack U.S. 19 out of a forest of mangroves and cabbage palms in rural Pinellas during the late 1940s and the early '50s, Davis knew that kind of money would have built God knows how many miles of highway when he was a young man. Road building was different back then. A crew waded into the wilderness, chop-

ping a ragged right-of-way past swamps and rickety
Cracker homes until it reached civilization again.
There were no environmental impact statements, no
lawyers or real estate specialists stalking state dollars through a jungle of paperwork.

He allowed himself a half-smile. Things were
different back then.

Different, but about to change. World War II had
just thundered into history when Florida politicians
realized a new storm approached. They already
heard its rumble in other parts of the country as the
nation emerged from war and experienced a growth
boom. If West Florida didn't get roads built, and
soon, the boom would pass over Pinellas.

The road men—and they were all men back then
—got busy. They started work on a highway to replace the old U.S. 19, a thin, meandering line that
wiggled through coastal fishing villages and small
towns before furrowing into South Georgia farmland.

Jimmy Lairscey, a former DOT engineer now in
private practice with a St. Petersburg engineering
and consulting firm, remembers that first highway,
an uncertain blacktop that some say had its roots in
an old Indian footpath. Lairscey called it the Old
Dixie Highway.

Newspapers carried daily accounts of World
War II when Lairscey was a teen-ager. He and his
family would load the Model A Ford and head
north to visit their family in South Georgia, leaving
their Tarpon Springs home and going until twilight. Sometimes they traveled after dark, but that
depended on how adventurous they felt.

"Back then, there weren't any fence laws in
Florida," Lairscey recalled. "You could be driving
along in the dark and run up on a cow."

The road was already old, a project from the late
1920s, a narrow, limestone-and-asphalt ribbon that
tied Florida's Gulf Coast to the rest of the state. It
varied from county to county, its quality depending
on each county's commitment to travel.

"You could be driving along, doing fine, and
then you'd pass into another county. Then the road
would get real bad again."

By war's end, practically everyone knew the road was already inadequate to carry Florida into the next decade. A nation bursting with energy and pride was on the move, moving South. The faint booms grew louder.

Gov. Fuller Warren heard it up in Tallahassee. He contacted an old college buddy, Brooksville banker Alfred McKethan, and asked him to head the state Road Board, the five-member panel that decided which road jobs got priority.

Always a Democrat, Warren had polished his persuasive powers on McKethan when they had discussed politics while undergraduates at the University of Florida, recalled McKethan, now 81. The governor's time in politics had only added luster to his already silver tongue.

"Fuller was a great orator even back then, and he was better as the governor," McKethan said. "When he asked me to join, I couldn't say anything but yes."

When McKethan took a seat on the panel, the new Highway 19 was nothing more than a draftsman's bold lines. It arrowed straight across central Pinellas, clean on paper, but another matter altogether for the men charged with cutting that path through the forests and mangroves.

Earl Davis knew. When he returned to Pinellas County in 1944, he came from the U.S. Navy and a stint in the South Pacific. He wanted solid ground under his feet. He got it on the "new" U.S. 19. He was 19 years old.

Skinny, with a tangle of red hair, Davis signed on with the state in 1946. His boss handed him a machete.

By 1950, he swung it with confidence and ease that come only with practice. He and other road crews worked through Pinellas's jungle, hacking at a wilderness that officials said would be a new road. With a relentless sun beating on him as he cut through fields, swamps, and shaggy forests, Davis always looked ahead to the next leg of the project.

The legs were long, and stretched interminably. The crews made slow progress. Mosquitoes whined about their heads, and snakes thrashed away when the right-of-way crews stumbled across them. Some quit, thinking they'd never see an end to the wet, hot, dirty work.

It did have an end; in spite of what some crew members thought, the highway was more than an engineer's fancy. It became a road-builder's fact.

Michael Zembillis struggled to understand. He had a tougher time than others.

Zembillis, who now works for Pinellas County's Engineering Department, faced obstacles, and not just those growing in front of the surveying crew he joined that year. A recent immigrant from Greece, he didn't understand English.

But his uncle, who knew McKethan on the Road Board, did; he convinced the youngster to enlist in the army of laborers cutting a road in the wilderness. Tall, swarthy, and energetic, Zembillis made a quick decision. "I signed a sheet of paper saying I'd work for them," Zembillis said. "They had to point it out to me where to sign." They also pointed him to Davis, by this time an accomplished crew chief. The one-time sailor taught Zembillis the secrets of surveying. Davis also taught him English.

"You learn it pretty quick when everyone around you is speaking it," Zembillis said.

The politicians' turn to speak came on July 19, 1955. The new highway had reached St. Petersburg's city limits. The glistening blacktop rolled to a red-carpet welcome, and Pinellas reacted with civic pride and a smiling look to the future. Pretty 19-year-olds competed for the title of Miss U.S. 19, bands played, and everyone talked about a new era for Gulf Coast Florida.

But no one said what the road builders already knew: the fine new highway already was inadequate.

Florida had not stood still while the road crews inched toward St. Petersburg. Visitors and newcomers clogged the old highway, and the Suncoast exploded in a storm of development. By 1960 Pinellas's population stood at 374,000; in 10 years it would reach 522,300. In that same period, the

Tampa Bay region's population would jump from 878,400 people to 1.18 million. And the lines along U.S. 19 grew.

So did the rest of Pinellas as suburbs took root more quickly than the orange groves they had replaced. Shopping centers herded cows out from their pastures, and gas stations dotted crossroads. At the same time, merchants moved to the new highway. DOT put in more stoplights.

Zembillis, by then a crew chief, went to work on other projects. So did Davis and others who pushed those twin lanes through Pinellas. Draftsmen who drew those first lines across the county hunched over their tables again, adding lanes designed to double 19's capacity.

They had to work quickly, McKethan said. "We expected growth," he said. "But nobody—and I mean nobody—could predict it would be this much."

By the mid-1960s, the Highway Department knew its 10-year-old road was in trouble. With the four-lane plans in hand, the crews went back to the highway's shoulders, rerouted traffic, and began adding an extra lane on each side. They finished in 1975.

That wasn't enough. "As soon as it opened to four lanes, it needed to be six lanes," McKethan noted.

But federal highway money, previously plentiful as America gained momentum following World War II, had become almost as scarce as an open lane of traffic on U.S. 19.

"We didn't even have money to lay pavement; forget about building an addition to a highway," said Jim Kennedy, DOT's administrator for the Tampa Bay area.

New York-raised, Citadel-trained, a two-decade veteran of Florida's road-building program, Kennedy said any road improvements were no more than a flight of fancy until 1978, when the highway benefited from an unexpected $50 million from the federal Department of Transportation.

Former U.S. Rep. Richard Kelly that year had

the Pinellas-Hernando 19 corridor declared a priority primary road in an $8 billion federal highway-improvement package. That meant the road would be one of the first in the nation to get money.

Yet being on a list didn't mean the highway would get the money; that was just a step in the right direction. DOT took the second step that same year, applying for $50 million to six-lane a 19-mile segment of the highway. Federal highway officials reviewed the request, and sent back a message no one really expected.

"We got the money," Kennedy recalled. "It went like a greased pig; surprised the hell out of us."

They didn't let the cash collect dust. By 1984, almost all of the Pinellas stretch of U.S. 19 was six lanes wide. Only a segment at Ulmerton Road remained four lanes.

That intersection is one of six that DOT will make into interchanges—steel and concrete bridge overpasses that will take 19's traffic over other cars traveling on roads that now cross the highway at ground level. The interchanges are part of a plan to make the highway into a freeway, or a road where motorists can enter or exit only at a few spots.

Like the "new 19" that took shape in the 1940s and '50s, the freeway project hasn't fully moved from paper to pavement. The last of the interchanges won't be finished until late in the next decade, planners say.

Will that be enough? Lairscey, who moved from surveying crew to an engineer's office before retiring last year, isn't sure.

"It gets more crowded out there all the time," he said.

He oversaw the construction of the first 19 interchange where State Road 60 now passes under the highway. Lairscey has a photograph of the interchange in his office, a modern-day reminder of a vision that took shape in the early 1960s when photographs were almost always black and white. Like *The Wizard of Oz*, only dreams came in color.

The state's highway dream developed, though Lairscey isn't certain the highway now is what officials envisioned then. "Sometimes I'm not sure anything will help," he said.

Neither is McKethan, who watched the trickle of visitors become a flood. He avoids 19.

"Florida was discovered," he said. "We were behind when it happened. We didn't expect so many people."

Nor had Davis, but he'd learned. State population and traffic projections practically demanded a new intersection to handle the increasing flow of people and their vehicles, and DOT engineers chose an award-winning design already in use just a few miles north of the sprawling intersection where Davis stood.

They selected an interchange, an ornate junction where east and west came together with north and south—a pavement-and-asphalt-and-concrete compass.

Davis had reviewed the interchange's plans until he felt comfortable, and kept a 2-inch stack of graphs, maps, and charts in his office.

The plans detailed a crossroads in which the highway's northbound and southbound traffic would rise over the east- and westbound traffic crossing at East Bay and Whitney Road. Frontage roads, which allowed traffic to turn off to businesses located along U.S. 19, would run parallel to the highway.

Graphs showed frontage roads that would widen as they approached East Bay Drive and Whitney Road, offering motorists four options, depending on which way a vehicle headed: turn left, turn right, make a U-turn, or go straight.

All those lanes demanded space. Davis had seen some of DOT's land-acquisition documents, and had quietly marveled at the amount of land the project would take. He'd also reviewed the bridge-building plans. They, too, were a marvel.

A football team could play on the largest bridge, a 420-foot-long, six-lane creation. At its zenith, it would allow almost 17 feet of clearance for the traffic passing below. The 108-foot Whitney bridge, by comparison, could hold a basketball team but would be hard-pressed to find room at either end for the cheerleaders.

But those were just a few numbers; Davis had plenty more. He'd picked up his calculator one morning before venturing out to the job and punched in some figures. The small calculator yielded some big numbers, he told a co-worker.

For example, the dirt. The soaring, still-unbuilt, earth-and-concrete walls that would hold aloft the bridges would need 230,000 cubic yards of dirt. That amount of soil would require 20,000 big dump trucks, he'd noted.

And he hadn't forgotten the concrete: 2,000 dump-truck loads of it, just to build the bridges' decks and approaches.

He'd also figured the asphalt needs for the project, a total that would stun someone who had not spent years standing in or near the stuff. Engineers estimated the frontage roads, plus the rebuilt portions that would pass under the bridges, would need 70,000 square yards to make a base coating $1\frac{1}{2}$ inches thick.

Then there were the most pressing numbers of all: traffic counts. Engineers told him 85,000 vehicles pass through the intersection in a 24-hour period, or about one every second, all day long. Projections indicated more cars were on their way, too. A study one firm conducted for DOT concluded that 101,000 vehicles per day would cross East Bay and 19 by the year 2005.

Traffic had always been a problem at "Four Corners," Davis thought. That was the name the old-timers called the crossroads where East Bay Drive crossed the highway. For some reason, the drive, officially called State Road 686, also was called Roosevelt Boulevard. East Bay began on the highway's western edge, and Roosevelt ended on the eastern side. Davis never knew why.

He did remember the old crossroads, though. There'd been a gas station on two corners, a vacant lot on another. Woods had reached right to the edge of the hole where he now stood.

Davis listened to the traffic crawling past. The

four corners had become a four-way snarl as motorists suffered through the intersection, and now
that suffering would be compounded as workers
moved traffic to accommodate an interchange that
would rise in the sand. Davis, who had lived in
Pinellas County for almost 50 years, sympathized
and suffered with them.

The suffering wouldn't be over for a long time.
Plans gave Danis Corp., the private contractor the
state hired to do the work, two years to convert the
intersection to an interchange. And that was only a
small part of a larger design. The big plan called
for converting 24 miles of "Useless 19" into a freeway. When it was finished, U.S. 19 would be lined
with frontage roads and feature seven interchanges,
each resembling the job just beginning to stretch
out along the highway and East Bay Drive.

But that was years hence—small consolation on
a warming afternoon.

An afternoon growing short. Davis looked at the
sun, casting long shadows as it sunk over Largo.
He jerked his thoughts back to the present and
spoke over the traffic, building strength as another
rush hour approached.

"It looks all right," he said to the laborer standing below him. "Just make sure the hole's deep
enough."

DIGGING INTO PAPERWORK

Ronald Gregory paused, searching for the right
words as he worked on the findings of his first-
ever road environmental impact statement. He'd
promised to have the report finished by November,
and as October drew to a close in 1980, he wanted
to make sure he delivered the goods.

He found the right words. "Without significant
upgrading of the highway there would likely be
further violations of the estimated air quality standards, reduced safety for the traveling public, continued waste of petroleum energy resources, and
restricted economic activity within the corridor and
the county," he dictated.

He believed those words as surely as he believed that steel makes strong bridges. Sure, they were tough words, but why draw false conclusions? Pinellas County faced a tough situation.

He suspected as much when he began making the report two years before. The facts his co-workers at Greiner Inc. compiled only reaffirmed his belief.

Gregory had been at Greiner's Tampa offices for four years when his bosses asked him to oversee the statement, called an EIS in the trade. Engineering, like all occupations, had its own acronyms, and Gregory knew them all. He also knew another: he told his bosses the report would be OK.

State and federal regulations required the EIS, the first real step toward making the Pinellas stretch of U.S. 19 into a freeway. As his first step, Gregory closed his office door and began reading state plans.

Ambitious plans. DOT proposed adding two more lanes to the highway, making it six lanes wide, with parallel service roads. It also wanted to build bridges at six big intersections along a 24-mile stretch of the highway, including the East Bay/U.S. 19 intersection. State and federal traffic planners said they would limit access to 19, making the highway a freeway. Planners said the interchanges alone would probably cost $513 million.

He started with eight people—studious, digging sorts who didn't mind wading through courthouse records, yellowing maps, and overgrown creek banks. He dispatched them to Pinellas County, telling them to check with utilities officials, courthouse clerks, draftsmen, shopkeepers, landowners, wildlife and water specialists, and anyone else who might know about the highway and what it hid.

The findings came back in a trickle at first, then a flow as his co-workers began discovering 19's secrets. A few scraps of paper became a mound, then a mountain.

He hadn't feared that mountain, because he'd scaled a more difficult one almost 20 years earlier.

He had long hair and a boyish face back then, and Ron Gregory, college student, resembled one

of Beaver Cleaver's pals all grown up as he straddled a ten-speed across the University of Georgia
campus. He straddled a tough question in 1972.

The Ph.D. in engineering was almost in his grasp
that spring when he went home to Florida for a
week. He ran into a buddy in Clearwater who told
him about a firm looking for a few good engineers.

"My first reaction was that I wasn't interested,"
Gregory had recalled. "But out of curiosity I asked
how much they would pay—just because I was curious—and he told me."

That much cash for an engineer? The amount,
though not much by today's standards—slightly
more than $10,000 a year—never left Gregory's
thoughts for the rest of spring break. The salary,
like the warming spring sun, hovered and burned.
The week passed in turmoil.

The next week found him back in Athens. His
bicycle clattered as he pedaled across the university campus, seeking advice from an engineering
professor, a trusted adviser.

Should he forsake higher education for higher
pay? Or should he remain true to his determination
to be a collegian? Gregory laid out the facts in the
older man's office.

Like any good engineer, the older man assembled the story's pieces and tested the strength of
the offer handed to his young charge. The teacher,
who had watched Gregory develop from promising
pupil to possible professor, weighed academia's
loss against private enterprise's gain. Then he told
his student goodbye.

"He said, 'You can always come back and get the
Ph.D. later,'" Gregory would recall years later. He
sold his ten-speed. He still doesn't have that degree.

Gregory got a job with a Clearwater engineering
firm with home offices in Washington, D.C., and
learned the art of traffic engineering, a pseudo-
science that Pinellas needed. His duties brought
him in contact with engineers from Greiner, an engineering and consulting firm that had been in business since 1908 and looked like it would be around
for the next century. He joined Greiner in 1974.

His co-workers call him energetic. They also say he's affable, a diminutive man with a shock of brown hair and a perpetual gee-whiz look on his face. And he's shrewd.

Shrewd, as in erecting a first-ever project information center at DOT's Clearwater office. He watched as his firm installed maps, brochures, photographs, and provided a smiling co-worker who was always on hand to answer questions.

"The first thing you'd hear was, 'What are you doing out there?'" Gregory recalled. "The second was, 'How will this affect me?'"

People already felt the effects of a highway that didn't serve their needs, Gregory concluded. He dictated a few more conclusions into the report:

• Based on University of Florida studies, Pinellas's population had grown by 100.6 percent in 19 years—from 1960's 374,000 people to 751,700 in 1979. Researchers found nothing to indicate that trend would reverse.

• Thirty-eight businesses and six homes would have to be relocated. One home might have to go at the East Bay intersection.

• No significant archaeological sites would be affected by the project. Eighty-eight percent of the area was "man-dominated."

• Revising the highway would not significantly alter natural habitats, nor compromise water quality standards.

He made his deadline, and DOT started planning the first of many deadlines it would face as it struggled with 19.

Greiner sent the report to DOT's offices in Bartow, then headquarters for Tampa Bay area road work. Officials there passed it around, including those charged with acquiring the land for the state's ambitious undertaking.

In late 1983, men wearing neckties began visiting merchants and homeowners near the East Bay/U.S. 19 intersection. The state wanted their land for the next step in its freeway project—an interchange.

Observations and questions

1) Images of movement unify this article. Find each of them and see how it contributes to the flow of ideas.

2) Believe it or not, Davis defines the word "freeway": "The interchanges are part of a plan to make the highway into a freeway, or a road where motorists can enter or exit only at a few spots." How can we judge which terms to define for the reader?

3) Telling construction stories requires unpicturable numbers, as in this example: "The soaring, still-unbuilt, earth-and-concrete walls that would hold aloft the bridges would need 230,000 cubic yards of dirt. That amount of soil would require 20,000 big dump trucks, he'd noted." Watch how Davis repeatedly converts nongraphic measurements (cubic yards) into pictures (dump trucks).

4) Notice the exaggeration in this description: "The findings came back in a trickle at first, then a flow as his co-workers began discovering 19's secrets. A few scraps of paper became a mound, then a mountain." Logic tells us that a "flow" cannot become a "mound," but the passage describes psychological rather than topographical effects.

5) The author describes Gregory like this: "His co-workers call him energetic. They also say he's affable, a diminutive man with a shock of brown hair and a perpetual gee-whiz look on his face. And he's shrewd." Notice how Davis conjures up a whole person for the reader from just three details of appearance. He also brackets the physical details with psychological traits: "energetic," "affable," and "shrewd." Economy makes description work better.

6) Davis flags "man-dominated" as engineering jargon by enclosing the word in quotation marks. Should he translate it into reader language? When should we quote jargon?

Anatomy of a road, Part 2: Blueprints of lives and land

DECEMBER 6, 1988

The sprawl caught Elsie Berberich, and she was afraid.

They'd moved to Florida in late 1953. Elsie and George Berberich decided they could raise a family here, and they chose a wooded spot near a Largo crossroads in Pinellas County. The young family built a home and motel near the new highway.

Life was good at the house near the intersection of East Bay Drive and the highway—and quiet. George and Elsie stayed busy—he with their motel, she as a nurse—and three young children grew in the leafy back yard. Some evenings, the couple sat in the gathering twilight and listened to crickets, cicadas, and a score of other nighttime sounds as another day closed around them. An occasional car passed, or perhaps a truck clattered by, a farmer heading home. Florida dozed.

"It was very, very peaceful in our back yard," recalled Berberich, who now lives in Tucson, Ariz. "We were really quite removed from the road."

But the state awoke, and so did Pinellas County. By 1960, the somnolent county stretched as it shrugged out of its slumber, and the two-lane highway stretching north and south widened to four lanes. Pinellas hummed, and so did the highway, as more cars passed each day. Cars and trucks drowned out the night's cicadas, and the couple had to watch their children to make sure they didn't stray too close to the blacktop.

Then George died in 1968. That left their block-and-stucco home, a motel, and three children. The night sounds didn't seem so friendly anymore, and the hum of traffic turned into a hiss. The future coiled threateningly, something fearful in the dark.

Berberich managed. Her back yard, a source of comfort where she and her husband greeted darkness, remained a refuge. She tended her plants and

258

prayed for the steel to be a mother, motel keeper, and man about the house.

She suddenly had more space in the bathroom, and cooking wasn't quite the production it once was. The house vibrated with his absence.

She drew her children near, and reached for comfort in her Bible. There had been changes in her life. What was death but another?

Elsie was fresh out of the University of Virginia's registered nursing program when she enlisted. A war needed nurses.

"They accepted me just like that," she said. "They were in desperate need of nurses."

They were desperate times. Nazis had spread across Europe like a gray storm, and the Allies needed skilled nurses here and overseas. The U.S. Army sent her to Camp Lee, Va., for training. The young woman, more familiar with the relaxed life of a college dormitory than a barracks, found herself in the starched, stand-up, at-attention, and olive-drab world of the Army. It issued her everything but a husband.

She found one on her own.

Lt. George Berberich ambled into the camp hospital one day in 1941. A good-looking youngster from Ohio, Berberich told the nurse he was looking for one of his soldiers. The two smiled and talked, temporarily forgetting the obligation that awaited them across the ocean. Another wartime romance took root and flowered. Lt. Berberich found more than a missing soldier; he found a wife.

"You know how those things happen in war," she said. "We got married. I got sent off [to Europe], and I didn't see him again for two years."

They survived the war and got on with the business of being husband and wife in 1946. After working in other states for eight years, the Berberiches loaded their car with small children and big dreams and headed south to Florida. Life was going to be good.

And it was. They owned and managed the Mark Edward Motel, a four-unit complex they built on the edge of U.S. 19 in 1957. They derived its name from their two sons' middle names. She continued working as a nurse, and her three children grew.

So did Pinellas, and Berberich knew the state eventually might want some of her land to accommodate the crawling traffic. She wasn't very surprised when DOT acquisition specialist Everett Sutton contacted her in January 1985. He offered her $13,700 for a sliver of land on the eastern edge of U.S. 19. The department wanted 4,201 square feet of her property, and the state said its offer of $3.25 per foot was fair.

She wasn't as sure, and called Richard Barnhill.

Winter held Pinellas in a reluctant, slippery grip in February 1985 when Barnhill's secretary told him a caller on the line needed an independent appraisal. He said hello to his next client.

"We don't take everything they say as gospel," he told Berberich, and promised to check her land at the Pinellas County Courthouse.

He remembered that trip three years later. "Well, mistakes can happen," Barnhill said recently. Then he smiled.

A Clearwater property appraiser, Barnhill's name appeared on a list of state-approved land appraisers, and Berberich picked his name from a list DOT had given her. Since the state would pay for his services, Berberich thought she had nothing to lose.

Barnhill listened to her on the telephone, nodding his head and making notations. He'd seen enough land in the last two decades to realize that getting the truth sometimes takes a little scratching. And he is accustomed to scratching.

A Mississippi native, he's from Charleston, a small town that proudly proclaims itself the "Gateway to the Delta." And that's about all it can claim these days, Barnhill said. "It's just another dying little Southern town."

Barnhill decided 20 years ago that he didn't want to watch it die. He tried farming, but it didn't work.

He moved to Greenwood, Miss., in 1969 and

took a job with a real estate development company. He learned the art of land appraising there. His employer needed an accredited appraiser, and Barnhill, who had seen plenty of real estate from the vantage point of a tractor, said he'd take the course. "I looked at the books and said, 'Shoot, that ain't so hard,'" he said.

Barnhill learned. That education took him to a Texas firm, and ultimately to Tallahassee, where DOT hired him as a real estate acquisition specialist. He worked out of the department's Bartow office for two years before opening his own business in Clearwater.

He bought a small house and put a big desk in it. He swore off neckties and covered his office walls with reminders of home. A painting of a Mississippi turkey, standing in a Mississippi bean field, painted by a Mississippi artist, commands one wall; it shares space with an antique map of his home state. A calendar from the Tallahatchie Bank of Mississippi practically covers a corner, and Barnhill has marked in red ink the dates when he returned home.

A misplaced redneck? Not completely. His homegrown objets d'art also share space with a wooden bust of Michelangelo's *David*. Its sightless eyes stare west. Perhaps toward Mississippi, home?

He visited Berberich's home and land later that month. Motorists idling at the clogged intersection watched with mild curiosity as the pudgy man aimed his 35mm camera at the motel, home, and land surrounding it. He dropped the film off at the drug store and visited the courthouse for a market analysis and detailed map of his new client's holdings. That's where he found the mistake.

He ignored the ringing telephones and hustling paralegals as he looked once at her land on the county's plat maps, then twice. Barnhill stepped back and looked a third time. What he saw didn't match the land description the state had given his client.

According to DOT, Berberich owned a rectangular piece of land slightly north of the East

Bay/19 intersection that fronted the highway's eastern shoulder. County maps depicted a different shape—a more valuable parcel.

The records showed Berberich owned a piece of property shaped like an inverted L, with land fronting both the highway's eastern edge and the northern side of East Bay Drive. It encircled other tracts at the corner.

"In effect, that made it more valuable," said Barnhill. "She didn't know the implications that would have on the value of her property."

He told her.

Barnhill also compared her land with 11 other Pinellas transactions of parcels similar to Berberich's to illustrate that the tract's fair market value was worth more than DOT estimated. He also noted that Berberich would lose rental income from a billboard located on her property that would have to be torn down.

Based on his findings, Barnhill concluded the motel keeper should ask for $37,200, or $23,500 more than the state's offer. Berberich drew in her breath, checked his findings—and agreed. They showed their findings to Sutton.

The DOT appraiser got out his calculator and punched in some new numbers, based on the assumption she would take her claim to court if the department balked at paying her. DOT and Berberich differed by $23,500. Supposing a jury would force DOT to pay half that difference, or $11,750, he headed a list entitled ALTERNATIVE COST ANALYSIS with that figure. Under it he added projected court costs, attorney fees, additional appraisal costs, and interest charges. They totaled $19,055. His bottom line figure came to $30,815. And that wasn't including DOT's original $13,700 offer, so the total cost of fighting Berberich would come to $44,515.

In other words, meeting Berberich's demand would be cheaper—$7,315 cheaper.

"The agent was unable to overcome the points made by Mrs. Berberich and is certain she will not agree to any amount less than $37,200," he wrote.

He recommended paying her.

The deal concluded on June 14, 1985, and the state took official ownership on Sept. 9 that year.

"I didn't want to be unfair, but I wanted what I felt was fair," she said. "There's nothing wrong with holding out to get your price, is there?"

She still had her home and motel, but sold that later in the year when J.O. Stone, a millionaire Buick dealer and Pinellas entrepreneur, offered to buy it to add to the chunk he already owned at the corner. Again she paused, and recalled the quiet nights, good moments, and promise the home held.

But the home was just a shell of itself. The children had grown, and George was only a memory and collection of photographs. She told Stone he had a deal. She sold slightly less than two acres to Stone for $475,000. That was roughly two-thirds of the tract she and George had bought 31 years earlier for $4,300.

"That was a little upsetting, to sell your home," she said. "I'd lived there 31 years, and that was the longest I'd ever lived anywhere."

She took what she treasured and moved to Tucson. She has an apartment that overlooks a shimmering city in the sun, and prizes her shrubbery and flowers. She also prizes the grandchildren who live nearby. Two boys are growing as surely as the trees she once tended in her Pinellas County back yard.

Still, she remembers the home in Florida, and said her citrus trees should be enjoying the weather.

"Gardening—planting—was one of my hobbies," she said. "I planted three orange trees, a grapefruit tree, and a lemon tree in that back yard. I did that a few years before I left.

"They're probably just beginning to grow good now."

Construction workers barely noticed this past summer when the dozers jerked the first orange tree out of the ground. They didn't look up from their toils when the growling diesel's steel teeth ate the rest of the small grove. But they did pause as the machinery turned on the house and motel.

The block shattered, the roof collapsed like a punctured tire, and walls fell over like faded dominoes. The dust hovered for a couple of hours, mingling with the swirl of dirt on the nearby job site.

Then the trucks took away the debris, the last reminders of the young family that played in the grove.

J.O. Stone tries not to think of land in sentimental terms. He prefers to see it as a commodity—road frontage, access, view—that's better than money in the bank. He's made a fortune wheeling and dealing in Pinellas County.

"I wish I had some more of that land on 19," he's said before.

But others think he already has enough. J.O. Stone, car dealer, motel and golf-course owner, entrepreneur, is a small legend among DOT real estate people who have dealt with him. He owns 11 parcels (none from Berberich) that DOT wants and his lawyers have been negotiating with state-appointed lawyers for four years.

Though the state already has taken some of the land by "an order of taking"—a bureaucratic term meaning the state may assume use of land for a project before its ownership is legally settled—other Stone parcels are still unclaimed. They are conspicuous in their absence on DOT land-acquisition maps.

One state-appointed lawyer says he hopes DOT will settle with Stone by early next year. But Stone has said he doesn't understand the delay. He'll settle tomorrow—for the right price.

The "right price" is a term that has served him well. Stone has followed the simple and tested maxim of buying low, selling high. He owns about 50 acres, he said.

The dealership is still at the same spot, on a windy corner not far from the beaches. Stone is still at the same spot, too, running his company from an office across the main showroom. He watched as two salesmen scurried across the breezy lot earlier this year, and smiled. For Stone, the wheels of business are magnesium alloy and chrome, wrapped with radial tires. They roll daily as new cars leave his lot.

He understands the primary source of his wealth: the car dealership is the spring, and the other enterprises are tributaries that benefited from its flow.

"This is still the main business."

A business that began when J.O. was a youngster. His father ran a Buick dealership in Trenton, Mo., a city in north-central Missouri noted chiefly for its location at the confluence of the Thompson and Weldon rivers. He began cleaning daddy's cars, and, in time, moved from the cleaning lot to the sales lot.

He doesn't remember his first deal—it was too long ago, and there have been too many since—but he does recall that his father had to handle all the paperwork. "I was too young."

But he wasn't too young to learn the lessons that would serve him well in coming years: "In selling anything, you've got to analyze other people's wants and desires."

The lesson stuck, and Stone has built a small empire over the years. He's owner, or part owner, of a motel, an auto-leasing company, a golf course, and a shopping mall. The mall is his latest project. It's also his most visible as thousands of motorists pass by the Bay Area Outlet Mall on Roosevelt-East Bay near U.S. 19. The interchange project looms less than a quarter-mile from the crowded shopping center's main entrance, which opened in 1984.

"It may have been planned, but I think my mall forced the state to do something."

If he hadn't broken ground for the mall on the 34-acre site, well, who knows? "We didn't build a mall there because an overpass was planned, but it's a big intersection, and that's where the merchants want to be. They want to make sure the customers can reach them, too," he said. "If we hadn't built that mall there, they might not be working on that intersection now."

DOT officially disagrees, but some officials think Stone may have a point. Though the interchange already was on the books, the mall prompted planners from Bartow to Tallahassee to take a hard look at which project received priority.

Earl Davis and Stone are on a first-name basis now. He and Davis, who is overseeing the interchange job for DOT, have discussed access, egress, and the finesse with which the state and its contractor have handled traffic flow. Traffic is important to both of them.

Because the land is in demand, it's worth a lot of money, Stone has repeatedly told the state. He told Anthony Santoro.

A DOT area administrator of acquisition who works out of DOT's Bartow offices, Santoro visited Pinellas County and met Stone and the car-dealer's brother-in-law, attorney Ira Desper, on Sept. 14, 1984. The state wanted a southwest corner lot for a turn lane's right-of-way, and the session didn't get off to a good start.

Outspoken, occasionally blunt, Santoro was not the typical smooth-talking bureaucrat. "I explained to them the right a governing body has to take land from private citizens for public use under the law of eminent domain (with just compensation), which dates back to the ancient Romans," Santoro wrote in an eight-page memo to his bosses.

But Desper and Stone were not impressed with a vanished civilization. As Santoro talked, both men became increasingly impatient, he wrote. Finally, Desper told him to cut the speech. The two wanted to know "the bottom line—how much money" was involved, Santoro said. They also wanted the state to compensate them $50,000 in damages for "lost earning power" on the parcels DOT wanted.

Flabbergasted, Santoro said he'd be in touch. Stone's lawyers have stayed in touch with Santoro and his co-workers. As one DOT real estate employee noted, "You have to have patience when you deal with J.O. Stone." DOT would not discuss any dollar amounts in the Stone case.

But Stone isn't the only tough dealer; DOT appraisers in Bartow routinely click off the names of shrewd businesspeople who have not jumped at the first, second, or even third offers DOT has tossed their way. Because they are still negotiating for some tracts, DOT's lawyers prefer not to discuss how those dealings are going. Some cases are slated to be tried in court, and others are in a paperwork limbo as specialists review each file. Still others are filed in a maze of offices at a DOT real estate office in Bartow.

Despite the contested parcels, DOT moved on. In late 1986 it hired Danis Corp., an Ohio-based bridge- and road-building construction firm, to build its two-bridge bypass. The highway department installed a site office near the intersection's southeast corner. The battered mobile home squatted in a corner of what had once been a McDonald's restaurant parking lot.

Danis Corp. followed with two offices of its own, and the former restaurant's asphalt parking lot fairly crawled with activity in January 1987 as trucks, tractors, and trailers brought in the tools of construction. They were ready the next month.

Observations and questions

1) This piece has 14 characters: George and Elsie Berberich, their two boys and two grandchildren, Everett Sutton and Anthony Santoro from DOT, Barnhill the appraiser, Stone the Buick dealer and his brother Ira Desper, Earl Davis the overseer, a DOT employee, and a lawyer. Study how the author helps the reader keep them all apart (e.g., by introducing them one at a time, pairing them up, not citing all of them by name, etc.).

2) Look at the last word in this sentence: "and the couple had to watch their children to make sure they didn't stray too close to the *blacktop*." Why does Davis choose "blacktop" instead of "road"? Try substituting other nouns for different effects.

3) Davis links his characters by introducing new ones as the old ones develop needs. Elsie needs advice, Barnhill steps onstage, and the author gives his background at length. Study how Davis weaves all these characters without losing or irritating readers.

4) Elsie exults about the citrus trees she planted ("They're probably just beginning to grow good now"), and one sentence later, "Construction workers barely noticed this past summer when the dozers jerked the first orange tree out of the ground." This harsh juxtaposition will produce emotional effects in readers. Which ones and for what reasons?

5) Is the reader supposed to like and admire J.O. Stone, the Buick dealer? Study how Davis manages our emotions.

6) Davis stitches paragraphs together by repeating words and images, as in this transition: Stone "does recall that his father had to handle all the paperwork. 'I *was too young*.' But he *wasn't too young* to learn the lessons that would serve him well in coming years..." Study how Davis uses this stitching to unify his article and make it flow.

Anatomy of a road, Part 3: Rain, muck cause delays

DECEMBER 6, 1988

The job had started with little fanfare. The first month of work was a jumble of faces and new names, so most people were only mildly curious when Greg Bell showed up on the site on March 6.

This guy was different. So said Larry McLaughlin, the job's superintendent. The man in blue jeans and sun-red skin would oversee the job, McLaughlin told the workers. Bell smiled, but didn't say much.

Instead, he walked into his office, sat down, and collected his thoughts, an indulgence he allowed himself before he walked out on the job to get a good look at the roads taking shape.

He is a road builder, lean as a surveying rod, with a pavement-hard belief he could get these roads from desk to dirt. Bell considers himself a pro. "I'm a dirt and right-of-way man," he'd said before, and he'd earned the right to call himself that. He'd stood in the tangle of asphalt in downtown Atlanta and rebuilt Interstate 85 as it writhed through that city's concrete canyons. Bell had seen the worst of roads, the worst of traffic; Florida couldn't top it.

But it got close, he admitted. Job specifications recognized how bad the traffic had become, and allowed Danis Corp., the contractor on the two-bridge job, a year to build frontage roads running north and south along U.S. 19 on both sides of the bridges that would rise over Whitney Road and East Bay Drive. Such a task, normally no problem for an asphalt veteran, would be formidable; construction workers and cars would be competing for an uncomfortably small amount of space. He hoped no one got hurt.

The crews outside the company's job site office were learning just how closely they would have to work around the traffic. They had to widen East

Bay's eastern and western approaches and turn lanes on both sides of U.S. 19. Bell turned to those plans.

They looked simple on paper, too. First, the workers had to build a two-lane temporary road beside the existing drive; it would run east from the intersection on the Bay Area Outlet Mall side, and would end at the mall's entrance. That meant all traffic would be shifted two lanes over, allowing Danis to build a permanent westbound road on the other side of East Bay Drive. Those two lanes would allow traffic to travel under the still-unbuilt bridge, or turn right onto the frontage road that would lead onto the highway.

When crews finished there, they would simply reroute traffic to the new lanes and do the same thing on the mall side of the drive, making a turning lane for traffic coming off the highway that headed east on East Bay.

When they finished on that side, they'd just move over to the western side, in front of Tri-City Plaza, and repeat the whole process.

Simple? Yes—on paper. But paper is not pavement. A stint in the U.S. Navy's Construction Battalion, or Seabees, had taught Bell that making dirt and asphalt conform to expectations could be a task as unyielding as a chief petty officer.

But maybe he was just as obstinate. Making roads had satisfied something in him ever since he saw what big intentions and a bulldozer could do at a Virginia naval base.

When he got out, the Ohio native headed south to the Atlanta area, figuring the best place to learn road building would lie in a hot spot of blacktop construction. There, he'd met McLaughlin and Dallas Wolford, who later became a Danis vice president. He also met a Georgia woman who said she'd marry him.

Wolford hired McLaughlin, and then he picked up the telephone and made a call to Atlanta. Florida needs your skills, he told Bell, and the 33-year-old couldn't turn down an offer like that. He packed for Florida, promising his fiancee he'd return in June 1988 to marry her.

Bell looked away from the blueprints and walked out of his office to meet his co-workers. He hardly looked twice at Richlene Young.

March 6 was her first day on the job, too. Road work had changed since Earl Davis signed on with DOT, and highway work had become the province of women, too. As one of six females Danis hired, the 22-year-old filled out her paperwork and watched as everyone started another day at work. Like Bell, she also collected her thoughts before she joined the throng outside.

She'd come from another construction firm in Clearwater where the foreman had been willing to hire a single parent. And they'd been good to her, but Young wanted more than that company could offer; it didn't have the heavy machinery that captured her attention. When her mother told Young she'd heard Danis was hiring women and minorities, she figured she couldn't lose: she was a woman, and black.

Young applied March 5, and a Danis official hired her before she walked out of the trailer.

She reported to the same trailer the next morning, slightly nervous, the new kid, and a woman at that.

Another woman—there were few, she noticed—smiled at her and told Young she was a rough roller operator trainee, the person who drives the heavy rollers that compress asphalt and soil. Young grinned.

So did Danny Barney, her foreman and immediate boss. She looked up as he walked in. "Come on," he told her as she finished signing her employment forms. They stepped out of the trailer into an already bright and loud day. They took a step toward the job site, and their first steps toward becoming friends. Both said little during those first awkward moments that always happen when boss meets worker. The sound got louder as they crossed the road, and Barney almost had to shout when he motioned to a hunk of machinery squatting by a pile of dirt.

"This is it," Barney yelled. It was a roller, green, massive, with an empty operator's seat. She swung up into the bucket seat and wiggled in it, checking its feel against her jeans. Barney stuck in the ignition key, turned it, and smiled at Young as the machine's engine clattered to life. Young felt a powerful tremor underneath her, and she grinned for the second time that day.

"I loved it right away," she said later. "I knew I'd found what I wanted to do."

They went through the instructions as Barney pointed the levers that controlled the machine. He also noted that it had a control that shook the 15,000-pound roller. When it vibrated, the roller banged moisture out of the earth so asphalt would adhere more readily to the roadbed. Young was entranced.

They put the roller in gear, and it lurched as it chugged toward the southeast corner where workers dodged cars as they followed a barricade trail. Barney showed her where to use the roller, and she uncertainly aimed the behemoth toward the roadbed and curbing. Sitting eight feet in the air, her hard hat dazzlingly white in the canopy's shadows, she watched the traffic pass by.

She began to feel at home atop the clattering machine as she pushed levers and the machine, miraculously, responded to her directions. It tickled the bottom of her boots, and she enjoyed the sensation. It felt like home.

Home, as in finding a place to belong. She hadn't felt that in the past few years. Young had worked in a downtown, upscale department store in Clearwater where she had excelled at selling bras and brass-bottomed pans. "If it's Maidenform and Revere Ware, I can sell it," she'd once giggled.

But she knew there were other ways to make a living. She quit that and headed to Atlanta, thinking she'd enjoy work in what had become the capital of the South. But clerking at a grocery store was not what she wanted. Atlanta was too big, and she and her daughter, Gabrielle, were too alone. They came home.

Now, she knew what home meant. Young turned, to make another pass over some soil. The machine, plodding, growling, massive, ponderous, responded. She grinned for the third time that day.

They had their routine established by April 1987. The crews showed up at 7 a.m. and worked until 5:30 p.m., taking a half-hour for lunch in a 10-hour work day. By then, everybody knew everybody else. Some uncomplimentary nicknames even took hold as the project dug itself into the soil.

The merchants dug in, too, grudgingly accepting the workers' presence. Motorists had learned to allow even more time to get through the interchange on their way to work, and some hard-hatters on the job site watched every afternoon for their favorite barmaid as she drove to work. Even the airborne morning traffic reporters had learned to expect the morning crawl at the tangled intersection.

But no one expected the polluted dirt.

Bell's radio crackled late one April morning, and he answered. The voice on the other end said it needed him now.

A crew digging a storm-water pipe drain discovered it. The earthing machinery turned up soil in the crossroads' southeastern corner that smelled suspiciously like gasoline. Probes in the soil survey at the southwestern and northwestern corners also revealed dirt that probably held high concentrations of gasoline.

The message spread along the official and unofficial lines of communication: the dirt was polluted. Bell, who had learned to expect almost any surprise from the soil, was nonplussed. So were state officials, who didn't expect the dirt to have too-high levels of gasoline and its derivatives.

The word reached Earl Davis, DOT's representative on the job, who walked 50 yards to the nearest site. He said nothing, and he wasn't surprised. Service stations once operated on two corners, and the spot on which he stood had been a gasoline storage area.

He and Bell nodded to each other, spoke briefly, and then each retired to his trailer—Bell for talks with McLaughlin and Danis engineer Estil Phillips; Davis for a talk with Doug Moore, DOT's resident engineer for the Tampa Bay area.

DOT engineers got on the phone and contacted Environmental Science and Engineering of Tampa, a company specializing in testing soil for pollutants. An engineer said he'd have someone visit the job site in early May and take samples to determine just how polluted the soil was.

That meant a delay, but what could anyone do? There were enough other tasks demanding attention, so the crews ignored the corners. But they didn't ignore the soil engineers, and everyone was curious as the soil engineers poked core-sample borers into the dirt and took notes early the next month.

But something else happened to divert their attention.

Again, Bell got the news through his radio. A crew needed him across the highway. Bell's four-wheel-drive whined as he drove through the dust and congestion.

They stood beside the northeastern edge of Tri-City's parking lot, on a tract that the state had bought, and pointed at the hole.

Muck. A short word for the undesirable leftovers of another age that occasionally come to light, a dark brown morass of dead vegetation, mud, and fossil remains. Muck is not a curse word in the road business, but it's not a welcome one, either.

Bell didn't welcome it, but, as he recalled later, "You have to deal with it. You dig it out."

Though it had been acceptable for a parking lot, the muck would never serve as the base of a turning lane, and they all knew it. The crew stood in a clump, looking at the goo. Shoppers leaving a nearby discount store paused, wondering why all those workers were doing nothing.

An unexpected delay and expense, Danis officials told DOT officials.

Davis, who'd checked out the peatlike bog, had returned to his office. He had to smile; muck was as much a part of Florida road-building as mosquitoes.

"Muck is all over Florida," he said later. "If you dig, you're going to find it."

Danis estimated removing the muck would cost an extra $24,683.02, a sum based on labor, machinery, and fill-dirt costs. When DOT officials got the estimate, they almost immediately recommended that the state pay it so everyone could get on with the job.

In a display of bureaucratic alacrity, DOT authorized Danis June 2 to dig up the goo and replace it with 5,000 cubic yards of solid fill.

Danis was just as fast; it had six workers at the site the next day, and trucks rumbled with new dirt to replace that which had been taken out. The muck was gone by July.

They finished just in time for the rains.

Larry McLaughlin hated delays, but who could stop the rain? He tried to ignore the downfall as it pelted the mobile office's roof. It reminded him of the traffic outside at the crossroads: seemingly ceaseless, an endless flow. Only the rain was faster.

But a wet Wednesday, July 15, 1987, gave him time to catch up on paperwork. That, like the rain, seemed without end. He picked up a pen to write a rough draft of a letter, but paused. The rain thrummed.

He'd known earlier in the morning that the crews wouldn't get anything done. They stood outside, awaiting orders, when the sky opened. The rain was uncertain at first, errant plinks on the trailer's roof, and McLaughlin hoped it would pass over and into the Gulf. Instead, the drops increased and the crew standing outside his mobile office sought shelter. He sent them home.

Some seemed pleased, quietly tickled to have a day off in the middle of the week. Others looked unhappy, because a rainy day means no pay. McLaughlin permitted himself a wry smile; he knew which workers had families.

He was pleased with the workers who had signed on when Danis began advertising for laborers and equipment operators earlier that year. Danis had won the contract for the interchange in late 1986, submitting a $17.6 million bid for the job. The company, based in Dayton, Ohio, sent McLaughlin from its Orlando offices to oversee the newest job, and put the word out in Pinellas newspapers: Danis needed workers.

That's how McLaughlin got started, as a laborer on the business end of a shovel in the hills of West Virginia. He'd worked up and down the Eastern Seaboard since leaving the state in 1969, and by the time he unlocked the office doors at Danis's Largo job site, he'd built bridges in West Virginia, North Carolina, and Florida.

They were basically all the same, yet each job has its own personality, and this one was no different. It had opposed them at first, turning up tainted dirt when soil specialists probed the crossroads' corners. He'd waited patiently as tractors tilled the dirt, allowing the gasoline to dissipate in air as the environmental testing company had suggested.

Then there were the utilities that his crews and other companies were digging up and moving; he and the guys in the DOT trailer had dealt with that since the beginning of the year. The muck across the road was still a dark brown and vivid memory. So was the aging water main a subcontractor had accidentally cut weeks earlier, and he wouldn't forget watching the crews hustle to put a "Band-Aid" on the old pipe.

While some marveled at the oyster shells, McLaughlin pondered what else the earth held. At this job, the dirt had surrendered 12,400-volt power lines, surprisingly small to carry so much current. The power crews moved them as the job progressed, and not once had they cut off the juice—a fact that amazed some Danis hard-hatters.

St. Petersburg was installing a new 48-inch main, and McLaughlin had waited for its crews, too. A gas company had lines in the soil, and GTE Florida's engineers had started charting their excavation the previous November and planned to move and improve their telephone lines until October 1988.

They all took time, and even the mighty utility companies weren't above nature's caprices. The same rain that stopped McLaughlin's crews that morning also sent a power crew back to its warehouse.

The rain continued, and McLaughlin turned his attention back to the letters and memos before him. Had all the jobs been this full of paperwork? He thought for a moment and answered himself: yes, all government jobs contained red tape, paper trails longer than the bridges he knew would rise over the soggy crossroads outside.

The crossroads had been wet for more than a week. Florida was in the middle of another steamy, soggy summer, and that meant sudden showers. It also meant work slowdowns as crews ran for shelter and scurried to cover equipment. And a rainy day invariably set his crews back a day and a half.

Too many setbacks meant morale problems, and McLaughlin didn't need that. He'd told the bosses back in Orlando that the job was going well, and it was; still, a break in the rain would help.

The summer came at a bad time in the project. Construction workers like to see their work, or, as McLaughlin had noted, "They like to step back and look at what they've done at the end of the day." But a construction job this big sometimes required everyone's patience.

The underground crews had started work first, cutting into the dirt Feb. 14, Valentine's Day. They peeled away the soil like old skin and began laying new concrete piping. The white pipes would handle the runoff water sure to splash off the new bridges and roads. The piping crisscrossed like so many arteries in a human body, and, like arteries, they were designed to give the maximum flow. But—again, like arteries—they operated out of sight, and crews were hard-pressed to see the actual toils of their labor.

"They would dig a hole just to bury their work," he'd say later. "They knew what they'd done, but they couldn't see it."

He couldn't see the end of the memos, and he

sat back in his chair as he read the latest. It came from Davis, who sat 30 feet away in his own office. The letter asked Danis to correct a faulty drainage pipe that wasn't channeling water properly, causing a pool to form whenever rain fell.

McLaughlin picked up his pen and replied, asking for patience as Danis tried to work around power, telephone, and gas crews toiling in the dirt. He made a notation for the letter to be typed and mailed back to Davis, who was probably at that moment writing him in his office.

McLaughlin sighed. Paperwork.

Bell looked up from his desk at Danis's other site trailer. He'd just finished a short passage in his diary, noting the day had been rained out. Bell kept the diary, not out of a love of writing, but of necessity. Still, rereading an old job diary never failed to make him smile.

But he wasn't smiling at the moment. He'd come to build the roads, but how could he? The road grades weren't at the right levels, and that caused pooling. It also upset the merchants, who blamed Danis for traffic snarls, the dust, and now the mud that would follow this latest downpour. He anticipated the next storm—a barrage of complaints from merchants who said the contractor wasn't doing enough to keep puddles off the roads.

Bell sighed. No work.

Chet Harbison looked beyond his inventory at the cars crawling past in the rain. They moved slowly, as slowly as the sales of his recreational vehicles.

He blamed the job outside—for the slow traffic outside, for the nonexistent traffic inside his showroom. Crews had started tearing up old pavement and digging in front of his business as they readied the area to build the first segment of frontage road on the highway's western side.

His company, just north of the crossroads, felt the change almost immediately as lumbering RVs had trouble entering and leaving his parking lot.

And though he knew something had to be done to ease traffic at the intersection, Harbison also felt more than the earth had been gouged. He felt hurt, too.

"There is something of a manhole out front," he complained to a visitor, "if you can find the entrance."

The rain kept falling. Harbison looked through the plate glass at his RVs. Their headlights seemed to stare back.

Observations and questions

1) Davis describes the boss, Greg Bell, like this: "He is a road builder, lean as a surveying rod, with a pavement-hard belief he could get these roads from desk to dirt." Are the similes ("lean as a surveying rod") and metaphors ("pavement-hard belief") arty and decorative, or do they help the reader picture Bell?

2) Highways are as hard to describe as wrestling holds. Study all the devices Davis uses to make this passage clear: "First, the workers had to build a two-lane temporary road beside the existing drive; it would run east from the intersection on the Bay Area Outlet Mall side, and would end at the mall's entrance. That meant all traffic would be shifted two lanes over, allowing Danis to build a permanent westbound road on the other side of East Bay Drive. Those two lanes would allow traffic to travel under the still-unbuilt bridge, or turn right onto the frontage road that would lead onto the highway." Cultivate friends in graphics!

3) Davis spends five paragraphs describing the roller. Notice how we see it through Richlene's senses and reactions. Why is this technique more effective than straight description?

4) The author uses an attribution that would send most editors into apoplectic shock: "'If it's Maidenform and Revere Ware, I can sell it,' she'd once *giggled*." What would you say to an editor who wanted to change "giggled" to "said"?

5) Davis occasionally writes sentence fragments, e.g., "Muck. A short word for the undesirable leftovers of another age that occasionally come to light, a dark brown morass of dead vegetation, mud, and fossil remains." Should we avoid incomplete sentences? What are they good for?

Anatomy of a road, Part 4: Bridging lives with steel

DECEMBER 7, 1988

The rain eased briefly in late July, though the crews had come to expect the sudden torrents that usually came late in the day. In Florida, the only thing more predictable than November's flood of Michigan RVs is July's storms.

The crews and the state and the merchants and the residents and the motorists had an alliance. It was a forced partnership, a sort of shotgun marriage. And like a necessary union, that alliance sometimes chafed.

Carmel Ceraolo felt that rub. The road crews had knocked off work for the weekend, but hadn't knocked down a pile of dirt near Tri-City Plaza in Largo. The mound was unsafe, unsightly, and unsuitable for a busy weekend of business. He also noted that construction crews had cracked the pavement of his parking lot at the mall's East Bay Drive entrance.

His tires screeched slightly as he wheeled into a parking place near his realty firm at the plaza. Normally a placid man, Ceraolo almost growled as he dictated yet another letter about the traffic project slowly stretching in front of Tri-City.

"I am distressed with the pace of the construction of this project," his letter to Largo Commissioner James Miles read. "There are many days I have observed that there is no one working, and when they do work, they move one pile of dirt from one spot to another!"

He also sent a copy to DOT's Jim Kennedy, who passed it along to Glenn Ivey, DOT's District VII construction engineer.

After checking with DOT employees who visited the site routinely, Ivey dictated a response on Aug. 10. The utilities' relocation and preliminary roadwork try everyone's patience, his letter read. "The utility work lends itself to the appearance of limited progress and certainly involves the moving of piles of dirt," he wrote. In a following paragraph, he asked Ceraolo to be patient, for better times—and traffic flow—would come as Danis Corp., the firm building the interchange, made progress: "The completion of the access roads will alleviate some of this distress."

Ceraolo read the letter and filed it with the rest he'd received from DOT. The state couldn't tell Ceraolo anything about distress. He saw it on his tenants' faces as they bemoaned the traffic snarls that kept away customers. A trip around the shopping center distressed him.

He was still distressed when he replied to Ivey's letter two weeks later. He and his tenants suffered "unnecessary burdens" at Danis's hands, he charged. When the letter arrived on Ivey's desk, the engineer ordered it placed in the fattening file containing East Bay/19 memos and correspondence.

Ceraolo didn't know it, but his letter had the desired effect. It caused a splash in the DOT pool of people who get things done, and DOT project superintendent Earl Davis dictated a letter to the company responsible for the mess.

Davis had been reviewing Danis's work progress, and didn't like everything he saw. He'd narrowed his eyes when he saw some new pipes filling with silt, and he especially didn't like watching cars splash through puddles at the crowded intersection during the last rain. He'd also seen Tri-City's parking lot.

Danis seemed to "wait until the DOT gets a complaint and then you have to be asked to fix the condition and then in some cases it is not repaired in a timely manner," he wrote.

Though Davis could kick an oyster shell from his office to Danis job boss Larry McLaughlin's trailer, he obeyed protocol again. Davis mailed the letter.

McLaughlin didn't argue. He'd learned the art of trying to get along years earlier, though he sometimes tended to forget his lessons. But he didn't this time; a crew moved the dirt and patched the pavement. He also patched relations with Ceraolo.

Ceraolo is proud of his shopping center, a vision he held when everyone else said he and his younger brother, Albert, must have been a little nuts to buy the brush- and pine-dotted, 20-acre tract north of St. Petersburg. They paid $175,000 in 1962 for a piece of land on both the eastern and western edges of 19.

Nuts? The purchase turned out to be a wise investment. Albert built a produce shop on the highway's western edge, and followed that with a frame house that hid behind some trees. He walked to work in the morning.

But he tired of the traffic and the noise. He realized just how weary he'd become of life on 19 when a motorist blocked him from leaving his home one afternoon in 1985. In 1987, he sold a sliver of land to DOT for $43,000 and moved north to Inverness. The worst traffic he's encountered since then has been tailgating boats on Tsala Apopka Lake.

"It kept getting worse and worse there," he said. "I finally decided it wasn't worth it and left town."

Carmel, however, stayed.

He took the other side of the highway and, in 1967, watched with satisfaction as workers erected a plywood sign announcing a new shopping center would locate at the East Bay/U.S. 19 crossroads. The shopping center opened a year later.

The memory still brings a smile to Carmel Ceraolo's face.

"When we bought that land out there, people told us the real estate market had already peaked, that we were too late," Carmel has said before. "But look at a map of the county: this is the Main Street for Pinellas County."

And a piece of Main Street is never cheap. If DOT's lawyers had doubted it, they'd suddenly changed their minds in January 1987 when a Pinellas County Circuit Court jury awarded the developer $1.05 million for current and future business losses. In the beginning, DOT had offered Ceraolo slightly less than a quarter-million dollars for a slice of land totaling one acre along the mall's eastern parking lot.

DOT appealed the decision, so when Ceraolo had not received the cash, the summer of 1987 found him waging a letter-writing campaign for his shopping center.

He wandered out to the site one afternoon in late August and watched the figures toiling in the dust. The sun cast long shadows across his parking lot, and Ceraolo scraped the dirt with his shoe. The traffic, as always, rolled.

He'd done well in real estate, but Ceraolo tried to keep land in perspective. He knew there were secrets in the earth, and he found himself wondering about those beneath his feet.

"If I didn't do this [real estate and leasing]," he once said, "I'd be an archaeologist. I'd like that."

The soil was yielding, but slowly, to Danis. It would yield even more soon.

Greg Bell felt good that afternoon. Oct. 23 had been sunny and windy, a perfect time to open a new road. He'd driven along the first segment of the frontage road, the shining blacktop north of the intersection along the western edge of U.S. 19. The quadrant marked one of the big steps in the construction job, for it signaled the moment when southbound 19 traffic would be shunted onto the frontage road. That meant they could get busy building the walls that would elevate the bridges.

He drove the new road one last time at about 1:30 p.m., then circled back to the barricades that kept southbound highway traffic from taking the new road. He reached for his radio and grinned into it. "Open it up," he said, and a construction worker complied. They moved the barricades away, and a flashing sign pointed traffic to the right, toward the new road. They all paused for a moment, waiting for that first car to make the turn that would direct all traffic onto the new pavement. The car turned, and Bell smiled at his reflection that flashed in the passing windows.

He wrote again in his diary that night—a simple

passage noting that the interchange had reached a passage of its own. Still, they had to perform the identical task three more times before the frontage roads would circle traffic completely away from the center of the intersection. But the first step was the hardest, and it was done. No one doubted they could, and would, make the other three.

Richlene Young gave up. She'd tried the expensive sun blockers, but nothing slowed summer's sun from her perch atop the asphalt roller she guided 10 hours a day. The sun baked her, and her already brown skin got darker. The folks at church said so.

She enjoyed the hymns, but didn't enjoy the looks she saw some people give her as she walked into daylight after the services. She wondered why, and a friend pulled her aside. Pointing at her skin, her friend told her she had a tan—a deep, dark one. Richlene blushed under her tan.

"I'm already dark enough," she told her grandmother later as they ate lunch, "and I don't need any tan."

Then Young remembered the sun blockers she'd sold at the department store; she'd moved cartons of the stuff to youngsters and dowagers both when Florida's sun reached its summertime zenith.

She came to work armed with a tube of the best. It rolled in her battered purse. She applied it liberally that Monday morning, slathering it on her face as a bold summer sun climbed over the buildings and distant trees. She didn't know how the cream would react to her skin, but she wasn't surprised at her co-workers' reaction. They howled when they saw the white cream on her dark face.

"Ain't nobody going to notice a tan on you," one said, and they all laughed some more. She laughed with them, but remembered the looks at church. Even her daughter had seen the difference. Richlene lived with the giggles.

But she couldn't live with what the white stuff did to her. "It makes me look purple," she complained to her mother. Ever the optimist, Young switched brands, and her next purchase sat like a gel on her arms and face.

But the gel was custom-designed to attract dirt; even the slightest breeze carried dust and sand, and she imagined that every breeze headed her way. The dirt settled like a fine carpet of grit on her arms and face, and their crystals magnified the sun. She burned, and quickly. Young threw that tube away, too, and by late fall, a very dark young woman guided the roller along the southwest segment of the intersection as crews hustled to open that next frontage road.

She steered her roller around the crew building the dirt-and-concrete earth wall north of the intersection. They needed her on the southwest side now, because Danis wanted to open another frontage road segment by early 1988. Her roller, which she now called "Baby," seemed to chuckle.

Roger Bloomfield watched the green roller march up a distant hill of dirt, but he didn't give it a thought. He had come down to Florida for three days to get Danis started building the walls that would lift U.S. 19 above the traffic on East Bay Drive and Whitney Road. He didn't have much time for idle thoughts.

He stood at the project's northern end, not far from the point where the Whitney bridge would begin its rise out of the dirt. A vice president of VSL Corp.'s retained-earth division's regional offices, Bloomfield worked just outside of Washington, D.C., but welcomed the chance to visit Pinellas County. He ignored the heat and instead looked south toward the crowded intersection, piled with dirt and people, punctuated with traffic. He also envisioned a Frenchman on the beach, playing with pine straw.

That image was in his head, and was the basis of his living. A Frenchman vacationing at the shore 30 years ago had constructed a wall of sand, making a rise that resembled a thick shark fin. On a whim, he'd interlaced the sandy ridge with horizontal strands of pine straw.

As the fin got higher, he continued laying the sand on the meshed straw that he'd placed inside the growing mound. The result was a surprisingly solid swath of sand and straw. The Frenchman didn't know it, but he'd created a retained-earth wall.

Three decades had not improved the retained-earth wall, though contractors used concrete panels instead of sand, and steel mesh took the place of the pine straw that kept the sandy walls standing straight.

A civil engineer, Bloomfield had made retained-earth walls before. It was all a matter of numbers, he thought, and the numbers already were coming together.

A Tampa concrete firm had begun making the estimated 5,800 six-sided panels that would hold up the dirt. A trucking firm waited to bring the first of an estimated 20,000 cubic yards of fill dirt the walls would need, and the mesh had been stacked at the site.

The wall, Bloomfield told Bell, would stand for a century.

Bell nodded his head. He'd built retained-earth walls, and appreciated their simplicity and strength. As a road builder, he viewed them as something that would hold aloft his work—a frame that holds a picture, perhaps—but he also knew that some engineers had the souls of artists. When Bloomfield noted how the sun's shadows would enhance the hexagonal panels' design, Bell nodded, thinking about his roads.

Bloomfield left, and the small crew he trained began building a test wall for DOT's inspection. It failed.

A DOT inspector took one look at the partially built wall and shook his head. As the trucks dumped fill dirt against them, the soil's weight had pushed the panels too far, and they leaned like an old barn over the road below.

"It doesn't look right," Bell acknowledged, and they tore it down. On the second try, they added an extra inch of "batter," or tilt, to the wall. When the trucks dumped their fill, the dirt pushed out the panels until they began forming a wall standing at an almost exact 90-degree angle from the ground.

The crew had been anxious as it laid the first line of panels. Had they done it right this time? The DOT inspector came back for a second look. This time he smiled.

The walls rose in eight weeks. The new year saw two humps rising out of the sand like a sea serpent playing in the surf.

January got started, and the crews shook off the lethargy that grips everyone between two big holidays. The people toiling at the road's edge south of the intersection could see they neared another milestone, and everyone worked harder.

Segment No. 2 of the frontage road opened Jan. 11. The traffic had been routed onto the new pavement just south of the intersection, the stretch running parallel to the highway's western edge. That meant all of 19's southbound traffic now moved on a new roadway, and the crews shifted their attention to the eastern edge.

Bell made another short notation in his diary that evening after the crews had gone home. He listened to the swish of traffic outside, and smiled as he put his diary back in his desk. The roads were coming together.

So was the job, and Davis, who also usually spent a few moments reviewing plans and paperwork in the evening, approved. The drainage wasn't such a problem anymore, and the merchants, who'd sweated as the Christmas shopping crunch neared, hadn't complained too loudly lately.

On paper, the company was slightly ahead of schedule. But the bridges weren't done. The dirt-and-panel walls outside seemed bare without the bridges' steel and concrete and pavement. They looked like a failed project—big notions abandoned.

The pile driver standing at the edge of Whitney Road offered proof that nothing had been abandoned. A gangly collection of gears and levers and cables, the pile driver looked incapable of mustering enough force to drive an 18-inch concrete pole into the ground.

But it did, and daily; it thumped and whumped at the concrete pilings, and every slam drove each piece farther into the ground and closer to completion.

The piers would be the foundations, or footings, for columns that would hold aloft reinforced concrete beams at Whitney. Plans called for a 108-foot bridge, a small thing in the road-building business.

Small, perhaps, but it slowed motorists who almost stopped when they realized the project they navigated daily actually was taking shape.

Still, the traffic crawled. Davis and others had gotten used to the ceaseless flow of cars, but he sometimes caught himself detesting all the vehicles.

So did Jim Mazzaferro. He had fired his son, and he blamed the traffic.

The snarl of vehicles outside Tri-City Shoe Repair at the plaza had frightened away customers. Who would risk his life to resole his wing tips?

Mazzaferro had watched the flow of customers become a trickle, and in early March 1988 he reluctantly let 23-year-old Jim Jr. go, promising to bring him back when business improved.

He mused, standing in the splash of sunlight that spilled through his glass door. The door opened. A friend, another merchant just down the plaza, entered.

Each repeated what the other knew: times had indeed been better.

"It's the highway," Mazzaferro said, and pointed a calloused, thick finger at the crawl a few yards distant. "Business is off for us—has been since they began working on the road."

His friend nursed a cup of coffee. Mazzaferro shook his head and picked up a shoe he was making for a man with a misshapen foot. He squinted into it with a practiced eye.

He'd squinted at his records, too, and estimated his store was averaging about $400-$500 less per month than he had made a year earlier. What else could you do? You raise your children to fend for themselves. He scowled. Who would have thought there would be a hole in the shoe market?

Shoes had served the Mazzaferros well. Mazzaferro learned the craft from his father, an immigrant who brought a knowledge of shoemaking from northern Italy. His father had learned the trade from Mazzaferro's grandfather, who had learned it from his father. The enterprising Italian who had first learned to mold leather into footgear was Mazzaferro's great-grandfather, and every Mazzaferro took quiet pride in making good shoes and passing the knowledge to the next generation.

Jim Jr. had shown a flair for the craft, and that had tickled Jim Sr.

Mazzaferro brooded for a moment. Perhaps they had seen an omen two years earlier.

Mazzaferro and his wife, Lillian, crossed the Florida state line on Jan. 28, 1986, whistling south on Interstate 95. A silver cylinder had risen into the sky as if greeting them, and the space shuttle *Challenger* left a billowing contrail in the blue heavens. Lillian said the craft was their omen—a roaring welcome to the Sunshine State. If it could challenge the unknown, so could they.

Then it boomed into small pieces, and their good-luck omen crashed into the sea.

Lillian must have been wrong, they concluded. The two had intended to retire, but instead bought a business at the plaza after Jim started working there part time. "People like good shoes," he told his wife. "They'll come."

And they did, but Mazzaferro noticed the decline in business not long after the utility crews began putting new pipes and lines in the dirt around the plaza. Then Danis began diverting traffic flow as crews made new roads. That diverted the flow of customers from his shop, and Mazzaferro found himself dusting unused stacks of leather, Cat's Paw heels, and taps.

But the Mazzaferros had weathered other misfortunes, and the road would improve. So would business. Then, perhaps, Mazzaferro told himself, he could get his son back in the shop where he belonged.

A shadow paused in his shop, and Mazzaferro looked up. A customer?

The shadow moved on.

Observations and questions

1) "The crews and the state and the merchants and the residents and the motorists had an alliance." Rewrite this sentence as a comma series rather than five nouns linked by "and." Which works better? Why?

2) Davis begins a section like this: "Carmel Ceraolo felt that rub." But the reader waits five sentences to learn that Carmel is a realtor and not one of the builders. Puzzled readers don't trust us. Rewrite the section to orient the reader instantly.

3) Davis reminds the reader of very basic information, "Danis Corp., *the firm building the interchange,*" although four previous stories have talked about Danis constantly. Why?

4) The author occasionally uses "human" measurements instead of more precise units: "Though Davis could kick an oyster shell from his office to Danis job boss Larry McLaughlin's trailer, he obeyed protocol again. Davis mailed the letter." How far can you kick an oyster shell? Why not just say "*x* feet away"?

5) Davis introduces his explanation of "retained-earth" construction like this: "He also envisioned a Frenchman on the beach, playing with pine straw," followed by six sentences on the Frenchman who invented the process. Do you find this flashback "arty," or a diverting way to supply "BBI," Boring but Important information?

6) "The snarl of vehicles outside Tri-City Shoe Repair at the plaza had frightened away customers. Who would risk his life to resole his wing tips?" I doubt that customers, fearing for their lives, stuck with holey wing tips. What does the question tell us about Mr. Mazzaferro's state of mind?

Anatomy of a road, Part 5: Pushing toward the finish

DECEMBER 7, 1988

Larry McLaughlin wasn't given to flights of fancy; he liked to focus on the job at hand, an approach that had served him well.

"In bridge building, you look at each job, one at a time," he'd said before. "That way it all comes together." It was like making a puzzle. He'd take one piece and made sure it fit before he picked up another.

He handled a lot of pieces these days. In addition to overseeing the interchange project at U.S. 19 and East Bay Drive in Largo, he also headed a couple of other Danis Corp. jobs elsewhere in the state. He seemed to spend almost as much time on the road as he did on his yet-to-be-finished bridges. That left his No. 2 man, Greg Bell, and engineer Estil Phillips to handle the day-to-day stuff, though he often called them during his travels and when he reached his home in Port St. Lucie on Friday nights.

McLaughlin liked the progress reports he got from the two. Danis had erected the concrete girders at the Whitney Road bridge, and the construction company also had opened the third leg of its frontage roads on Feb. 16, 1988, a year and two days since it started its job.

This leg started south of the main intersection, and diverted all northbound traffic onto a new blacktop. That opening had been followed March 30 by the opening of the final stretch of frontage road. That had been a big day on the job—the completion of Phase I in a two-phase job.

Bell practically giggled for most of the afternoon after the motorists, used to the changes and rearrangement of their traffic lanes, had followed his truck as he drove the last segment and led them northward. Everybody had felt pretty good, in fact.

The morning drive-time helicopter pilots now

292

saw what Danis and DOT intended: all north- and southbound traffic veered away before it reached the still-unbuilt bridge. That freed crews to drive the next set of pilings for the 420-foot span, the big stretch reaching across East Bay Drive.

Pilings are a bridge's foundation. At the East Bay Drive/U.S. 19 bridge, 10 pilings were driven into clusters, forming a pier. Each pier would hold aloft a concrete column, and the columns held up the steel girders.

The pile driving started in mid-January. An ungainly, unlikely-looking assortment of boom and gears and cables, the driver beat a steady, if monotonous, cadence. Motorists slowed, pedestrians paused, and hard-hatters stood back as it whumped each piling into the earth. They shut off the driver for the last time on April 7, and McLaughlin cast an appreciative look at their labors. The piles, driven in clusters, stood together like friends at a small party.

Richlene Young reached down and gave her daughter's hand a quick squeeze. The 4-year-old wore her best yellow dress, and they strolled outside Bay Area Outlet Mall among a swarm of last-minute shoppers looking for the right clothes to wear the next day, Easter Sunday. A warm wind played tag with their hemlines.

The wind also carried sounds of construction, and Young saw "Baby," her roller, crawling up a dirt wall leading to the big bridge. Some Danis employees took advantage of the dry, warm weather to work overtime, and the roller passed among the pilings like a large animal in a forest. Young looked down at her daughter and grinned. Why not?

She held her daughter's hand more tightly as they walked across the hissing roads and into the swirling dust. She smiled at the man on the roller, and pointed at her daughter. He understood immediately and stepped off the thundering machine.

Young clambered on, and reached for her daughter. She sat Gabrielle on her lap and put "Baby" in gear. She'd learned a few roller moves since her first trip on the machine, and it responded smoothly.

Gabrielle wasn't so calm. She squealed happily as "Baby" rumbled, the dirt flattened, and the air filled with noise.

Motorists passing by saw her yellow dress atop the green machine, a daisy bobbing on a hillside.

The steel started arriving in June.

When it hired Allied Steel of Chicago Heights last October to make its girders, Danis had specified three different lengths of steel. The girders had to be 73, 76, and 122 feet long, and plans called for six spans to cross over East Bay Drive. Each span, or five girders, would total 420 feet. The steel weighed 912 tons.

OK, Allied said. The firm, a subsidiary of Trinity Industries of Montgomery, Ala., ordered the steel from a Gary, Ind., plant, in October 1987. Winter already whispered icy promises when the first panels arrived by rail. A crane carried the dark, dull expanses of sheet metal to waiting welders who began fabricating trapezoidal, or tub, girders. The gray steel shone red as the welds took hold, and the four-sided girders slowly grew. They stacked them like felled trees in a nearby yard.

Trains took them away. They hissed under their load and clanked south to Montgomery. Heavy-duty trucks waited there, and hauled the girders from there to Largo, where a crane lifted each girder as if it would break.

Made of panels three-eighths of an inch thick and 5 feet 9 inches tall, the girders would no more break than they would fly, George Vardaman realized. But Vardaman, Allied's southern representative, had worked in steel all his life. Sometimes, metal—and the men who handled it—could be capricious.

"A piece of steel is like a woman," he liked to say. "You never can predict what it can do."

If that was true, this shipment had been an agreeable one, though not everyone else had been so accommodating. There'd been that squabble with an engineer for Law Testing Inc., the firm

DOT had hired to make sure the steel met all qualifications. He hadn't liked the welds on some beams, and that had slowed the job briefly until Vardaman asked Allied's welders to weld two smaller pieces together. He'd had that sent to Law's Jacksonville offices, along with a hydraulic machine that bends steel. There, he'd invited the firm to watch as the machine tried to break apart the two panels at the welds. The welds held, and the two panels bent together like a taco shell.

The steel had no more problems after that, and the workers for Mulberry Construction Co., the firm Danis hired to put the beams in place, fairly flew. They used two cranes to lift the first girders in place on June 23, bolting the 73- and 76-foot lengths together. They'd started on the southern end, pointing the girders northward and laying them across the columns. After the crew finished the southern edge, it repeated itself on the northern side.

When the men finished on both edges, a distance of 122 feet separated the southern and northern girders. Then they lifted the 122-footers into the final spaces, affixing them with bolts thicker than a finger, and as long.

The Danis crews had watched with quiet respect as the muscular men clambered on the steel like cats. In October, they bolted the last 122-footer in place and crawled down.

Bell, who waited most of the day for the last girder to fall in place, walked out to thank the men as they packed their tools. "You're welcome," the foreman replied, and almost pushed Bell out of the way. But Bell wasn't insulted.

The steel job's end signaled the start of a "set-out party," a tradition among those who work in steel.

They watched the truck leave, trailing dust and banging as it headed for the blacktop and a cold beer—or several—for the men who'd hung 912 tons of steel in the air. The girders hung overhead like a cold canopy.

The hanging of the steel, more than anything,

served as a sign that the job would end, and gave new purpose to the work at the intersection. Crews are pouring concrete on the "deck," or bed of the bridge that spans the sprawling intersection. Other trucks are spraying final coats of asphalt on the frontage roads, and all the utilities are buried and forgotten.

The shape of U.S. 19's future? It's a highway that rises and falls and dips and twists past former farms, vanished citrus groves, and swamps that made way for Florida's march into the future. It's a road that planners say won't solve the anticipated continuing onslaught of visitors and new residents who see something good in Gulf Coast living.

Thousands of them will hurtle over East Bay Drive and never know what it took to make a road over another road. The DOT engineers will, and are quietly pleased with the project. Though it's just another bridge project, the East Bay job highlights a commitment to make 19 a road for the future—a concrete, steel, and asphalt monument that dwarfs those who devised it.

"This bridge will be here for a long time," Davis said. "Almost everybody else will take it for granted. But we won't."

Observations and questions

1) The lead for this story also forms the lead of the end of the series. Evaluate Davis's opener for both these functions. What other leads drawn from material inside this story can you think of ?

2) Davis explains complex things with step-by-step description, e.g, "Pilings are a bridge's foundation. At the East Bay Drive/U.S. 19 bridge, 10 pilings were driven into clusters, forming a pier. Each pier would hold aloft a concrete column, and the columns held up the steel girders." How else could you describe this structural component?

3) "Motorists slowed, pedestrians paused, and hard-hatters stood back as [the pile driver] *whumped* each piling into the earth." What kind of verb is "whumped"? We call it "onomatopoeic" because it imitates a sound. How about the picture?

4) Davis fills this article about steel with nature imagery. Find all the instances and think about why he uses them.

5) This piece describes very precise steel work: "When the men finished on both edges, a distance of 122 feet separated the southern and northern girders. Then they lifted the 122-footers into the final spaces, affixing them with bolts thicker than a finger, and as long." Amid such precision, Davis uses imprecise measures: "bolts thicker than a finger, and as long." Why?

6) This series won the ASNE award for government reporting. Think about how we would normally report such a story, which, after all, deals with the construction of an intersection. Borrrrring. How does Mark Davis transcend our unfortunate tradition of tedious government stories?

A conversation with
Mark Davis

DON FRY: Do you like reporting?

MARK DAVIS: Some days I enjoy it more than others. Reporting is an honest thing to do. When I was a public relations man...[Laughter] You've got to remember, I've been on both sides of this fence. Every reporter ought to be a PR man for a month.

And a copy editor another month.

Yes, that's right, to keep everything in the right perspective. When newspaper reporting is done right, it's the only time you're going to get paid to do what people ought to do for free, and that's to know the truth and find out what's happening. I've never made apologies for being a reporter, and that's what I mean by "honest."

What makes a good newswriter good?

Well, good editors. You can get lazy sometimes, and you reread it and say, "That's not bad." And you turn it in, and the editor says, "Come on, Davis, you can do better." For good newspaper writing, you have to be your own worst critic absolutely always, and the older I get, the tougher I am on myself, which tells me I'm getting better.

What else, besides not being lazy?

Well, it takes an eye for detail. Sometimes you lose sight of what you're writing about. You sit in some old county commission meeting, and they're talking about developmental impact or some old crummy ordinance, and you forget that basically they're dealing with people. Somebody's going to be affected, and you have to keep your eye on those details: who the people are, how it's going to affect them for better or worse, and how they view it.

Do you mostly work on your own story ideas or take assignments?

It's about 50-50. Lately, I've been getting more assignments because of all this ballyhoo about the prize. Suddenly everybody says, "We need Davis to do this." [Laughter]

Davis to do a "writing job." We call that the "sow's purse syndrome." [Laughter] So how do you get your own ideas?

Well, you've got to talk to people and, more importantly, you have to listen to them. I have to work on that constantly.

How do you work on listening?

Everybody has something worth saying, and everybody is owed the courtesy of being listened to. If you do it like that, then sometimes you run across very nice little nuggets of information. A million things happen out there that the newspaper never gets around to writing about. You have to just listen and winnow through it.

How do you know who to interview?

First get the nugget of information that's available to all the media. Then you ask, "How does this affect others around this event? To whom should I speak to get a larger and more multifaceted picture of this event?"

How do you know when you've got enough?

[Whistles] Don, I don't think you ever really know that. Sometimes you know because you can see that second hand sweeping. Normally, on a daily beat, you grab as much as you can. You should have some idea of how quickly you write, and at the very last minute, start writing.

Are you fast or slow?

I'm fast. That's AP training.

What makes you fast?

Well, I start assembling the parts of the story as I collect them. I'm constantly reshuffling and lining up in priorities what my story should be. Quite often, when I'm driving back from somewhere, I'll start putting it together in my head. Even when you're talking with other people, there's part of your brain back there, the reporter's cerebellum or something, shuffling the cards. And sometimes when I sit down in front of my screen, that thing's already just about written.

When you're "shuffling the cards," do you mean trying out sentences or sections or paragraphs or ideas?

I'm talking about ideas and sections. If I get those in the right order, the sentences are going to line right up and tumble out, usually without a lot of trouble.

Do you work from an outline?

I did on this series, but I never have on a daily basis.

Why did you use one on this series?

Well, I'd never written anything that long. And my editors wanted to see how I was going to do it. I worked harder on the outline than just about anything. That was tough.

Do you normally discuss the structure of a piece with an editor before you write it?

Sometimes. If we get a story with a couple of interesting angles, a lot of times I'll stick my head in my boss's door and bounce a lead off him real quick.

And he'll look at it and say, "That's not bad..."

**The highest praise in journalism: "Not bad."
[Laughter]**

...then I'll throw him another one, and I trust my editors so implicitly that if they select Lead A over Lead B, I'll go on that tack, unless I feel very strongly otherwise. [Laughter] And they haven't led me wrong yet.

Why does that help? You're the guy who knows the information, not the editor.

Well, it helps me to help my thoughts. It might be that Lead B was clouding my judgment. Sometimes, once you get over the lead, the rest of it's really pretty easy. That's what they teach you in school: get your lead and then you worry about the rest.

This will shock you, but I write the lead last. I write the body of the piece, and then I write the lead...

[Whistles] That does shock me.

...because I want to write a lead that perfectly introduces what follows, and that's easier to do if what follows already exists. OK, once you've got the lead right, do you write in blocks, or just sentence by sentence?

I write by thoughts, which I guess is another word for "blocks." Sometimes one sentence will handle the thought, and other times, it's going to take four or five, so I jump from block to block.

Do you save stuff for the endings of your stories?

Sometimes, yes. I'll hold that conclusion just like an ace in a draw poker game. And sometimes, I've been known to squawk a little bit when they want to shorten the story. They'll say, "We'll just cut off the bottom." And I'll say, "For God's sake, no, take it out of the middle." [Laughter]

Do you have a "notes mode" so you can send notes like "Please protect this ending"?

Yes. I can message the desk, and they are quite aware that reporters take pride in what they do. When they have to shorten something considerably, they will message, saying, "We need help. We can shorten it, or you can shorten it." And invariably, the reporter will do the shortening. And I appreciate that a lot.

Do you revise as you go along?

I revise as I go along most of the time, especially in the longer pieces. I get down about four or five paragraphs, and I start saying, "That's not quite right." Then I ignore it for another two or three paragraphs. It's like a dog scratching to get in, and finally you can't ignore the scratching any longer, and you go out there and correct it.

Do you revise a lot?

I do some revision, yes. I've yet to meet an editor who revises my copy as much as I do, which is a good sign. My best editor is my wife, Hagit.

Do you get somebody to look a piece over before you turn it in?

Well, I can't, really, not anymore. My wife didn't read any of the U.S. 19 stories. But I'll talk with her about ideas for stories, and I'll bounce leads around. Hagit can unerringly pick out the right ones, and say, "Baby, this is the one." And I appreciate that.

Are you edited much?

Yes, I am. I think I have a pretty good coterie of

editors downtown. They're committed to making sure it's correct, and they want it to read well. They'll edit some sentences, but they assume that if I put it a certain way, that that's probably the way it should be. Just about always, I agree with them when they do make a change.

When copy editors do something wonderful to your copy, do you thank them?

Yes, I do. I probably don't thank them enough. For every time you thank a copy editor, there are 10 people cussin' him or her. They want to do as good a job as they can, but the nature of what you do puts you in adversarial roles. One dog in this corner and one dog in that corner fighting over the same bone. Sometimes one dog needs to thank the other dog.

Has a copy editor ever saved you?

Yes, absolutely. Funny thing about little words: they tend to vanish, words like "not." You say somebody was not arrested, and something happens to that "not." I've had copy editors, good, sharp, astute people, catch those things. Or I'll make a suspect out of the wrong person. I did that once, and the copy editor caught it, and I appreciated that.

Did you thank that copy editor?

You bet I did. And she was so pleased and a little flustered. I said, "Donna, you got me out of a sling, and I appreciate that very much." And she said, "Well, you're welcome. That's my job." But you could tell when she hung up the phone, she felt a lot better.

She probably fainted. [Laughter]

We all think our copy is sacred, the next thing to be chiseled in stone. But anything can be improved, and those people keep you out of trouble. I suspect

I thank copy editors more than most reporters, just because I've been around a little bit longer.

Maybe they've saved you more. [Laughter] Was this U.S. 19 series your idea?

No. The managing editor had this idea. One day, he was idling out there on Highway 19, which was just a morass of barricades and heavy machinery and guys leaning on shovels, and a lot of activity going nowhere. And he thought there'd be an interesting story, to write about one road project, to use that as an example for how roads always have been built, to get to know some of the folks involved with it. He let this idea simmer back there for a while. When he interviewed me, he mentioned that he was looking for somebody to write a particular story over in a nearby county. Then the *Tribune* hired me and stuck me in a bureau in North Tampa. I'd only been there about a month when they told me *what* they wanted, but they didn't tell me *when* they wanted it. So about a month later, I went out to the job site and introduced myself around to some of the hard-hatters.

Now wait a minute. You'd only been on the paper four weeks, and this intersection is 25 miles away from your beat. Why did they pick you?

They saw something, I suppose, in my writing that they liked. When they offered me the job, they said, "We've got some road project stories in mind. We might want you to do one of them." Well, I wasn't going to say, "I'm not going to write about a road." I said, "OK. I'll do it."

How long did you spend on the whole project?

A year, but I didn't work on it the whole time. One of the facets of bureau work is you're always surrounded by alligators, and they're snapping at you all the time. Your boss has this tendency to say, "Mark, while you're waiting for a phone call from somebody at DOT, can you make a quick call to find out about this fire?" [Laughter] And before you know it, the project gets set back and set back. So sporadically, I would go out there and talk with the people who were building the road. And all the time, I was taking a lot of the notes home and working on them there. Notes can go cold after a while, so whenever I did some interviewing, I wanted to go ahead and put them in the system as quickly as I could, while I still had some recollections and thoughts and colors that could fade.

What were you doing on the beat?

I did cops, general assignment, you know, the mayhem that seems to fill papers so frequently. [Laughter] I was covering an area that's really prone to weird and sudden and violent things, so that took a lot of my attention. But I always kept coming back to the project. I'd snatch a week here or a few days there, and I guess they were getting kind of ticked off at me.

Were you talking to editors as you went along?

Yes. I would check in with my bureau chief to make sure I wasn't getting off track, because we're talking about a tremendous investment of time.

He, of course, had not assigned the story.

Well, I had two bureau chiefs working on it, Cindy Spence and Warren Johnston. Warren helped me whip it in shape. He was the one who said, "We need to do this and this and this," and I owe him a lot for that. You get so close to something, you can lose your perspective, and it helped to have a disinterested party read through it.

Did you have enough time for this project?

When you've been a daily newspaper reporter for a long time, you're used to rushing, hurry, hurry, push, push. That second hand is sweeping, and the end of the world's at 4:00! [Laughter] But with an assignment the magnitude of the one they handed me, suddenly time is not so much a factor. There's a clock there, yes, but it's a far distant clock. You have to fight the urge to be complacent. At the same time, you have to fight not to rush too much.

For example, one of the characters in one of the segments is a shoe merchant. I spent half a day with him. I had to train myself to sit back, take it easy, and let the salient facts come to me. Sometimes you can't chase it. Having come up on small newspapers as I have, where you're always pushing and hurrying and hustling to the next task, that was a challenge for me sometimes, because I felt like I wasn't earning my living. I said, "Oh, my God, I've spent four-and-a-half hours with a shoe merchant. What have I done for the *Tribune* today?" [Laughter]

For the first six or seven months, I probably donated no more than a week every month and a half to just doing some work on "U.S. 19." That's what we called it, "U.S. 19," but, after a while, one of my co-workers called it "Product 19." [Laughter]

Did you record your interviews?

I rarely record interviews, because it seems to slow me down so much. There's no tape recorder made that will record a shadow moving across the floor. That's something you've got to see and write down.

Reporters who depend on tape recorders tend not to take good notes. Were you writing as you went along, or did you do all the writing at the end?

I did most of the writing at the end. By the time it came time to lock and load it, I had piles of notes, and I started going through them. But the actual writing took place over about a four-week period at home.

How did you organize all that stuff?

Normally, with a smaller piece, I won't outline.
But with something like this, I would no more
dream of driving across America without a map.
This was the verbal equivalent of trying to negotiate the Rockies. I didn't know where the Donner
Pass was. I had to write it all down. And the outline changed as I went along. Most afternoons and
evenings, when I'd sit down to write, the first thing
I'd do is call up the outline and reread it and see
where I'd stopped.

I had given my bureau chief my rough draft of
the first third. It was printed on a continuous roll of
paper, and it stretched from here to that hedge out
there. I rolled it all up and handed it to him like
parchment. He rolled it all out and said, "Well, I can
tell this is too long for one day." [Laughter] So
based on how much I had written, we decided there
would be somewhere between five or six segments,
and it came out as six stories over three days.

**But you had written part one before you made
the decision on the total...**

Yes, my first part one, the parchment that stretched
from here to the hedge, actually turned out to be
parts one and two in print. I had written it all as
one long narrative, and it was too long. I had to go
back and edit it. When I finished what I considered
part one, my editor said, "This is all well and good,
but it's too long. I'm going to have to split it in two
pieces, and it's a little fat here and there." I'd held
this one so closely and so dearly for so long, that
hurt a little bit to hear, but Warren was absolutely
right. We engaged in the slash-and-burn technique
of editing. He'd wade in, saying, "Get that verb
over there, will you? Hack that one out." [Laugh-
ter] And an adverb would scoot by, and we'd snag
it and throw it out. The end result was much more
readable, and reading over it now, I see places
where we probably could have done some more.
We showed part one to our senior editors, Donna

Reed and Tom Sherberger, and they said, "Hey, this isn't bad."

Argghh! That minimalist compliment again!

Yes, but it fired me with new resolve. You pat me on the head, and I'll run around the building three or four times for you. You kick me in the butt, and I might go halfway around the building and growl at you as soon as you're out of range. [Laughter]

What caused you the most trouble?

Well, the hardest part, Don, was leads. I've never had a lot of trouble with leads, but I'd never written anything this long. And I thought to myself, "What kind of a lead do you put on something like this?" [Laughter] And I wrestled with that for a while, and after I'd gotten the lead done, I wrote a lot of the history of the highway. I also had trouble making a conclusion for each piece and starting anew with a decent lead for the next part. It's like writing chapters in a book, I suppose.

Why did you write it at home?

Warren said, "You're going to have to start writing it sometime." And I said, "Warren, I can't write it here. Every time I start, something happens, you want me to make a phone call, or there's a disaster. Why don't you let me have about a month off, and I'll finish my research at home."

So the first week in October, I reported to work by getting up and walking into the kitchen and having a cup of coffee and playing with the cat, which was really quite nice. Most mornings would find me doing research and tying up loose ends and going places. In the afternoons, I'd do some writing, maybe 30 to 50 inches. And then I would go back and tear out probably a third of what I'd written each time. And I suppose I read and reread and reread that thing about a hundred times. Then I inadvertently killed the first draft of part one...

You lost the whole draft?

Yes. I had to rewrite it, every word of it.

Anybody ever teach you to back up files?

Well... [Laughter] The rewritten version was actually a little better, but that was the low moment in the project. My wife fussed at me for not making a hard copy, and I was growling at her and slamming the door, and the cat ran away, and I was no fun at all that evening. [Laughter] But by this time, I was writing pretty seriously, because I began to see the end.

After about four weeks, I had all the copy basically done. I knew that some of those stories needed to be rearranged and whittled down. They needed to be slashed and torn at, because there was just too much there.

I worked until 4 a.m. Sunday, tearing and slashing and burning and rewriting. By the time Monday rolled around, I was one scabrous-looking individual. I called my boss, and I says, "Warren." He says, "Mark." I says, "I have it for you." He says, "Well, bring it in." So I put on my best Italian suit, double-breasted, got out a starched, all-cotton shirt, one of those outlandish, garish Italian ties, and shined my shoes and went to work, unshaved. I looked like a bum who'd rolled a rich guy. And that evoked some comment in the newsroom and some laughs and finger pointing. But I didn't really care, because I had made deadline. And then it rolled into our mainframe system, all 400 inches of it...

Four hundred inches, yike! What did they say?

Well, they said, "Take the rest of the day off. You look like hell." [Laughter] And it sat in the system for several days. I made sure it wasn't going to expire on me, and we set the kill date for 1999. [Laughter] I was too close to it. You have to sit back and let your passion, as it were, cool, and then you can look at it in a far more sensible light. After three or four days, oddly enough, I was a little reluctant to go in there and start reading. But I waded into it and started slashing and tearing again.

Were you revising with an editor, or by yourself?

By myself. I had asked my editors to let me have one last crack at it, and they agreed. They knew that I tend to edit myself pretty hard.

Was this edited in the main office or in the bureau?

Both places. The first editing was done in the bureau. Warren would print a hard copy out and take it home to read. He'd make notations and highlight things he thought needed work, fleshing out or deleting. We finally finished it, and Warren said, "I think it reads pretty good, and we'll send it on up."

How long did the two of you spend on it?

We spent a week on it, not constantly, obviously, because when you're in a bureau, things are happening. People are dying, houses are burning. But in the afternoon, when the fur and the dust had settled, we'd slug our way through it.

Who edited it downtown?

We turned it over to Tom Scherberger and Donna Reed, and the more people who read one of these things, the better it is, I think. Tom went through it and found areas where he thought it needed strengthening, and I didn't always agree with him on those, but to his credit and mine, there was compromising all the way around.

Did he let you rewrite it, or did he rewrite it?

He preferred that I rewrite it. And when he did rewrite it some, he wanted me to sit right down and watch him, which I appreciated a lot. Ideally, that's the way it should always be.

Indeed. How long was it edited downtown?

Oh, they had it for two weeks. They turned that thing upside down and shook it to see what fell out. They turned it sideways and held it to the light. And by the time it was ready to print, it had been read by four editors. Later, they asked me to come in every afternoon and make sure each story jumped properly.

That's a great privilege. You and David Finkel of the *St. Petersburg Times* are the only reporters I know who get that kind of treatment.

Well, I've never gotten that treatment before or since! [Laughter] I'd check it to make sure the cutlines were right, the names, the IDs. I rewrote a couple of cutlines, because they needed them shortened, and they figured the best person to write a concise cutline would be the guy who'd been out there.

Let's look at your first lead, which depicts Earl Davis looking down into a hole full of oyster shells, essentially down to "...not on the job itself." That's a long lead, even for a long series.

Indeed. I was trying to get into his head, so to speak, and ease people into the fact that I'm writing about a road. They're out there toiling away at this modern-day concern, and they run across something from eons ago. My original lead started 70,000 years ago, with the sea receding....

A James Michener lead! [Laughter] Too hard.

Yeah, it was too hard, but that was my favorite. I thought that was interesting, and I thought maybe other people would find it interesting, too. If you're going to get somebody to read something this long, you'd better bring the bear out of the woods pretty quick.

I notice that you link paragraphs by repeating words and concepts. Listen to this sequence of beginnings and endings: "His boss handed him a machete." Next paragraph: "By 1950, he swung it..." That paragraph ends: "...Davis always looked ahead to the next leg of the project." Next paragraph: "The legs were long..." That paragraph ends: "Some quit, thinking they'd never see an end to the wet, hot, dirty work." The next paragraph begins: "It did have an end..." I call that technique "stitching."

I call it "transitions."

When journalists think of "transitions," they tend to think of transitions between sections, not between paragraphs. You write transitions between paragraphs.

Is that all right?

Well, it works. [Laughter]

OK. A well-written piece should flow. Too many newspaper stories have Paragraph A, Paragraph B, Paragraph C. You have to take a mental leap to get to the next graph, and I don't want my readers to have to do that. My editors say my stories are hard to shorten because of that. "We take out one paragraph," they said, "and the whole thing stumbles." And I said, "So take a paragraph out of somebody else's story." [Laughter]

Think of it as a defense against samurai editing. [Laughter] One of the hardest things in here is describing the intersection itself. Listen to this: "He'd also reviewed the bridge-building plans. They, too, were a marvel.
    "A football team could play on the largest bridge, a 420-foot-long, six-lane creation. At its zenith, it would allow almost 17 feet of clearance

for the traffic passing below. The 108-foot Whitney Bridge, by comparison, could hold a basketball team but would be hard-pressed to find room at either end for the cheerleaders." The only thing harder to describe than roads is probably wrestling holds. [Laughter]

Well, that was tough to do. At first, I used a hypothetical couple, two motorists named Fred and Sally, but it just didn't work. I thought, "How can I describe this in the simplest terms possible?" I labored quite a bit on these graphs, trying to get them as absolutely simple as I could.

That intersection is hard enough to drive through, much less describe. [Laughter] Where did those sports metaphors come from?

Well, I thought to myself: "I'm going to say something is 420 feet long. What's even remotely close that somebody can relate to that figure? Obviously a football field, 300 feet, 100 yards. I'll put a football team on the big bridge. The Packers and the Lions could go at it out there." Then I thought: "What about the smaller bridge?" I called the sports department and found out that a basketball court is 90 feet long, and I said, "Hot dog. We've got it."

Wonderful. These stories work because they aren't organized around agencies and trends and documents and numbers, but around people.

Well, we go along with professional blinders on, dealing with bureaucrats. We tend to forget that these bureaucrats are affecting other people who have never walked into a DOT district administrator's office. The closest they ever got to the EPA is passing a dump out on the interstate. But they're the people who are affected. Not only that, Don, but on a much more basic level, I'd rather go talk to regular folks than I would to some guy behind a desk, with a $40 haircut on a 10-cent head. I like to talk to people.

Every reporter talks to people. But it's quite something else to make people the main focus of the story, as opposed to roads and machines and money. See what I mean?

Well, roads are made for people, and there's no way in the world I could have written 370 inches on a road! [Laughter]

Were these tricky descriptions accompanied by graphics and maps, or did you write it to stand alone?

I wrote it all to stand alone. All writing should be able to stand by itself. If you have a graphic to go along with it, that's great. There were challenges throughout this series, usually having to do with descriptions of roadways. How do you describe moving traffic? Even the guys who described it to me had a hard time. Usually they ended up drawing it on a piece of paper.

One of the justifications for graphics is that some things are easier to represent graphically, so you don't have to write it. But you don't count on the graphics. Suppose you had a good graphic artist. Would you still do that?

Well, we do have a good graphic artist, and I still do it. It's not my job to assume that somebody else is going to do what I ought to be doing.

Yes, yes. I never assume anybody's going to do anything.

No, no. You're going to end up with egg on your face that way.

I like your step-by-step descriptions. Listen to this one in Part 5: "Pilings are a bridge's foundation. At the East Bay Drive/U.S. 19 bridge, 10 pilings were driven into clusters, forming a pier. Each pier would hold aloft a concrete column, and the columns held up the steel girders.

"The pile driving started in mid-January. An ungainly, unlikely-looking assortment of boom and gears and cables, the driver beat a steady, if monotonous, cadence. Motorists slowed, pedestrians paused, and hard-hatters stood back as it whumped each piling into the earth. They shut off the driver for the last time on April 7, and McLaughlin cast an appreciative look at their labors. The piles, driven in clusters, stood together like friends at a small party." Nice.

Thank you. I kinda grinned at that one myself.

It isn't just that image at the end, it's the clarity of the presentation. We're talking about a rather complex structure.

And a dry topic too.

Yes, a big problem is how to deal with "BBI," Boring But Important stuff. You humanize it and turn it into actions, as you've done here very well.

Thank you. At this point, I was pushing towards the finish. A horse smells water and runs a little harder on the last stretch. At this point, I had to fight against myself not to just push it all together, not to hustle up and do a half-ass job toward the end. That was tough.

Well, you had been at it for a whole year. But at the very end, your leisurely telling speeds up. It's even a little abrupt, if I may say so.

Exactly. We did not have quite as much space as I had anticipated. I had another conclusion, but it was too long. The last four graphs were revisions. I had to take five inches out of it, and five inches sometimes can make a whopping difference.

You bet. Novels can end well because no one

ever tells a novelist to cut five inches out of the ending. Look at your very last paragraph: "'This bridge will be here for a long time,' Davis said. 'Almost everybody else will take it for granted. But we won't.'"

How early did you know that quotation was going to be the kicker for the whole thing?

It was the front-runner for a long time. I had run across several different conclusions. Earl said that to me as he was sitting at his old desk at the office. I was just scribbling away, and a little bell went off when he said that. I put a star beside it. I had started with Earl, meandered all around the topic, like a rabbit trail, so I decided I'd end it with Earl, too.

So the government story ends with people, just as it started with people. Whom do you picture as your reader? I'm not asking about demographics. I'm asking about the reader in your head.

Well, I picture someone similar to me, because whenever I write something, it has to be agreeable to me first. I suppose it's the supreme mark of egoism to write for yourself, but I suspect the ideal reader most writers have in mind is probably someone with similar tastes and thoughts.

The problem with writing for yourself is that you know too much about the story.

Well, that's true. I'm always cognizant of who might be reading my stories, but I purposely do not write down for some common-denominator reader. I like to write about just regular folks. I think people who read what I write probably have similar interests. And I try to write honestly. I'm not quite sure what that means, but I know honest writing when I see it.

So does the reader.

St. Petersburg Times

Thomas French
Finalist, Non-Deadline Writing

Thomas French lived all over Indiana, and graduated with a journalism degree from Indiana University in 1980. French joined the *St. Petersburg Times* in 1981 to cover police, then courts, and eventually politics. He now works as a general assignment reporter in news features. French was a finalist in 1987 for his series "A Cry in the Night."

French likes to write about younger people in stressful situations. He composes tightly chiseled vignettes to present people whole, with their edges raggedly human.

Adventures in babysitting

OCTOBER 2, 1988

Forgive the new world history teacher if he's a little nervous.

His name is Mr. Samsel, and for him, this is baptism-by-fire time. It's Aug. 25. Just after sunrise on this muggy Thursday morning, the fall semester officially opened at all Pinellas County schools. Samsel, a short, wiry young man wearing a tie and a hopeful smile, is standing at the front of a classroom at Boca Ciega High, his school. This is his first class of the day—the first class of his career.

It's only a homeroom, filled with a bunch of bored seniors yawning their way into another year. Samsel doesn't have to teach them anything. He just has to make sure they fill out some forms and don't tear apart the room with their bare hands. But as he gazes at the rows of blank faces before him, something happens. His voice develops a hint of a tremor. His eyes dart from one student to the next. And he can't seem to stop his feet from walking back and forth in front of the blackboard.

"Why am I pacing?" he says out loud.

The seniors don't answer. The future leaders of America sit silently, some of them slumped forward, staring into space through half-closed eyes. Over to the side sits a boy. He is wearing a crucifix, blue jeans, and a T-shirt. On the front of the shirt is a big smiley face. In the center of the face's forehead is a bullet hole, dripping blood.

This boy is giving his friends a detailed review of *A Nightmare on Elm Street 4*—he was particularly moved by a scene in which a supernatural dog urinates a stream of flames on a grave—when the voice of the principal, Barbara Paonessa, comes over a loudspeaker on the wall.

"Good morning," she says," and welcome to school year 1988-89."

A chorus of moans rises across the room.

"At Boca Ciega High School, we begin each school day with the pledge to the flag...."

The students struggle to their feet and face a flag hanging in the corner. Paonessa begins reciting the familiar words. "I pledge allegiance to the flag of the United States of America and to the republic for which..."

The students stand, saying nothing. Some swing their arms. One boy belches.

With his hand over his heart, Samsel quietly speaks the pledge along with Paonessa. When she is done, he turns to the class and introduces himself. Earnest almost to a fault, he begins the day with a pep talk for the seniors. He reminds them that this is their final year of high school, that they've almost made it to graduation. It would be a mistake, he says, for them to mess up now with drugs or alcohol or discipline problems. He wraps it all in a sports metaphor.

"So all you've got to do," he says, "is bat your baseball home."

The seniors stare at him as though he were a visitor from another planet. A sullen-looking kid near the front throws out a question.

"Why are we here?"

Samsel looks confused. "What?"

"Why are we starting school on Thursday?"

"Would you rather have come yesterday?"

The kid doesn't answer. Samsel pushes on. He takes attendance and passes around some of the forms that need filling out. A few feet away, the boy with the smiley face on his T-shirt goes on talking to his friends. He is telling how he and some others filmed a drunken buddy.

"He was running around the house nude.... We got him sleeping with a dog and everything. We were going to tattoo him, but he didn't fall asleep fast enough."

Around the room, students begin writing.

"Isn't this great?" says Samsel. "Just like real life—forms and everything."

Smiley Face looks at one of the sheets in front of him. He reads aloud as he fills it out.

"Please list medical problems."
He stops.
"Brain dead," he says.

It promises to be an exciting year filled
with opportunities to positively assist our
students as they continue to shape their des-
tinies.

*—from the introduction to the Boca
Ciega High School Faculty Handbook*

Wish the new world history teacher good luck.

His full name is August H. Samsel III. But in
class he keeps quiet about that. When he introduces himself to his students, he sticks to "Mr.
Samsel." Only a fool tells teen-agers his first name
is August.

Samsel is no fool. A former tank commander
who served in the Army for three years, he also is
no stranger to adversity. He knew teaching was going to be hard. But until he stepped in front of that
first class at Boca Ciega, he could not possibly
have understood just how hard. On that Thursday,
he began to learn.

That day, Samsel entered one of the most important and least appreciated professions in the world
—a profession that can bring immeasurable re-
wards but that also holds staggering challenges. In
Florida, which has the lowest graduation rate of
any state in the nation, the state Department of Education reports that only about 65 percent of those
who start high school actually make it through
their senior year to graduate with their classmates.
Though many students still work hard, learn well,
and show a remarkable creativity and drive, an
alarming number of others guard their apathy and
ignorance with fierce determination—sleeping
through class, paying little attention to teachers.
Even among those who aspire to something more,
many cannot spell the word "college."

Consider the situation at Boca Ciega, which has
a dropout rate similar to that of other Pinellas high
schools. In the past three years, between ninth

grade and the start of 12th, Boca Ciega's class of 1989—this year's seniors—has been virtually cut in half, to a great extent because of dropouts. Paonessa, the principal, bemoaned that fact at a recent senior assembly.

"Look how few are really here," she said, gazing out at a half-empty auditorium. "You started with a class of about 600, and there's just about somewhere around 300 left."

Somehow, teachers are expected to turn this problem around. They also must arrive at school before dawn, grade assignments late into the night, buy many of their own supplies, wade through stacks of paperwork, play hall monitor, play babysitter, keep administrators happy, deal with angry parents, break up fights, and interpret school board policies so confusing that they make tax forms look simple.

What are they paid for all this? In Pinellas County, the standard starting salary for first-year teachers is $20,250. The top teaching salary—paid to someone with a doctoral degree and at least 16 years of classroom experience—is $34,900.

This does not particularly bother August Samsel. He likes money as well as the next person. But if he had been dying to get rich, he would not have become a teacher. Instead, he says, he went into the profession because he loves kids, loves history, and wants to make the schools a better place. He grows a bit starry-eyed when he talks about teaching. He says students are like young hunters who need tutoring before they head into the forest.

"I want to be part of that guiding force for the next generation," he says without a trace of irony in his voice. "I want to be part of that force to turn education around."

Samsel is 28 years old—ancient by the standards of most high school students. Still, with his smooth face and small frame (he claims, not very convincingly, to be 5 feet 6), he could easily pass for 18. He is married to an accountant. He likes to run four or five miles at a stretch. Not jog—run. At full clip. When he's driving, he sings off-key to the songs on the car radio. His all-time favorite movie is *National Lampoon's Animal House*. This is kind of funny, because Samsel seems about as straight-laced as they come. His hair is short, his jokes are corny, and he is probably the only man under 35 who still wears an undershirt beneath his button-down.

"Were you ever a tour guide?" a girl in one of his classes asks him one day in a deadpan voice. She is studying him through her sunglasses, which she has worn throughout his lecture.

"I've been many things in my life," Samsel says. "But never a tour guide."

"Have you ever smoked marijuana?"

"No."

"Come on. Never?"

He ignores her and moves on.

On his right hand, Samsel wears a class ring from the Citadel, a military college in South Carolina, where he performed thousands of push-ups and tried to avoid being called "slime" by the upper-classmen. He went to the Citadel partially on an ROTC scholarship, and when he graduated, he satisfied one of the scholarship's requirements by going into the Army. His stint as a tank commander was not a barrel of laughs. He was stationed in Fort Riley, Kan. It was freezing cold in the winter, hot and dirty in the summer, and the tanks almost always smelled of diesel fuel. Plus, Samsel was horrified by the fact that many of the soldiers around him could barely read or write. He asked himself what would happen if they were ever forced into combat. Would they be able to read their orders?

Such questions only strengthened his desire to become a teacher. He'd thought about it ever since he was a kid. When he was growing up, his mother taught reading at an elementary school in New York City for more than 15 years. Night after night, he'd hear her come home and talk about the pupils in her classes.

Now, Samsel wants to follow in her path. But as a new teacher at Boca Ciega, he starts at the bottom of the ladder. For instance, he is what is known as "a floater": he does not have a classroom of his own. As he teaches his daily schedule of five world history classes—a required course for sophomores—he floats among four different rooms.

"I am the wind," he says good-naturedly.

He does have a desk in one classroom that he can call his own. But he is only allowed to store things inside the desk, not on top of it. Another teacher uses that room—and that desktop—when he's not there.

Two of Samsel's classes are in rooms normally used for teaching science. They are cluttered with lab tables, lab equipment, and colorful wall hangings that show, among other things, the digestive system of the tapeworm—not exactly ideal surroundings for teaching about democracy in ancient Greece.

Samsel has been assigned to lead two "basic" classes—a term used to describe classes with kids whose grades and test scores are lower than average. Some of these students are attentive and try hard to improve their grades. But others are so undisciplined that they make it difficult for anyone in the room to learn. Disruptive and lacking motivation, they can be a teacher's nightmare. It's not surprising, then, that basic classes are often given to the newest teachers, who have the least seniority.

Still, Samsel can't help but wonder if it's the kids who suffer most from this system. Don't struggling students, more than anyone else, require the experience of a veteran teacher?

"Somewhere, someplace, they got behind the eight ball," he says, "and they need that expertise."

Not that students in other classes don't need help as well. This became clear to Samsel during the first few days of school, when he asked his kids to tell him something about themselves on a written information sheet. Listed below are some of his questions, and some verbatim answers from kids in both his regular and basic classes:

Favorite leisure activities?
"Not yet."

"Sleep."
"Lestion to the radio."

What are your plans after high school?
"Colleage."
"Going to collage, and law school."
"Go to Colleageal & Army."
"Collage, tour operater."
"Be a prof. Modle, Bueatiion."
"To go to traid school and take up a traid."
"To be a weder or plouming."
"Avertizement Executive/Actress."
"Surf around the world for a year, then go to college."
"I don't no."

What do you like most and least about history classes?
"Nothing."
"I don't like anything about History."
"I don't like anything about any class."
"Least are test's, eassay's."
"They have us mimiries all the capitols."
"I Least like test. Take lot of think."
"I don't like it at All."
"I don't care."

Any other additional information which you may think is useful?
"Your doing alright so far. I skate for a living there for my knees are bad so I must stand from time to time."
"I am not verying good at taking test."
"I'm scared when I take test. (Really)."

Samsel shows his sophomores a color photo of the planet Earth. "Anyone recognize what that is?"
"Jupiter!" someone says in one class.
He shows them a drawing of some cavemen.
"They still living?" says someone in another class.
He shows them a photo of the Sphinx in Egypt and asks if anyone can identify it.

"King Tut!"

He tries to explain how the centuries have been divided into "B.C." and "A.D." One of the boys gets a confused look on his face.

"This is A.D. now?" he asks.

"Yes."

Another boy, learning about B.C. and A.D. in another class, has a different question.

"What's this got to do with the studying of history?"

"We're going to get into that," Samsel says.

He asks if anyone can name a religion.

"Like a cat running behind a car or something?" says one kid, who apparently has mistaken religion for superstition.

He asks if anyone has heard the word "prehistoric."

"Like *Flintstones*?" says someone.

He talks about the components of culture. He asks if anyone knows what the word "component" means.

"Is that, like, *The Price Is Right*?"

He does not make fun of the girl who has said this. He asks if she's thinking of "opponent." She nods, and he goes on, explaining the difference.

In these early days, as he learns to feel his way as a teacher, Samsel takes it all in stride. He jokes with his students and encourages them to speak up. He tells them there's no charge for wrong answers. He tries to make them see that history is alive, that it's made up of people who had flaws and obsessions and moments of stupidity mixed with moments of genius—people who weren't that different from us, even though they had never heard of MTV. He tries to make the students see that the past is part of them and that, one day, they will be part of the past.

"You're history," he says, a big grin on his face. It's one of his cornier lines.

The kids don't laugh. Most of them don't even flash him a polite smile. Merciless, unsympathetic to the terror of standing in front of a room of teenagers, some of them are openly hostile to his attempts to fire their imaginations. They snicker at him. They patronize him. And should he happen to misspell a word on the overhead projector, they mock him.

Most of all, they assault him with indifference.

"You finished?" says one of them.

"Is that it?" says another.

One afternoon, Samsel sights a boy yawning.

"Bear with me," he tells him. "I realize it's hot."

The boy smirks. "That's not it," he says.

Not all of the students act this way. Many sit at their desks, paying attention, taking notes, contributing to the discussion. They ask good questions about the Hanging Gardens of Babylon. They speak intelligently about Hammurabi's Code and listen intently as Samsel describes the rise of the pharaohs in ancient Egypt. Sometimes they actually seem grateful for their teacher's efforts.

"Thank you, sir," a boy says one morning as he leaves a basic class.

Other students, however, seem to linger through class in a state of benevolent distraction. They fix their eyes on Samsel and appear to be hearing what he says. But when they speak up, it's clear they're thinking about anything but history.

"Mr. Samsel?" one kid says to him. "You just get out of college or something?"

"What kind of music you listen to?"

"Where you from?"

"You like teaching, man? You ain't going to get no money."

Then there's the class when a boy notices the ring from the Citadel on Samsel's hand.

"Hey, man. That's a chill ring. You want that?"

Samsel is good-natured about such things. The off-the-wall questions do not faze him. The insults do not stop him. He is relentlessly cheerful.

"I want you to learn," he tells the students. "You don't learn, I feel bad about it."

He gets tough when he needs to but tries not to come on like Attila the Hun. Above all, he remains calm.

One day he goes to a class and tries to take attendance. But when he calls out the first few names on his list, no one answers. He calls out another name. No answer. Another name. No answer. He switches to another list and calls out another name. Still no answer. Finally, as he calls out what must be the seventh or eighth name, a living, breathing student responds.

"Here!"

He tries to show this class some color slides but finds that this particular room has no screen on which to show them. He sends someone to find a screen, but when the screen arrives, he cannot make it stand properly. And when he tries to write on the blackboard, he cannot find any chalk.

Somewhere in the room, a girl giggles.

"Okay," Samsel says. His voice is steady. A steely determination has entered his eyes. "We'll have chalk tomorrow."

* * *

The worst comes during the first week, on the second day of school. This is the day when Samsel tries to teach his third-period class and cannot find the class.

Samsel has never been to his third-period class before this day. (On the first day of school, he had his homeroom during third period.) The class is supposed to be in Room 12-7. But when he arrives there, the room is already filled with another teacher's class. This teacher tells him to try Room 10-10. Samsel goes to 10-10, but it's also filled. By now, the bell has rung. The minutes are ticking by. Where are his students? Are they wandering the halls, too?

The teacher in 10-10 walks over to the intercom on his wall and presses a button to call the administration office. Maybe someone there will know what's happening. He and Samsel wait for a response. Nothing. So the teacher in 10-10 tells Samsel to try 10-8. He tries 10-8, but it's filled, too. The teacher there walks over to his intercom and tries to call the administration. Still nothing.

The teacher in 10-8 is smiling.

"This is perfect," he says.

Samsel is not laughing. By now, he has grown very quiet. He walks into the hall and finds an assistant principal, who checks a schedule sheet and informs Samsel that he is supposed to be in 12-7 —his original room. Samsel follows the man. It turns out that there has been a breakdown in communication. The room Samsel was told was 12-7 was not 12-7 at all. Now, the assistant principal takes him to the correct room. The members of his third-period class are sitting in their seats, waiting to see if their new teacher will ever show up. They look disappointed to see him.

Samsel apologizes for the delay, introduces himself, begins taking roll. He calls out a name. There is no answer. Another name. No answer.

Fourth period, that same day. Samsel picks up his folders and papers and heads for yet another classroom. This is one of his "basic" classes. He tries to give the students a pep talk. World history, he assures them, will be fun.

"We'll be spending 18 weeks together," he says ."This should be a pleasant and very enjoyable learning experience."

Sighs float down the rows. Samsel goes on. He is trying to teach them this business of B.C. and A.D.

"This is all we're going to study is, like, B.C. and A.D.?" says one boy.

"No," Samsel says. "That's where we've got to start it."

He hands out a worksheet. One of the girls stares at him.

"I really don't want it," she says.

"Ohhhhhhh s___," says someone else.

A girl belches. Another girl stares out the window. One of the boys scowls.

"Can't learn nothing from dead stuff," he says.

Fifth period. Samsel has no class—just a planning period and a lunch break. He takes a few spare minutes to talk to the head of the social studies department. He tells her about how he couldn't find his third-period classroom and how two teachers tried unsuccessfully to contact the administration office through the intercoms. He says this worries him. What if there were an emergency and someone in the class needed help?

The department head gives him a faint smile. She has been at Boca Ciega for more than a decade.

"It's happened before," she says. "That's life."

Sixth period. This class is held in a chemistry laboratory. The kids sit in desks that are crammed together off to one side of the lab tables. Moments after the bell rings, a boy and a girl in the middle of the room are already arguing.

"Is there a problem here?" Samsel says.

"Yeah," says the girl. "He's messing with me."

"You better move her," says the boy. "She laugh at me, I'm gonna knock her out, man.... I'm gonna chop on her head."

Samsel tells them to stop it and pay attention. He goes on. He's talking to these students about B.C. and A.D., too. This is his toughest class. It's a basic class, and veteran teachers have already advised him to not bother assigning homework to his basic students. They won't do it, the other teachers told Samsel. They won't even try. This class is particularly hard to control, partially because of the room. It's hot and stuffy, and the fact that it's a chemistry lab only adds to the distractions.

"What is so funny back there?"

Samsel stops his lecture to say this. The boy and girl in the middle are still arguing.

"She's so stupid," says the boy.

"She is not stupid," Samsel says. "If she was stupid, she wouldn't be in this class."

The girl stares at the boy.

"You make me sick," she says.

"Shut up," says someone else.

"Why don't you shut up?"

Half of the kids in the room are quiet. They are trying to listen to what Samsel is saying. But the other half make it almost impossible to concentrate. The boy who has been arguing with the girl continues interrupting. He tells Samsel that teachers talk too much. He hums and makes plopping sounds with his lips. When another kid appears to have fallen asleep at his desk, this boy gets up, sneaks beside him, and claps his hands.

"Wake up, man," he says.

Samsel stares him down. "Stay in your seat."

The boy returns to his seat. He begins playing aloud with Samsel's name.

"Mr. Sling-o," he says, bouncing the syllables down the rows. "Mr. San-so."

Samsel keeps telling him to be quiet. He keeps trying to return to the lesson. He is talking about the beginnings of civilization. Around him, the arguing continues.

"What you looking at?"

"F___ you, boy."

"You hear her cuss?"

It is difficult to describe how frustrating it is to sit through such a class. Suffice it to say that most people, even reasonable, law-abiding people, probably would have been tempted to rip out these students' tongues.

Not Samsel. When the class ends, he is as unperturbed as ever. He knows he has a problem. He seems to have no doubt he will solve it. That's his job, isn't it? Besides, he didn't think the kids were that bad.

"They were pretty good," he says calmly. "Just playing the games."

Ken Fuson
Finalist, Non-Deadline Writing

Ken Fuson grew up in Granger, Iowa, and graduated from the University of Missouri. He worked at the *Columbia Daily Tribune* for four years before joining *The Des Moines Register* in 1981. Fuson was also honored as a finalist in 1981.

Fuson lets the 1,180 souls of State Center, Iowa, stand for all of us. He brings us as readers up close so we can see them and ourselves.

It's a new day in State Center

MAY 22, 1988

STATE CENTER, Iowa—As the first light of a fresh spring dawn brushes the new water tower and the old grain elevator, a small town stirs to life.

"I'm gonna die!" a boy groans at the high school, where track team members sprint in the morning chill, thick puffs of frosty air trailing them.

Nearby, Leland Weuve, 74, heads for the Trojan Inn, where men with calloused hands, seed corn caps, and bibbed overalls cram into wooden booths for a cup of coffee before they leave for the fields.

Along Main Street, at the elementary school, buses return from the six towns that feed the West Marshall School District. Alison Clark, a third-grader, hops from the Melbourne bus, ready for her spelling test.

Down the street, Olaf Klomsten sweeps the Main Street Tap. The regulars—Ralph Moody, Duwane Miller, Ubbe Rops, and the rest—will straggle in soon for another day of playing cards, drinking beer, and cursing friends.

Here comes Ralph Moody now, in his rusty green pickup truck with the cracked window (he hit a pheasant). Like most of the town, Moody, 65, rises before the sun, a habit acquired during 20 years of owning the garbage business. These days, he's either buying rounds at the Main Street Tap, feeding the 300 sheep he bought "just for something to do," or introducing his town to strangers.

There's much to see. Spring is a time for churning soil and planting corn, for mother-daughter banquets and school proms, for sitting on benches during the day and shooting free throws at night, for cooing at babies (Erik Eckhardt was born on the first day of spring) and wondering what the future holds for a town that 1,180 people call home.

"I love this town," Ralph Moody says. "I'll die here."

332

He swings past the funeral home on Main Street and looks at the sign above the door. If the red light is shining, somebody has died during the night.

The light is dark.

Spring beckons in State Center.

STRUGGLING FOR A PLACE

This cool morning, with skies the color of a swimming pool and clouds as plump as pastries, finds State Center neither thriving nor dying. It is, as its name and location suggest, somewhere in the middle, one of 832 towns in Iowa with fewer than 2,500 people that are struggling to find their place in a new era in rural America.

A year in an Iowa farm town is no different from a year in a Texas oil town or a West Virginia coal town or any other small town where economic forces have assaulted a way of life. It's the daily battle of proud people who believe they have a tradition worth protecting and a community worth saving—but don't know where to begin.

The backbone of the country, the rural towns were called, first as outposts for Western expansion, then as collection centers for the nation's food, always as custodians of the most cherished American values: hard work, fair play, respect for the land, service to the church. Places worth keeping. Home.

Then it changed.

"Everything's big business now," says Butch Horn, 39, who owns the Steak Center restaurant in State Center. "That's where our country's going, whether we like it or not. I hate it. I loved it when it was all small towns. That's what made this country."

Today, grain prices and land values are rising, thanks to government farm payments. Mike Eckhardt, Erik's father, says the tax returns he prepared in April for area farmers were some of the healthiest in years.

Yet apprehension reigns, scars still tender from the farm crisis. State Center has lost 10 percent of its population since 1980. Selling a home takes an average of six months. School enrollment will decline by 30 students next fall. One of four people in town is a senior citizen.

Those are only numbers.

They don't tell how the State Center Garden Club was forced to cancel its flower show because members are too old to lug the heavy displays.

They don't tell how Kristin Robinson, graduating senior, star athlete, and homecoming queen, got so sick she couldn't eat when her parents lost their farm two years ago.

And they don't tell how Nelda Grage waits for customers to visit her year-old crafts store, Aunt Jane's Attic. When she and her partner held an open house, three people came.

No longer master of its own universe, the town is wrapped in a straitjacket of confusion and indecision. "To be honest with you, I don't think we have any planning for the future in this community," says Mayor Larry Bohnsack, 39.

In the season of rebirth, does State Center have the energy to recover?

Inne Taylor and Roxanne Goecke publish the *State Center Enterprise* and the *Melbourne Record*— "the only newspapers in the world that really care about the West Marshall area," the mastheads read.

Taylor, 39, writes the stories. Goecke, 36, sells the ads. Each earns about $150 a week.

Two years ago, they came within hours of locking the door on the 120-year-old *Enterprise* and the 90-year-old *Record*.

"You think, 'If it folds, it's my fault,'" Taylor says. "It's up to me. I think people feel that way about the town. There's a pressure you feel all the time. How much can you give before it crushes you?"

HEART OF THE HEARTLAND

From a distance, State Center's new water tower stands as a beacon of progress, the most visible symbol of the town.

The old tower was shaped like the Tin Man's head; the new tower, built last year, looks like a

334

bloated egg plopped atop a giant golf tee, gleaming white, as slick as porcelain.

But somebody goofed. The logo on the tower —a rose surrounded by the words *State Center, Rose Capital of Iowa*—is too small to read from the highway. No matter. Few people happen upon State Center by accident.

Boxed in on all sides by some of the world's richest farmland, the town sits along U.S. Highway 30 between Ames and Marshalltown, 45 miles from Des Moines, 30 miles from the nearest interstate highway, and 13 miles from the nearest McDonald's. If Iowa were a dart board, State Center would be the bull's-eye.

The town is small enough that no presidential candidates campaigned here last winter, but large enough that residents can rent R-rated movies from the Gutekunst Library (although the most popular rental is *Grease*).

State Center has produced few notable sons or daughters in its 121-year history. Oh, Debbie Sue (Weuve) Rohrer was crowned Miss Iowa in 1975. Larry Poling, a city councilman, portrayed Nikita Khrushchev in *Miles From Home*, the movie filmed in Iowa. And Bob and Dennis Baker smashed the state record for average soybean yields last year. But that's about it.

"I wouldn't call it a progressive town, but it's not as dead-set against new ideas as some small towns," says the Rev. Ken Stuber of the First United Presbyterian Church.

When he arrived three years ago, Stuber's sermons tackled sensitive issues: foreign policy, racism, gossip.

"I had some people very upset with me," he says. "I've learned to be more diplomatic."

Word travels fast. When Roger Evans, the high school guidance counselor, rented an apartment one night, the first person he saw at school the next morning asked him about it. Melissa Billman, 12, says she enjoys small-town living "because you get to hear stuff you're not supposed to know."

Ask the people in State Center to describe their

town and they haul out the familiar traits: safe, clean, friendly. Sure, petty jealousies exist, but there's an understanding, as in any family, that what you hear stays here. As more people and businesses leave, small towns grasp even tighter to their image of pastoral wholesomeness. It's their one drawing card.

Moderation is king. Don't make too much money, or get into too much trouble, or act too different, and everything will be just fine. Evans says the first boy who wore an earring to school nearly had it yanked from his head by another student.

"The problem is our kids aren't tolerant of differences," he says. "There isn't a good appreciation of people who look different or dress different or think differently."

State Center is white, mostly Republican, and of predominately German heritage, the telephone book filled with Henzes, Hillemans, and Riemenschneiders.

The railroad gave birth to the town—even now, some 50 times a day, freight trains rumble through without stopping—but farming supplies the lifeblood. When President Reagan needed to mend relations with farmers in 1982, he chose the Dee Brothers farm outside State Center. He said he particularly enjoyed the homemade peach ice cream.

There are six churches, one for every 200 people, but you still can find a dice game at night if you know where to look and promise not to tell.

Three of the churches are Lutheran. A fire on New Year's Day in 1945 destroyed St. John's Lutheran Church. Half the congregation wanted to rebuild in the country, half wanted to rebuild in town. So each side built its own.

Fires have played a major role in State Center's history. Much of Main Street burned in 1895. Perhaps that explains why the town has such a strong volunteer fire department, capturing the state championship 10 times, finishing second the past four years.

Many of the fire department members belong to other civic groups. As small towns lose population, and those who remain get older, the demands pile on the people who are left.

Margaret Hemphill, 65, a librarian, watched the seniors leave town when her late husband was the school superintendent. Most of them, she knew, were gone for good.

Earlier this month, her son Jim, 27, who had been living at home while he worked at a Marshalltown television station, left for a magazine job in San Diego.

"You know how mothers are," Hemphill says. "I went in and cleaned up his room and cried the whole time."

For every Jim Hemphill who leaves, a Jim Maish must pick up the slack or watch the town slide.

Maish, 63, who owns a plumbing and heating business, belongs to the Lions Club, the Commerce Club, the Methodist Church board, the Marshall County Conservation Board, and helps his wife, Dorothy, with the Welcome Wagon. He also prepared the lemon chicken dish for the church's mother-daughter banquet this spring.

"You think about a laid-back, rural community and it isn't like that at all," Maish says. "You're stressed and pulled in so many different directions, trying to do the right thing.

"There's a feeling that everybody has to take their turn."

Reinforcements are needed. Boyd Van Metre, the real estate agent, says enough vacant housing exists for 20 families.

But where would they work?

MAIN STREET

In April, the City Council postponed Roger Yeager's request to put a billboard along the highway, lamented drag racing on Main Street, and approved a new toilet for the City Hall restroom.

Then Mayor Larry Bohnsack dropped a bombshell. He had talked with a businessman who expressed interest in building a manufacturing plant in town, he said. Maybe 40 jobs. He declined to say more.

Like most in Iowa, the town is desperate for new business. When the Des Moines City Council rejected a loan for a condom factory, Irma Henze, 50, who owns a clothing store, and other business leaders joked that State Center should offer a site. It was just as well they didn't. The last thing a town whose school nickname is the Trojans needs is a condom factory.

If State Center were an Army camp, Henze would be its sergeant—cajoling, pushing, and begging people to open businesses, support civic groups, and promote the town. But even she is wary of the mystery factory.

"I'm always hopeful, but I'll believe it when I see it," she says.

One reason for the town's lack of enthusiasm is that hopes have been squashed before. Another is that State Center hasn't decided how much development it wants.

Probably half the town, including Bohnsack and three of the five councilmen, works in Marshalltown, Ames, or Nevada.

"People don't come here to find a job," says Don Goodman, who owns Goodman Milling, the grain elevator. "They come to live."

The debate is an old one. Years ago, the town spurned advances by Maytag and Fisher Controls to build plants in State Center.

"Maytag begged to get in here," says Ernie Westphal, 78. "The people running this town wouldn't let them. They said niggers would come to town, that's just what they said."

Today, State Center pays for that attitude. Only five new homes have been built since 1979. Last year's retail sales were the lowest in 11 years.

"I'm fearful of what the next 10 to 20 years will bring to Main Street," says Jim Jorgensen, president of the Central State Bank.

But some say Jorgensen's bank stifles progress by not investing enough in local business. Mayor Bohnsack banks in Melbourne. So do the newspaper publishers and several store owners.

"We had many business opportunities that we

turned down for what we considered to be strong economic reasons," Jorgensen says. "If that's a deterrent to economic development, I guess I have to look at our business first. It's more important to this town to keep the bank open."

As a result, the Central State Bank reported troubled debts of only 11 percent last year; the Melbourne bank's ratio was 152 percent. That bank was sold this spring.

Economic efforts sputter. One group, State Center Development Inc., was formed years ago to loan money to promising ventures, but the $9,000 account sits largely untapped. Bohnsack organized another development group last year, but it fizzled. Only the Commerce Club, representing the town's 41 businesses, shows signs of life.

At the April club meeting, members discussed whether to build a float for the summer's Rose Festival parade. The vote was 3 yes, with 13 abstaining.

Nothing stretches the limits of town and business cooperation more than the event for which State Center is best known, if it is known at all: the Rose Festival.

THIRTY YEARS OF ROSES

Bill Haesemeyer was hot.

"It's not supposed to look like this," he says, pointing to the dandelions and brown stems that littered the beds in the town's rose garden.

"This one's dead. That one's dead. This one. This one. Over here. Here. Here."

Haesemeyer, 74, the bank owner, played a major role 30 years ago in State Center's coronation as the Rose Capital of Iowa.

This June, as it does every summer, the town will be the host to about 10,000 people for the three-day festival.

The trouble is, the people who started the event want the young adults to take over. The young adults say they're busy—and they're still bitter.

Years ago, a swimming pool was planned for the area where the rose garden now sits. "We still want a swimming pool," says Deb Horn, 35.

A handful of volunteers keeps the Rose Festival afloat, with the responsibility for cleaning the garden and planting fresh roses passed like a virus among the City Council, the Jaycees, and the Rose Board.

The great rose crisis of 1988 was short-lived. City workers mowed the grass, volunteers transplanted fresh rose bushes, and, says Irma Henze, who serves on the Rose Board, "the good Lord gave us sunshine."

SURE COULD USE SOME RAIN

Of all the seasons, spring is the most unpredictable, nature's 2-year-old. Three examples:

March 22—Alison Clark and her third-grade friends toss their jackets in a pile on the school playground. Eighty-two degrees. Branches rock gently, leaves dance in the street.

At the Gutekunst Library, 4-year-old Anthony McGrew breaks from his mother's hand and races for the twisting slide.

Across town, Leland Weuve, the Trojan Inn regular, pushes a tiller along a patch in his front yard. The blades spit chunks of soil the color and size of coal.

Weuve sold his 700-acre farm to his son-in-law and daughter years ago, but he returns each spring to help.

"I like to see things grow," he says. "I like being out there. I just like the smell of it."

In the country, grass stands in ditches like hair on a punk rocker's head, its color changing slightly each day, from yellow to greenish yellow to green. Broken stalks of corn, last year's soldiers, await the disc.

Farmland values have rebounded. Soybean prices are higher. It's time to plant.

March 24—A bruise-colored mange spreads across the sky. The radio warns of tornadoes.

Blackbirds hide on the ground. Grass ripples in nervous shudders. Quick as a lizard's tongue, the storm strikes with a burst of rain and hail.

340

Just as quickly, the rain and hail stop, the blue skies return, and the sun bathes the town in a soft butterscotch light.

The economic storm of the farm crisis also has abated in State Center, but the victims are easy to find.

In town, Jackie Henchal, 48, works as a deputy city clerk. She and her husband, Larry, 50, lost their 600-acre farm two years ago.

"The economy's got to get a lot better before it can heal all the wounds," she says. "Your dreams are broken. Your hearts are broken. Your spirit is broken. You're just broke."

May 4—Soil crumbles in the hand. Rainfall during April was four inches below normal.

"We need rain just to know it can rain," Don Goodman says at the elevator.

As each dry day ends, the plea becomes a mantra. Rain. We need rain. Wish it would rain.

"There's just fewer farmers to do business with," says Goodman, 48. "It was nice for everybody when there were lots of farms and lots of people."

By the end of the week, the skies open with a vengeance, unleashing almost an inch of rain and some hail.

"That was a lifesaver," Leland Weuve says. "The hail gave the corn a haircut, but it'll be all right."

FUTURE OF STATE CENTER

The largest buildings on Main Street are occupied by Goodman Milling and the schools, appropriate given the importance of agriculture and education. But Don Goodman, elevator owner and school board president, knows which comes first.

"The school's what keeps this town," he says.

In that case, the future of State Center gathered on an April afternoon to color ducks, sing about eensy-weensy spiders, and practice standing in line for recess.

Kindergarten round-up was a success. A total of 69 children attended, more than Superintendent

Jerry Nichols had expected.

Nichols, 54, who watches enrollment trends as closely as Goodman monitors grain prices, has seen the number of West Marshall students decrease from 1,300 in 1969 to the 780 expected for next fall.

The impact is seen in everything from the high school chapter of the Fellowship of Christian Athletes, which has three members, to sporting events. West Marshall will compete in a new sports conference next fall with smaller schools.

Nichols worries that if Iowa legislators force school districts to maintain a minimum enrollment of, say, 1,000 students, State Center could lose its high school.

"Ultimately, we're probably going to have to restructure," he says.

Right now, Tyler Dose, a freckle-faced, tow-headed 5-year-old, only cares about the duck he's coloring during kindergarten round-up.

"I know what color their feets are supposed to be," he says. "Orange. Because that's what color the baby chicks' feets are."

Upstairs, the 17 students in Dolores Horn's third-grade class also are discussing birds. Alison Clark, a pixie-faced 8-year-old, says her brother saw an owl holding a snake. Gross, the kids say.

The class protects Alison. In March, her father, Dan Clark of rural Melbourne, was killed in a truck accident near Tama.

Horn, a teacher for 31 years, took doughnuts and a plant to the house. Several students brought presents for Alison.

"The whole class was real sweet," Horn says. "They still are. Everything she does, they pull for her."

In music class, when Alison misread the song "Old Dan Tucker" as "Old Dan Trucker" and began to cry, several students hugged her.

And sometimes, Horn will find a note at the bottom of Alison's spelling test, such as, "I hope my Dad is all right."

"I'm sure he is, honey," Horn writes back.

342

THE TIE THAT BINDS

West Marshall High School enjoyed a productive spring. Gita Nason's trumpet-playing won an outstanding performance award at the state solo and ensemble contest. The mixed chorus received a top rating at state. And both performances of *The Music Man*—whose cast included townsfolk to supplement the students—received standing ovations.

But sports is the tie that binds the school district.

On the west side of the elementary school, Brian Winkler and his eighth-grade friends shoot baskets far into the night, their silhouettes outlined on the pavement.

Winkler, 14, who was born with cerebral palsy but stars on the basketball team, jumps and dangles from the chain net.

"We're talkin' serious hang time now," he says.

Winkler's father, Ken, has coached the football team to the state playoffs the past four years. This spring, the boys' track team won four first-place trophies and set several school records.

Wade Baker was a member of the relay team that broke one of those records. But the 17-year-old junior is best known as one of two boys who broke into the high school two years ago, causing about $50,000 in damage and outraging the town and students.

Baker returned to school last fall after spending 11 months in a Fort Dodge boys' home. "I noticed some of the teachers looked at me like, 'Oh, boy, he's back.' But I think it had mostly been forgotten or forgiven," he says.

With brown hair, braces, and a winning smile, Baker says he's trying to behave better, but trouble seems to find him. If it finds him too often, he risks violating his probation.

He and his classmates minded their manners prom night, the boys sharp in their black and gray tuxedos, the girls elegant in their satin strapless gowns and puffy bubble dresses.

At the dance, Principal John Dotson, 31, stood

sentry in the door, with the slightly uncomfortable look of a man whose sole goal in life was to last until dawn without hearing from the county sheriff.

For the 89 seniors, the last of the large West Marshall classes, prom represented the final rite of high school before graduation ceremonies this afternoon. College or trade school awaits most of the graduates. Few will find jobs in State Center.

"They have to leave," Don Goodman says. "There's nothing for them here."

CARDS, BEER, FRIENDS

The Main Street Tap is a dank, dark sanctuary, a place to belch, scratch, and solve the world's problems, but mostly a place to play cards and drink a few beers. Or a lot.

"Drink, Vince?" Ralph Moody asks.

No answer.

"Drink, Vince?" Moody asks louder.

"Why, sure."

"Need a draw, Kenny?" Moody asks.

He does.

There's Moody, 65, war veteran, former boxer and baseball catcher, who started the town's garbage business 20 years ago with three customers and sold it last fall.

There's Ernie Westphal, 78 and ornery, who played billiards there when he was a kid, dropping the pool cue through a hole in the floor when his father walked in.

There's Duwane Miller, 53, who everyone calls Cooter, a retired Navy veteran. He has blood and kidney problems, but that doesn't stop him from drinking shots of brandy, which he orders with a glass of water, or smoking Chesterfield cigarettes, which he places atop a package of Vicks cough drops.

"This used to be quite a town, by God," Westphal says. "We had four implement dealers at one time, and two or three car dealers and three or four grocery stores. There were two movie houses in town. We used to sneak into the Princess Theater. You could always tell when the train was coming through because the screen would shake."

All day long, the regulars sit in front of the only window in the bar and play Queens, an incomprehensible card game in which diamonds are trump, tens beat kings, and queens are better than everything. The men keep score by trading kernels of corn and cuss worse than prison inmates. The constant dealing of cards has worn a white cross in the tabletop.

"It could be a pretty good town if people wanted to change it," Miller says. "But they don't want to change it. They want it to be like it was 25 years ago.

"This town has to change in order to get disparity —whatever they call that word, disparity, diversity. Improve, improve, improve."

Later, at night, after a full day of cards and beer, Ralph Moody leans close, showing pale blue eyes, flushed cheeks, and hair parted almost in the middle, the style in old movies.

"I'm proud of State Center," he says. "This is a good little town. I'm so satisfied here."

When the bar closes, Moody swings past the funeral home for one last look above the door.

The light is still dark.

State Center has survived another day.

The Miami Herald

Arnold Markowitz
Finalist, Deadline Writing

Arnold Markowitz has worked at *The Miami Herald* since 1967 as a general assignment and investigative reporter, assistant city editor, and now as lead rewrite man for what he calls "crisis news." Earlier he worked for three New Jersey papers: the *Milltown Sentinel*, the (Newark) *Star-Ledger*, and the *Ocean County Observer*, the last as managing editor. He was a Nieman Fellow in 1975.

Markowitz creates three-dimensional characters and realistic settings by his meticulous placement of details.

Reverend discovers wife dead

NOVEMBER 2, 1988

When Ella Hickman sang at the church next door, her soaring alto voice was unmistakable. It was silenced as she arrived home from grocery shopping Monday afternoon. The nearest neighbors told her husband, the Rev. Donnie L. Hickman, that the only scream they heard was his, when he found her stabbed to death in her bedroom.

Ella Hickman, 49, was killed for the money in her purse—an unknown amount, but not very much after a grocery shopping trip, the minister said—and for a gold necklace with her name on it and the contents of a coin bank where she put her loose change each evening.

Supported by his faith and by friends who had been at his side since Monday evening, Rev. Hickman, 54, sat Tuesday on a metal folding chair in the shade of his driveway canopy at 6524 N.W. 26th Ave. in Liberty City, trying to sort things out.

"If I was on the other side of the fence, out in the world, I would take matters in my own hands," he said. "Being on this side, I leave it in the hands of the law and the Lord. If the law doesn't give me justice, the Lord will."

He is a thin man with a sparse goatee and dark-framed spectacles. His home is small, carefully kept, with a weedless lawn garnished with neatly tended ferns and dracaenas sheltering a litter of newborn gray tabbies at play. The Hickmans' grown son Chris, a warehouse worker, sat alone on the front bumper of his mother's gray Cadillac, watching the kittens.

The house, surrounded by a chain-link fence, has iron bars over the windows and Luck, a mixed Doberman-shepherd, in the back yard. Burglars had broken in three times in two years. After the third time, last Nov. 5, the Hickmans had an alarm system installed. Uneasy in the home they had lived in for 25 years, they were thinking of moving.

A little more than two years ago, Hickman became pastor of the 300-member New Hope Missionary Baptist Church in Hollywood. His wife sang in the choir there and was a member of the board of deaconesses. Sometimes she would sing next door to her home at the tiny Fellowship Missionary Baptist Church, founded by her husband and still full of old friends.

Two weeks ago, she sang "Lord, You Brought Us From a Mighty Long Ways" at Fellowship, and spoke to the congregation. Amelia Seldon was there.

"She made the remark that you never know where death is, and you have to be nice to everyone," Seldon said. "She could sing until tears came out."

Joyce Reese, who also goes to the church next door, sat beside Rev. Hickman on Tuesday and spoke about the friend she had lost:

"She was a loving person, always willing to help others. She loved to go to church, to sing and praise the Lord. I met her more than 20 years ago. I heard her singing in church, and the next day I went over to see who had been making that beautiful sound. We sort of adopted each other as sisters, and we've been like sisters ever since.

"Sure, she was worried about crime in the neighborhood. We all are. Our church and our houses have been broken into. We're all afraid."

For almost 20 years, Ella Hickman worked as a housemaid for a family in Coral Gables. On Monday, her day off, she backed her car out, locked the driveway gate, and drove away to buy groceries.

The market is no more than a 15-minute drive from the house. Her cash register receipt was stamped 1:37 p.m.

When Rev. Hickman arrived home at 4:30 p.m. Monday, he noticed his wife's car across the street in a vacant lot. That was odd, he thought. Ordinarily she stopped there only long enough to go in the house for the key to the driveway gate.

Hickman also saw that the diamond-shaped window in his front door was smashed. When he opened it, he saw a rock the size of a melon on the floor. His wife's purse, eyeglasses, and shoes were on the living room carpet. Her wallet and credit cards were there. The alarm box was torn off the wall, its wiring cut.

Hickman began looking into bedrooms. The door to the fourth one was ajar. He pushed it open.

Ella Hickman lay there dead, her ankles tied with an electric cord cut from a radio and the telephone wire around her neck. Her glass coin bank had been dumped out. The pennies were on the floor. The missing change could not have amounted to more than $20, the husband said. Closets were open but the house was not ransacked. Nothing else seemed to be missing.

Rev. Hickman ran outdoors, calling for help. A stranger driving by stopped, went into the house with him, and called police. Later he questioned the neighbors. They told him they had not heard the dog bark or noticed a stranger at the house.

He admitted that it is hard for him now to hold on to his faith, but he can do it. He wondered about the robber who murdered his wife:

"If they find him, I will do everything in my power to see that he gets time, and money won't get him out. Amen. He'd better have faith. He's going to need faith."

The Hartford Courant

Lynne Tuohy
Finalist, Deadline Writing

Lynne Tuohy left the University of New Hampshire four credits short of a B.A. in English and political science to work for the Newburyport (Mass.) *Daily News,* and moved on to the Springfield (Mass.) *Daily Advocate* and the *New Haven Register.* She joined *The Hartford Courant* in 1984 as a court reporter and later became criminal justice editor, coordinating court coverage and training of new reporters.

Tuohy lets the players in her courtroom drama do the talking, with quotations carefully selected, lightly attributed, and clearly framed.

Crafts denies he killed wife

JUNE 17, 1988

NEW LONDON, Conn.—Richard Crafts took the witness stand Thursday in the most dramatic moment of his 12-week murder trial, and calmly denied killing his wife and using a chain saw and wood chipper to dispose of her body.

"And do you know whether Helle Crafts is alive or not?" defense attorney J. Daniel Sagarin asked his client.

"I certainly hope she is," Richard Crafts replied. "I believe she is."

Crafts testified in a courtroom so crowded with more than 65 spectators and reporters that a sheriff stood at the door turning away late-comers. Despite the crowd, the courtroom was silent except for the exchanges between Sagarin and Crafts.

The 50-year-old airline pilot—who prosecutors say killed his wife by unknown means, cut up her body with a chain saw, and disposed of it with a wood chipper—testified with a voice and manner that was so calm it bordered at times on nonchalance.

Sagarin seemed to leave no stone unturned, from the intimacies of the Craftses' marriage and Richard Crafts's infidelity, to point-blank questions about whether Crafts shredded his wife's body in a wood chipper he had rented.

Helle Crafts was last seen Nov. 18, 1986. Richard Crafts testified she left their Newtown home in the early morning of Nov. 19, 1986, and her last words were, "I'm leaving now."

"She was all right the last time I saw her, the morning of Nov. 19, 1986," Crafts testified.

Regarding his marriage to Helle Crafts in 1975, Richard Crafts said, "Helle was pregnant at the time we were married. We both knew she was pregnant. She was too far advanced for a doctor to perform an abortion." The oldest of their three children, Andrew, was born five months later.

Asked if he was faithful to Helle Crafts during their marriage, Richard Crafts replied, "Not exclusively, no." He said he believed his wife was aware of his philandering.

"She had occasionally asked me when I was going to grow up and stop my foolish wandering around," Crafts said.

In an apparent effort to address inflammatory evidence introduced by prosecutors about bloodstains on the Craftses' mattress, Sagarin asked Crafts if he had harmed his wife.

"No, I've never raised a finger in anger to Helle in my life," Crafts said. "No sir, I've never done her any harm, ever."

Danbury State's Attorney Walter D. Flanagan said he was not surprised that Crafts testified, and does not believe Crafts's testimony damaged the prosecution's case.

"I think Mr. Crafts is the type of individual who thrives on challenge, and I have judged him to have a very large ego," Flanagan said outside of court. "This is a way for him to keep up with his own personality.

"I think the person who tries to commit the perfect crime... implicit in that design is a desire to deceive the jury, too," Flanagan added.

It was impossible to gauge the effect of Crafts's testimony on the jurors, who remained attentive but expressionless throughout the day. Even the dramatic moment at the start of court, when Sagarin announced his first witness by saying, "Mr. Crafts, would you take the stand," elicited no visible reaction.

During breaks, when the jurors filed in and out of the courtroom past Crafts in the witness box, only one of the 12 jurors and three alternates turned to acknowledge him. Crafts, however, turned his body fully toward them, craned his neck, and smiled.

Asked why he did not assert his constitutional rights to remain silent and have an attorney present during interviews with state police in December

1986 and January 1987, Crafts said, "I didn't think it was necessary. I wasn't trying to conceal anything. I had no indication that she was anything but alive."

Jurors learned through Crafts's testimony that he has been incarcerated since his arrest Jan. 13, 1987, unable to make bond. That is usually concealed from juries so that it does not prejudice their deliberations.

Crafts testified on a range of subjects, among them that:

• He has never been on River Road or the Steel Bridge in Southbury with a U-Haul truck or a wood chipper. Both locations are considered crucial evidence scenes in the state's case. River Road is where fragments of bone, clumps of hair, and a tooth believed to be those of Helle Crafts were found.

• He took the old freezer the Craftses owned to the Newtown landfill after picking up a new one two days after Helle Crafts disappeared. The whereabouts of the old freezer is considered a mystery by police and prosecutors, who believe it is somehow tied to the disposal of Helle Crafts's body.

• The fall of 1986 was not the first time Helle Crafts broached the subject of divorce with her husband. Richard Crafts said it was discussed in 1981, but "we patched up our differences and continued the marriage."

Crafts said he believed there were other discussions about divorce between 1981 and 1986, "but I'm not certain of her degree of sincerity. She would mention it as a means of attempting to induce me to change my behavior. She would say, 'Don't you want to be married to me anymore?' or 'Is something wrong with our marriage?'"

• While friends and neighbors testified about the radical change in Helle Crafts's appearance in 1986, from robust and beautiful to gaunt and haggard, Richard Crafts testified, "I assumed it was another one of those diets she embarked on.

"I'd noticed that she lost a great deal of weight. She looked very tired most of the time. She was a lot more moody than she'd ever been," Crafts said. However, he said he never discussed these changes with his wife.

• The family's live-in nanny, Dawn Marie Thomas, testified about a phone message Richard took days after Helle Crafts disappeared, in which he wrote: "Helle called."

Richard Crafts explained Thursday that that message referred to a friend of his wife's, also named Helle, who had phoned from Copenhagen, Denmark, for her.

• Crafts said he rented the wood chipper Nov. 20 and 21 to get rid of brush that had accumulated on a wooded lot the family owned in Newtown.

• The last night Helle Crafts was seen, Richard Crafts testified she had returned home from an overseas flight while he and the children were having dinner.

"We put the children to bed....We talked a little.... She asked me if I had any time that week to receive the papers from the sheriff pertaining to the divorce. I put her off a little; asked if maybe we could talk about it tomorrow.

"She persisted, asking me if I was going to discontinue the manner in which I was behaving [meaning] my girlfriends," Crafts testified. "I put her off a little, saying maybe we could talk about it tomorrow. She turned over and read her book."

Sagarin said during a court break that there was never any question Crafts would testify.

"Richard getting on the stand says to the world, 'Ask me anything you want to....I'm going to answer all your questions. I'm telling the world I didn't kill Helle Crafts, I don't know where she is, and she was all right the last time I saw her.'"

But Sagarin concedes the testimony is not without risk, and Crafts knows it.

"Richard opened himself up," Sagarin said. "He has agreed he will take whatever risks in testifying, and those clearly include a wide ranging cross-examination." Flanagan will cross-examine Crafts today.

Sagarin's last round of questions went to the

credibility of a man who is either a murderer or an abandoned husband maligned by a murder prosecution.

After giving Crafts the opportunity once again to say he never used a chain saw, wood chipper, or U-Haul truck to dispose of his wife's body, Sagarin asked Crafts about his own veracity.

"What I've told you today and what I've told the Newtown police and state police is true," Crafts said.

"So help you God?" Sagarin queried.

"So help me God."

The Washington Post

Henry Allen
Finalist, Commentary

Henry Allen graduated with a B.A. in English from Hamilton College. He worked for the *New Haven Register* and the New York *Daily News* before joining *The Washington Post* in 1970. He served as a writer and editor in the Style section, and an editor for Outlook. He was also a finalist last year.

Allen can turn a phrase. He specializes in seeing through hype and American mythology, but without losing sight of real and legitimate feelings rising from deep within our culture.

JFK: The man
and the maybes

NOVEMBER 22, 1988

If Jack Kennedy had lived...

It's horrible to imagine the change. He'd be 71 now. His neck would be swollen like Frank Sinatra's, his gorgeously hooded eyes would be so fleshy they'd look tired and sly. His hair would seem old-fashioned, an anachronism from the '60s the way Ronald Reagan's hair is an anachronism from the '40s. He'd have the quality of a relic, like Richard Helms or Robert McNamara when you see them around town.

Who knows? Maybe he'd have made a great elder statesman, like Averell Harriman or Clark Clifford. Maybe he'd be one of those institutions people stand up to applaud without quite remembering why, like Helen Hayes. But he wouldn't be Jack Kennedy, our Jack Kennedy.

In 1982, John Gregory Dunne wrote that "there are no new facts about the Kennedys, only new attitudes." Instead of growing old and fat, Kennedy has come to hover in our collective psyche like a hologram, three-dimensional and eerily transparent, the generic man of destiny, the template of the bright-young-man-as-public-figure. He is an idea.

By 1984, Ronald Reagan could get away with invoking Kennedy like motherhood or the flag. Ronald Reagan! The essence of the rumpus room Republican, the small-town power-of-positive-thinker, everything that Kennedy had promised to liberate us from! By 1988, Bush had claimed Kennedy's foreign policy, Dukakis had his haircut, Quayle had his youth, and Bentsen had his friendship. Everybody was grabbing for a piece of him in a feeding frenzy that finally left Bentsen snapping at Quayle in the most memorable line of the campaign: "You're no Jack Kennedy."

Who was?

The Kennedy we knew has become the Kennedyesque we know. As in: Gary Hart and Jack Kemp in politics, Ted Koppel on television, Martin Sheen in the movies, and Bob Forehead in the comic strip *Washingtoon*. As in the movie *The Candidate*. Or Hart adopting that hand-in-jacket-pocket gesture Kennedy used to make. As in a million massive-forelock haircuts, such as Richard Gephardt's, all those baby-grand smiles like John Tunney's and the calculated breeziness of John Kerry. As in whatever it was that George Bush saw in Dan Quayle.

If Kennedy had lived, all the Esques wouldn't be around, or if they were, Kennedy would be laughing at them the way he laughed toward the end of his life, showing some lower teeth, the sides of his mouth stretching out far enough that the corners turned down a little, not just sardonic but self-consciously sardonic. That was part of his charm—the tease, the magician saying "it's only smoke and mirrors" and then making you believe it anyway. Kennedy once said: "Bobby and I smile sardonically. Teddy will learn how to smile sardonically in two or three years, but he doesn't know how yet."

The odd thing about the Kennedyesquery has been that we want the style but not the substance. Lyndon Johnson never understood this. When some of the Kennedy faithful attacked Johnson like children attacking their widowed mother's new boyfriend—as if no on else had a right to carve the roast or put up the Christmas tree—he got so frustrated. Wasn't he not only telling them bedtime stories of the New Frontier, but actually taking them out there and putting them on horseback? *That wasn't the point.* What about the civil rights legislation? The space program? What about all the other presidents who pitted themselves against the bureaucracy with the aid of a band of brothers, in the mode of the Kennedy White House: Ehrlichman and Haldeman, Carter's Georgians, the conservative true believers, whatever it took to get things done. *Not the point.*

We seem to resent not only success where Kennedy failed, but the idea of anybody else having those ideas at all. Jack Newfield of *The Village*

Voice attacked Johnson as the "Antichrist." And ever since, as the smiles and haircuts have proliferated, we have resisted comparisons of substance. Ronald Reagan may go to his grave wondering how Kennedy people could hate him for cutting taxes and raising military spending at the same time. And Washington is still full of Kennedy people waiting for the restoration or the resurrection with the ennobling fury of exiles who never feel the need to explain anything to anybody—aging Hamlets in pin-striped suits, best and bright at law firms and dinner parties and endless book signings, people who had once hoped to constitute what James Reston hailed as "a new class of public servants who move about in the triangle of daily or periodic journalism, the university or foundation, and government service."

The Kennedy White House spawned a giddy elitism based on a blend of potential, a look, and a certain crispness of attitude, as if the principles of undergraduate popularity had been inflated into a political philosophy. The Kennedy people were too fast for the State Department, too smart for Congress. There was a premise that one or two acutely excellent people in the right place at the right time could change the world, either Peace Corps style or James Bond style. It was a government of "informal consultation, anti-bureaucratic, round-the-clock vigils, the crash program, the hasty decision, the quick phone call," as Victor Navasky has written. Much slamming of phones and smoking of little cigars. Much conspicuous intelligence, which is the ultimate value of the rational, objective man of the future. "There's nothing like brains," Kennedy said once. "You can't beat brains."

It was as if he were an ironic messiah scaring us out of our middle-class Eisenhower complacency, as if a prophet had been written into the score of *West Side Story*—"I got a feeling there's a miracle due, gonna come true, coming to me. Around the corner, or whistling down the river, come on, deliver..." If existentialists had saints, he might be one, finding truth, as he did, in action, not contemplation—finding it in action for the sake of action, too. In a campaign speech, he said: "I don't run for president in the 1960s because I think it will be an easy time. I don't. I think it will be a very dangerous time for us all."

Much has been made of authenticity, Camelot, Weberian concepts of charisma, and so on: the wit, the cool, the Irishness, the aristocracy, the family man, the Regency rake, the war hero, the media manipulator, and our nostalgia for an era when everything was possible and nothing was quite real. But what lingers like an instinct in the back-brain of American culture is more basic.

To begin with, he was madly good-looking.

When you watch him now on television, 25 years after his assassination, it feels like your head moves when you follow him across the screen. Lovely. He runs on a lawn during a touch football game, enthralled with the chaos downfield; or campaigning on a Boston street, he turns away from an old couple and flicks his hand back toward the man as if to say everything from "Thanks" to "You and me, pal" to "We'll be looking for you at the polling place." Perfect. It was the kind of move Richard Nixon never, ever made. Not once.

Six feet one-half inch tall, 170 pounds when he died. Brown hair, blue eyes. That slight hunch to his shoulders, increasing with age and the pain of back problems, a posture that gives him a preoccupied air, which in turn makes whatever he's doing look as if his attention has just been caught, a gift.

A fabulous head. Like California hot rods of the early '60s, the scalp raked forward, a muscular momentum with no particular destination. Going my way? His eyes squinted a little, as if in surprise or second thought, and a slice of white showed under the irises. The eyelids sloped into crinkles suggesting anything from exhaustion to delight, whatever you wanted to read into them. He was one of those rare men on whom eye bags look good—a piquant contrast to his teen-ager's hairline—and he was the only president who ever looked right in sunglasses, which he wore a lot, tapping into the iconography of the Age of Cool, when sunglasses suggested a fashionable alienation. The lips were just full enough to hint at insolence, and his smile was thrillingly ambiguous, 4,000 teeth placed in just such a way that his S's would whistle a little, yet another of his arresting little acutenesses, along with that strange accent that for all the fat flatness of the vowels seemed to be in a hurry anyway. The chin was terrific, curving out and a little up, as if the whole face might just lift off and go soaring away all by itself, any second.

A dangerous face. It had moments of stillness that were a little menacing, or a little sly, as if he had a piece of gum in his mouth and didn't want to be seen chewing it. A face that looked to see if you knew what the joke was, and if you didn't, the joke was on you. The happily self-conscious face of a man posing for a portrait between phone calls. The kind of face that makes you want to attract its attention, like a glamorous zoo animal. A smile that could turn in an instant—Carl Kaysen, one of Kennedy's national security advisers, remembers how Kennedy would reach up with his finger and tap one of those teeth with impatience.

Ultimately a totally public face. Sometimes there's an accidental quality to the sighting of someone famous, like Jack Nicholson in a restaurant, for instance. It's like seeing a deer run across the road. Wow! you say. Not so with Kennedy. I saw him only once, at the Hyannis airport after he'd won the Democratic nomination. There was nothing accidental about him—it was like seeing a billboard, not a deer.

But as soon as he started working an audience, there was a pure animal speed to him, pure instinct. This is part of the image, too. At a White House press conference shown on television recently, he is asked why he has a Band-Aid on his finger. The smile. He hesitates, but not because it's none of the reporters' business. Instead, it seems he hesitates to show them he knows it's none of their business but he'll tell them anyway. He calculates for a microsecond. He knows that even if he tells the truth they'll suspect he lied. He savors this idea—what can they do about it, after all, and besides, maybe an obvious fib would be more charming than the truth.

He says, "I cut it while I was slicing bread...unbelievable as it may sound."

He lifts the hand to show it to them as an afterthought, a *conspicuous* afterthought, a gift, not an obligation. He knew where the press ranked. He once said: "The press is a very valuable arm of the presidency."

As a member of the upper class, he had grown up amid the received wisdom of long-settled questions. It was an atmosphere in which instinct counted for a lot in weaving through the subtleties: how the in-crowds and the out-crowds are shaping up, where the party is, where the money is, who's got what and who doesn't, how and when to get a little slack. Gesture was everything. A certain smile, a certain face could get you through.

If you liked Kennedy back then (or watching him now), you could come away from the television feeling as you might have after a Cary Grant movie—as if his grace, his quickness, his easy startlement and intelligence had transformed your walk and smile, conferring an intoxicating self-consciousness, like the first whiskey of the day. Then you'd trip over the dog or say something stupid and feel it fall away from you.

As Kennedy once said: "We couldn't survive without television."

On the other hand, if you disliked him, was it out of objective analysis or your envy of his charm? Being annoyed by people who were infatuated with Kennedy was easy, but you worried that in arguing with them you turned yourself into the sort of monstrous fogy who counsels young girls for their own good, advising them to break off love affairs that are, in fact, going to hurt them.

For a lot of us, Jack Kennedy managed to exist at precisely the point where love and hate converge. Almost everything written about him is touched with infatuation, resentment, or both, from

the praise of Schlesinger and Sorensen to the nastiness, soap opera, and psychoanalysis of books like
Nancy Gager Clinch's *The Kennedy Neurosis* or
The Kennedys: An American Drama by Peter Col-
lier and David Horowitz, not to mention the canon
of conspiracy theorists who have created an image
of American Evil just as the American public has
created the image of Kennedy. (If Kennedy was a
demigod, wouldn't it take a demidemon to kill
him?)

There were successes: pushing back the U.S.
Steel price hike, the Peace Corps, the Cuban mis-
sile crisis, the test-ban treaty, the enfranchisement
of the intellectuals—he wasn't afraid of bumpkin
opprobrium for being seen with Andre Malraux or
Robert Frost. Also, Kennedy looked comfortable
in white tie and tails, and he could shake hands
with Charles de Gaulle without making us worry
that he'd embarrass us.

But the failures were big: the Bay of Pigs, the
Berlin Wall, the lies about Vietnam. Later would
come the scandals: his chronically adolescent sex
life, the Castro assassination plan, and his tendency
to go slumming, politically speaking, with Mafia
types. Only the young die good, as it happens in
the real world, and he was young, but not that
young.

We don't forgive his failures as much as we ignore them. They are as irrelevant by now as his
successes. Like gods or royalty, the fallen Kennedy
wasn't accountable, he just *was*. As early as 1961,
Kenneth Crawford wrote in *Newsweek,* under the
title "Royalty USA," that "We don't like to have
our symbols making mistakes, so we don't acknowledge that they make them." As time went
along, and we kept working on the image in our
minds, we dumped his faults on other members of
his family—Teddy became the irresponsible, shal-
low one; Bobby was ruthless; and Jackie had all of
the moral debits of the upper class.

Good arguments can still be had on what
Kennedy might have done if he'd lived: made
peace with the Russians, pulled out of Vietnam,

passed the social legislation that Lyndon Johnson twisted arms to get. No matter. As far as the facts go, the revisionists have been revised and revised again. No likely end will bring him loss or leave us happier than before. We've even forgiven Jackie for marrying Aristotle Onassis, that shuffling human twilight of a man, Jabba the Hutt with a private yacht, the image of a devourer of virgins and beautiful widows. At the time, there was a popular rumor that explained it away: Jackie married him, it was said, because Kennedy was still alive, though a vegetable, and Onassis could hide him on his island where Jackie could be with him. Such are the many little corners of Valhalla.

There is a scared glow to Kennediana. A recent *Nova* program titled "Who Shot President Kennedy?" quotes a doctor on why no autopsy was done at Parkland Hospital in Dallas: "That would have been a little sacrilegious, I think, under the circumstances." As Walter Cronkite describes reports of a mysterious change in caskets, along with the fact that Kennedy's brain is still missing, it's hard not to hear echoes: *The stone was rolled away...we know not where they have laid Him.* Then Phil Ochs sings a song called "Crucifixion."

What else but archetypal emotion can explain 34 percent of Americans saying in a September poll that Kennedy had been the "most effective" president since World War II, compared with 17 percent for Truman, 14 percent for Reagan, and 3 percent for Lyndon Johnson, and 21 percent saying Kennedy was the best president *ever*, with Franklin Roosevelt and Abraham Lincoln running second at 17 percent each?

The facts don't support this degree of unambiguous enthusiasm. Neither did the image he had during his lifetime.

There were so many contradictions. Kennedy was an aristocrat, an ethnic, a liberal civil-rightser, a conservative tax cutter. He was a young man with more diseases, pain, and disability than any of the old men who have served as president since Roosevelt. He was known for both sleeping through concerts and being an intellectual. He derided Nixon for having "no class," but on the night of the 1960 presidential primary in West Virginia, he relaxed by watching a soft-core dirty movie in downtown Washington. He was a war hero whose brother Bobby would find it profoundly courageous of him to cancel a subscription to the *New York Herald Tribune*: "He did it deliberately and was glad. He was happy that he did it afterward. And he didn't cut off and sneak off, sneak away somewhere and read it."

All Kennedy's infatuees ever needed was an excuse to love him. And they remember him still the way a middle-aged wife and mother lies awake at night remembering a boy who rode his motorcycle into a bridge abutment, and how her father couldn't figure out why she cried so hard, she'd only gone out with him a couple of times, and he was never going to amount to that much anyway.

Ah, youth. You watch that gray footage of the casket being unloaded from *Air Force One*, of Jackie moving with the bewildered clumsiness of grief, and you feel the random, empty quality of things. It feels like now, you think—that's when *now* began. It is plain that before Kennedy was shot, everything was different: the colors were brighter, the world was smaller and full of purpose. Snug. Wrapped like a trick knee with the Ace bandage of intention.

This is not true—chaos and oblivion are always leering from the shadows. What began with Kennedy's assassination was not the present but the past. Bruce Duffy, who lives in Takoma Park and wrote a novel called *The World as I Found It,* said recently: "I was home sick when I heard he was shot. My mother had died the year before, and Kennedy's death was especially painful because it had the effect of moving her farther away from me. It put her into a whole different era."

This is not an age of character but of personality, and Kennedy gave us that. This is also not an age of darkness but of glare, as a poet has said, and Kennedy gave us that, too.

In the long view, he was a warlike young man of

great charm, ambition, and propensity for getting himself in trouble. We have a niche for men like that—Alexander, Alcibiades, Charles XII of Sweden, Napoleon, to mention the grander figures. Kennedy promised nothing less when he said of the American people in 1960, "They want to know what is needed—they want to be led by the commander in chief."

Who knows if he would have delivered? All we can do is believe.

As Lyndon Johnson said of Bobby Kennedy: "I almost wish he had become president so the country could finally see a flesh-and-blood Kennedy grappling with the daily work of the presidency and all the inevitable disappointments, instead of their storybook image of great heroes who, because they were dead, could make anything anyone wanted happen."

Anything anyone wanted—if Jack Kennedy wasn't that then, he is now.

The Sacramento Bee

Pete Dexter
Finalist, Commentary

Pete Dexter grew up in South Dakota, Michigan, and Illinois. He wrote columns for the *Philadelphia Daily News* for five years before joining *The Sacramento Bee* as a columnist in 1986. Dexter has published three novels: *In God's Pocket, Deadwood*, and *Paris Trout*, which won the National Book Award in 1988.

Dexter can tell a tale. He chooses little details and running routines to drive the story along through a beginning, a middle, and an end.

Parrot will leave
the wife speechless

DECEMBER 30, 1988

A lot of years have passed and the details are fuzzy now, but I think I remember enough to say that the last time I tried to buy my wife a parrot it didn't work out well for anybody.

I am not even sure we were married then, but I can authoritatively tell you it was her birthday and I'd spent most of Thursday afternoon with the finest gift consultant Dirty Frank's Bar in Philadelphia had to offer, trying to come up with something that would express the depth of my appreciation for this woman and the straight and narrow path she had chosen for me to follow.

And about 3 o'clock in the afternoon, one of us hit on the idea of a parrot. I would name it Dick, and teach it to say things that would indicate, to an outsider, that my wife and Dick had a relationship that was closer than women ordinarily have with their birds.

As soon as this had been decided, I finished the drink in front of me and headed for a pet shop.

The pet shop, however, didn't have much of a selection. The only parrot on the premises for less than $1,000, in fact, was in a bad way, medically speaking—leaking bodily fluids out its eyes and nose, drooling, and did not seem up to talking.

And so, dejected, I returned to the bar and consulted through the night with the finest gift consultant Dirty Frank's had to offer and finally settled on another gift, something in the same general family.

Which is to say that at the first light of day, we drove over to the Italian Market on 9th Street and bought a live chicken.

An hour later we purchased spray paint—I believe from an all-night convenience store that catered to the needs of inner-city youth—and then we drove to the apartment complex where my wife and I were living.

It seems to me that we took two cars—looking

back on it, my guess is that the gift consultant did not wish to intrude on the private moment a man and a woman share when he hands her a freshly painted chicken.

Which is to say that the bird was in my car and I had no help at all keeping it calm. Chickens, of course, are never calm, but put an unsupervised one in your front seat, and you understand the meaning of hysteria.

At any rate, I got the bird to the apartment complex and tried to spray-paint him there in the parking lot. But it turns out that if there is one thing a chicken likes less than a car ride, it is a paint job, and while I was trying to do the feet, it escaped.

Wings flapped, paint sprayed, and the animal ran directly under the wheels of a Volvo, which was advertising itself as the world's safest automobile.

Within a few minutes, a number of the apartment residents were gathered around the flattened bird, speculating on devil-worship cults. One or two noticed I was painted the same colors as the dead chicken, but, as my gift consultant pointed out, the first man on the scene has an obligation to help the victim.

So I left the parking lot, washed up, and later that afternoon bought my wife flowers.

And I never considered owning a parrot again until dinner last Wednesday, four days before Christmas. We were having baked chicken.

I looked at the chicken, I looked at my wife.

That fast, a done deal.

The bird is 2 years old and comes from the rain forests of the Amazon River. The woman at the bird store said it would probably live another 50, 75 years. I took it home in a box Christmas Eve, planning to name it Stan and hide it until morning. But it turns out that you can't hide a parrot.

I tried, though.

I lifted it quietly and carefully out of its box and began to coax it into its new home, but every time we got near the cage door, the screaming was just awful.

It bit me 16 times in 40 minutes.

Beyond that, the parrot hasn't opened his mouth.

When it does start to talk, though, it knows all the words.

St. Paul
PIONEER PRESS
DISPATCH

Ann Daly Goodwin
Finalist, Editorial Writing

Ann Daly Goodwin graduated from Carleton College with a degree in English, and from College of St. Thomas with an M.A. in education. For 16 years, she taught English and journalism in high schools and colleges in Minnesota. The *St. Paul Pioneer Press/Dispatch* hired her in 1983 as a columnist and editorial writer. This year she also won the Scripps-Howard Foundation Walker Stone Award for editorial writing.

Goodwin shucks the grey essayness of our editorial tradition to hit the reader dead-on. Who else would let a cigarette coo seductively, or cook up an eggode?

Your fatal attraction

I am your cigarette, seductive, waiting.

I am waiting for you to pick me out of the pack, bring me to your lips, light me up, draw my rich and satisfying smoke deep into your lungs.

I know your friends and family are worried about us. They think I'm bad for you. That's nonsense; what harm could come from our affair? You know you could end it, you could walk away from me any time you wanted. Haven't you done it a dozen times already?

I know about the "I Quit" campaign, especially the five half-hour "quit clinics" that start Monday on WCCO radio and WCCO-TV. They promise to help you pitch me out of the house—out of your life forever. Deep down, they say, that's what you really want. Ha! I'm not worried. We mean too much to each other. You're not going to fall for a line like that.

I know how angry you are about all the people who tell you there's nothing wrong with *you*, it's *me* they don't like. Piffle. If they *really* cared about you, they'd accept you the way you are. They'd accept you, my dear, as my steadfast friend, impatient with those who put me down, indignant at attempts to keep us apart, haunted by my memory whenever I'm not there, touching your lips. How could you stop loving me? Me—your enticing, richly satisfying seducer?

I know you will bring us together once again. Soon. Now. I'm waiting. I'm yours, my darling, whenever you want me.

Till death us do part.

An eggspressive ode

MAY 6, 1988

Oh, you egg.

Oh, you poached darling, you scrambled charmer, you over-easy taste-beguiler, you soft-boiled breakfast bliss.

You egg, you devil you, stuffed with unseen cholesterol that goops up our arteries and allows you on our plates a paltry twice per week.

Ha! Hear this, you oval Benedict Arnold. Now some hens are pecking chicken feed laced with fish oil and—if early studies prove true—soon we can gobble you down to our heart's content.

Oh, you delectable day-beginner. So you're a good egg, after all.

The Washington Post

Robert Barnes
Finalist, Gov't. Reporting

Robert Barnes grew up in Pensacola, Florida, and attended the University of Florida, where he majored in journalism. He stayed in Florida, working for the *Clearwater Sun* and the Associated Press in Tallahassee before joining the *St. Petersburg Times* in 1981, writing mostly about politics. He became political editor in 1983. In 1987, he moved to *The Washington Post* to cover Maryland government.

Barnes reports politics as drama, not as votes and trends. He lets his readers see and hear politicians clowning, whistling, barking, and even mooning.

Full moon brings out antics in Annapolis

APRIL 5, 1988

ANNAPOLIS, Md., April 4—They have barked like dogs and whistled like trains. And now the spectacle that is the Maryland General Assembly is drawing to a close.

Over the last 12 weeks, the 188 lawmakers have deliberated over issues as controversial as abortion and AIDS; debated topics as weighty as drugs, crime, and gun control; and agreed along the way that it will cost somewhere around $9.8 billion to educate, protect, and provide for the general welfare of Marylanders. But no one said they had to look like Jefferson and Hamilton while doing it.

The collegial atmosphere, the closeness of quarters, and, as one female legislator put it, the overwhelming "maleness" of the assembly led even its own members to describe the session as resembling at times a cross between a fraternity reunion and summer camp.

"Sometimes," said Del. Timothy F. Maloney (D-Prince George's), "it looks like reruns of *M*A*S*H*."

It is in the closing weeks of the session, when legislators sit through hours of voting sessions, that the jokes, pranks, and catcalls become more numerous. But no matter what happens between now and Monday's midnight adjournment, it is likely that the award for legislative antic of the year already has been claimed.

That occurred late one night when Del. Joseph V. Lutz (D-Harford) was struck by an amazing confluence of nature: a table filled with reporters in an otherwise empty restaurant and he, outside the window, on a deserted downtown street.

One greeting led to another until Lutz honored the reporters with the international salute of high school, which required the delegate to turn away from the reporters, loosen his trousers, and show the Fourth Estate a side of him not normally visible.

"It was not a full shot," Lutz said later, describing the incident as "just a high school joke."

Reporters, however, gleefully reported the happening to House Majority Leader John S. Arnick (D-Baltimore County), who rose on the chamber floor the next morning to tell delegates of a "serious problem."

As Lutz slunk to the rear of the chamber, Arnick, in mock seriousness, reminded delegates that the House dress code extends to the streets of Annapolis. But while the delegate in question might not have been at all times properly attired, his sentiments were, according to Arnick, "absolutely correct."

To the uninitiated, just the daily workings of the House and Senate must appear to be some sort of private joke. Those in the visitors' galleries often look in amazement at the frenzy on the floor, and Senate President Thomas V. Mike Miller Jr. (D-Prince George's) recently explained to a group of retired federal workers in the gallery about the process of bill introductions and committee reports leading up to final passage. "They will start paying attention then," Miller said of his chatting colleagues.

The Senate, though, is sedate compared with the rambunctious House. When delegates recently passed a bill protecting government "whistleblowers," it was accompanied by a collective pucker-faced chorus of whistles. Any bill that bypasses normal procedures on the way to passage results in the sounds of a freight train.

And most any bill this year dealing with animals has caused an outbreak of barking. Such was the case with a bill sponsored by Del. Leon Albin (D-Baltimore County) dealing with dangerous dogs. Its introduction also was greeted with the tape-recorded sounds of a vicious growling dog.

Presiding over all of this is House Speaker R. Clayton Mitchell Jr. (D-Kent), who tries his best to remain grim-faced but professes to be relieved to see some playfulness in his chamber.

"If those types of things didn't happen, you

would worry that the tension was too tight," Mitchell said.

Mitchell said he realizes that "people in the gallery must look down at times and think, 'This is what my tax money goes for?'" But he said that the few minutes of frivolity are outweighed by the hours of work legislators put in during the 90-day session.

"There's a line that you can't cross; you have to maintain a certain decorum," said Del. Maloney, whose budget subcommittee has spawned an extracurricular group known as the Ad Hoc Subcommittee on Awards/Pizza, which has jurisdiction over throwing parties for legislators and giving mock citations of merit.

Maloney maintains that the activities can serve a useful purpose. For instance, after Gov. William Donald Schaefer, angered over the defeat of several of his prized projects, declared that he and the legislature were "at war," the House Appropriations Committee held a ceremony to present Schaefer with an Indian feather bonnet and a peace pipe.

Later, committee members received a mug of artificial flowers and a note from Schaefer: "Peace pipe has been smoked. Happiness reigns. Look forward to big Pow Wow before next moon."

"It got him in a much better mood," Maloney said.

But perhaps the best summation of the subject came last Friday—April Fool's Day—from former delegate Robert Neall, who delivered the House's opening prayer.

"Grant us Your grace and wisdom," Neal prayed. "So that we be fools just one day out of 365, instead of the other way around."

Annual Bibliography

BY JO A. CATES

Once again, media coverage of AIDS was an important topic of discussion in the trade and scholarly journals. Other subjects of concern included the state of the English language, writing coaches, and beat reporting. In addition, William Zinsser, author of *On Writing Well,* offers his devoted readers more well-written words of wisdom in *Writing to Learn.* This selected bibliography of books, periodical and magazine articles, documents, and conference papers, all published in 1988, focuses on the art and craft of writing for newspapers. Also included are selected items on grammar, composition, and the teaching of writing.

BOOKS

Barry, Dave. *Dave Barry's Greatest Hits.* New York: Crown, 1988.

Blundell, William E. *The Art and Craft of Feature Writing: Based on the Wall Street Journal.* New York: New American Library, 1988.

Fedler, Fred. *Reporting for the Print Media.* 4th ed. New York: Harcourt Brace Jovanovich, 1988.

Ferris, Timothy, and Bruce Porter. *The Practice of Journalism: A Guide to Reporting and Writing the News.* Englewood Cliffs, NJ: Prentice-Hall, 1988.

Finnegan, William. *Dateline Soweto: Travels with Black South African Reporters.* New York: Harper & Row, 1988.

Friedlander, Edward J., and John Lee. *Feature*

Writing for Newspapers and Magazines. New York: Harper & Row, 1988.

Goulden, Joseph C. *Fit to Print: A.M. Rosenthal and His Times.* Secaucus, NJ: Lyle Stuart, 1988.

Kane, Thomas S. *The Concise Oxford Guide to Writing.* New York: Oxford University Press, 1988.

McQuade, Donald, and Robert Atwan, comps. *Popular Writing in America: The Interaction of Style and Audience.* 4th ed. New York: Oxford University Press, 1988.

Missouri Group. *News Reporting and Writing.* 3rd ed. Brian S. Brooks, George Kennedy, Daryl R. Moen, and Don Ranly, eds. New York: St. Martin's Press, 1988.

Murray, Jim. *The Jim Murray Collection.* Dallas: Taylor, 1988.

National Reporting 1941-1986: From Labor Conflicts to the Challenger Disaster. The Pulitzer Prize Archive, v. 2. New York: K.G. Saur, 1988.

Newman, Edwin. *I Must Say: Edwin Newman on English, the News and Other Matters.* New York: Warner, 1988.

Newsom, Doug, and James A. Wollert. *Media Writing: Preparing Information for the Mass Media.* 2nd ed. Belmont, CA: Wadsworth, 1988.

Quindlen, Anna. *Living Out Loud.* New York: Random House, 1988.

Safire, William. *You Could Look It Up.* New York: Times Books, 1988.

Sherrod, Blackie. *The Blackie Sherrod Collection.* Dallas: Taylor, 1988.

Stephens, Mitchell. *The History of News: From the Drum to the Satellite.* New York: Viking, 1988.

Thompson, Hunter. *Generation of Swine.* New York: Summit Books, 1988.

Zinsser, William. *Writing to Learn.* New York: Harper & Row, 1988.

MAGAZINE, PERIODICAL, AND NEWSPAPER ARTICLES

Alderson, Jeremy Weir. "True Confessions II: Confessions of a Travel Writer." *Columbia Journalism Review*, July/August 1988, pp. 27-28.

Ausenbaugh, James D. "How to Coach Writers: Part One." *The Coaches' Corner*, June 1988, p. 3.

——. "How to Coach Writers: Part Two." *The Coaches' Corner*, Sept. 1988, pp. 3, 11-12.

Ball, Diana Coleman. "Roving Reporters: The Charles Kuralts of Newspapering." *Editor & Publisher*, 24 Sept. 1988, pp. 14-15.

Baron, Dennis. "Our Presto-Changeo Language." *Righting Words*, Jan./Feb. 1988, pp. 15-17, 20-21.

Brecher, Edward M. "Straight Sex, AIDS, and the Mixed-up Press." *Columbia Journalism Review*, March/April 1988, pp. 46-50.

Brooke, Robert. "Modeling a Writer's Identity: Reading and Imitation in the Writing Classroom." *College Composition and Communication* 39 (Feb. 1988): pp. 23-41.

Burkhart, Ford N. "Disaster Journalism Gets Mixed Reviews." *Editor & Publisher*, 13 Aug. 1988, pp. 64, 53-54.

Campbell, Larry. "Reporting With the Senses." *The Coaches' Corner*, March 1988, pp. 1-2.

Caughey, Bernard. "The Popularity of Obituaries." *Editor & Publisher*, 23 April 1988, pp. 46, 146-147.

Childers, Doug. "Media Practices in AIDS Coverage and a Model for Ethical Reporting on AIDS Victims." *Journal of Mass Media Ethics*, Fall 1988, pp. 60-65.

Clark, Roy Peter. "Coaching Writers: The Human Side of Editing." *Washington Journalism Review*, Nov. 1988, pp. 34-36.

——. "10th Anniversary of Recognizing Stories That Cry Out, 'Read Me!'" *ASNE Bulletin*, March 1988, pp. 27-29.

——. "The Writing Process: How It Really Works." *The Quill*, Feb. 1988, p. 31.

Cranberg, Gilbert. "Can We Keep Newsrooms Honest in a Society Rife With Plagiarism?" *ASNE Bulletin*, May-June 1988, pp. 4, 6.

Davis, Foster. "'Making Me See' Is the Key to Visual Writing." *The Coaches' Corner*, Sept. 1988, p. 7.

deView, Lucille S. "The Computer: Help or Hindrance?" *The Coaches' Corner*, Dec. 1988, p. 9.

"Editorially Speaking." *The Gannetteer*, Sept. 1988. (Issue devoted to newspaper writing.)

Elliott, Deni. "Identifying AIDS Victims." *Washington Journalism Review*, Oct. 1988, pp. 26-29.

Estrin, Herman A. "A Dozen Suggestions to Improve Journalistic Writing Effectiveness." *Community College Journalist*, Fall 1988, pp. 6-8.

Ettema, James S., and Theodore L. Glasser. "Narrative Form and Moral Force: The Realization of Innocence and Guilt Through Investigative Journalism." *Journal of Communication* 38 (Summer 1988): pp. 8-26.

Fry, Don. "An Exercise to Teach Editors How to Coach." *The Coaches' Corner,* March 1988, pp. 7, 10.

——. "Attribute, but Try Not to Slow Flow." *APME News*, April/May 1988, pp. 11-12.

——. "How to Form a Writers Group." *The Quill*, March 1988, pp. 25-27.

——. "What Do Writing Coaches Do Anyway?" *APME News*, June/July 1988, pp. 9-13.

Garneau, George. "Get Serious About the Sports Pages." *Editor & Publisher*, 7 May 1988, pp. 16, 37.

Garrison, Bruce. "Rules of the Game for Beginning Sports Writers." *The Coaches' Corner*, June 1988, pp. 1, 8.

Gersh, Debra. "The 1988 Pulitzer Prizes." *Editor & Publisher*, 9 April 1988, pp. 13-15, 50, 55-56.

——. "The Subway Beat." *Editor & Publisher*, 23 April 1988, pp. 44, 144-145.

Giblin, James Cross. "A Nonfiction Writer Is a Storyteller." *The Writer,* April 1988, pp. 13-15, 46.

Gibson, John. "AP Coverage Shines as Bright as 'Skins." *APME News*, April/May 1988, pp. 5-6.

Givens, Murphy. "Keep the Reader Interested." *The Masthead*, Winter 1988, p. 24.

Glassman, Robin. "Suburban Reporting: Pioneering on the Frontier." *The Coaches' Corner*, June 1988, pp. 1, 9.

Gomme, Ted. "In Support of the Paragraph." *Content*, July/Aug. 1988, p. 13.

Gould, Whitney. "Editorials: Smile When You Write That." *The Coaches' Corner,* Dec. 1988, pp. 5, 8.

Greenberg, Joel. "Telling the West Bank Story." *Columbia Journalism Review*, July/August 1988, pp. 40-42.

Gwin, Louis. "Prospective Reporters Face Writing/Editing Tests at Many Dailies." *Newspaper Research Journal* 9 (Winter 1988): pp. 101-111.

Haughton, Jim. "Covering Spring Training." *Editor & Publisher*, 16 April 1988, pp. 18, 29.

Johnson, Dirk. "Part of Reporting Is Simply a Matter of Asking Questions." *The Coaches' Corner*, March 1988, pp. 1, 3.

Karim, Karim H. "Covering Refugees With Figures of Speech." *Content*, Jan./Feb. 1988, pp. 30-31.

King, Barbara. "Preparing a Workbook for Each Reporter." *The Coaches' Corner*, June 1988, pp. 2, 9.

Kirtz, Bill. "Editors Tell How to Avoid Bland Writing." *Publishers' Auxiliary*, 28 Nov. 1988, p. 3.

Klein, Julie. "The Story of Sage." *The Quill*, March 1988, pp. 28-34.

Klooster, David J. "How to Make Students Better Writers." *Editor & Publisher*, 17 Dec. 1988, pp. 48, 37.

382

Kramer, Staci D. "AIDS and Anonymity." *Editor & Publisher*, 12 March 1988, pp. 9-11, 43.

Krasnow, Bruce. "Coaching the Writer of a Series." *The Coaches' Corner*, Dec. 1988, pp. 1-2, 6.

Kritzberg, Barry. "Fire Ants, Doublespeak, and the Vox Populi." *English Journal*, March 1988, pp. 43-44.

Laermer, Richard. "AIDS Obituaries: Death as a Rewrite." *Editor & Publisher*, 13 Feb. 1988, pp. 64, 47.

Lander, Estelle. "AIDS Coverage: Ethical and Legal Issues Facing the Media Today." *Journal of Mass Media Ethics*, Fall 1988, pp. 66-72.

Langley, Monica, and Lee Levine. "Broken Promises." *Columbia Journalism Review*, July/Aug. 1988, pp. 21-24.

Larson, Richard L. "Selected Bibliography of Scholarship on Composition and Rhetoric." *College Composition and Communication* 39 (Oct. 1988): pp. 316-336.

Lesher, Tina. "The Writing Coach Movement." *Editor & Publisher*, 8 Oct. 1988, pp. 56, 45.

Levy, Mark R. "WJR Readers Choose America's Best Journalists." *Washington Journalism Review*, March 1988, pp. 23-38.

Lutz, William. "Fourteen Years of Doublespeak." *English Journal*, March 1988, pp. 40-42.

McNichol, Tom. "The Prose on the Prompter: Rating the Anchors' Writing." *Washington Journalism Review*, July/Aug. 1988, pp. 35-37.

Malerba, James F. "Rites for Righting Writing." *Editor & Publisher*, 16 July 1988, pp. 52, 43.

Maney, Kevin. "Writing Tight." *Writer's Digest,* April 1988, pp. 26-27.

"The Masthead Symposium: AIDS and the Editorial Page." *The Masthead,* Winter 1988, pp. 6-12.

Mencher, Melvin. "Editorials Failed to Analyze Hazelwood." *The Masthead,* Fall 1988, pp. 17-23.

Mollenhoff, Clark R. "Journalists Suffer Their Own Deadly AIDS." *The IRE Journal,* Fall 1988, p. 3.

Murray, Donald M. "Writing on Writing: The Craft of Description." *The Coaches' Corner*, Sept. 1988, pp. 1, 8-9.

Nicholson, Charles. "Big as All Outdoors." *The Writer,* June 1988, pp. 19-21. (About outdoor writing.)

Pitts, Beverly J. "How Writers Work: Research Into the Process." *The Coaches' Corner,* Dec. 1988, pp. 6, 8.

Reigstad, Tom. "Reporting on the Marketplace: Coaching Business Writers." *The Coaches' Corner,* Sept. 1988, pp. 2, 12.

Riordan, Carol Ann. "Covering AIDS." *presstime,* May 1988, pp. 26, 28, 30.

Roberts, Eugene. "The Finest Reporting Is Always Investigative." *The IRE Journal,* Winter 1988, pp. 12-14.

Rodriguez, Ginger Gundersgaard. "Drafting Language Into the Law." *Righting Words,* Sept./Oct. 1988, pp. 22-25.

Rogin, Richard. "True Confessions I: Confessions of a Stakeout Artist." *Columbia Journalism Review,* July/August 1988, pp. 25-27.

Romano, Tom. "Breaking the Rules in Style." *English Journal,* Dec. 1988, pp. 58-62.

Rosenstiel, Thomas B. "Press Didn't Mistreat Jackson; It Treated Him Too Much Like Other Candidates." *ASNE Bulletin,* May-June 1988, pp. 7-9.

Rykken, Rolf. "The Police Beat: Not Exactly a Dead Beat." *presstime,* Sept. 1988, pp. 6-9.

Sachsman, David B., et al. "Environmental Risk Reporting: Hypotheticals Teach Skills." *Journalism Educator,* Summer 1988, pp. 57-59, 77.

Salsini, Paul. "Reflections on the Richness of Writing." *The Coaches' Corner,* March 1988, pp. 4-5.

Scanlan, Christopher. "Riding the Roller Coaster: The Emotion in Good Writing." *The Coaches' Corner,* Sept. 1988, pp. 1, 4-5.

Sibbison, Jim. "Covering Medical 'Breakthroughs.'" *Columbia Journalism Review,* July/August 1988, pp. 36-39.

Spear, Michael M. "Feature Reading Adds Dimension to Feature Writing." *Journalism Educator,* Winter 1988, pp. 26-27.

——. "The Man Who Would Not Freeze: And Other Tales That You Ought to Tell." *The Quill,* July/Aug. 1988, pp. 26-29.

Stein, M.L. "Advice on AIDS Coverage." *Editor & Publisher,* 7 May 1988, p. 45.

Strickland, Bill, comp. "The Secrets of Our Success." *Writer's Digest,* Dec. 1988, pp. 24-32.

Thomas, Jo. "Bloody Ireland." *Columbia Journalism Review,* May/June 1988, pp. 31-37.

Timbs, Lawrence C., Jr. "Put More Romance in News Reporting, Writing Courses." *Journalism Educator,* Winter 1988, pp. 23-25.

Walker, Ruth. "Editorial Writing Demystified." *The Coaches' Corner,* Dec. 1988, pp. 1, 3.

Walton, Thomas W. "Let's Hang Cliches Out to Dry." *ASNE Bulletin*, Jan. 1988, p. 32.

Ward, Jean. "The News Library's Contribution to Newsmaking." *Special Libraries* 79 (Spring 1988): pp. 143-147.

Waxman, Maron L. "You and Your Copy Editor." *Writer's Digest,* April 1988, pp. 28-30.

REPORTS AND CONFERENCE PAPERS

Coulson, David C., and Cecilie Gaziano. "How Journalists at Two Newspapers View Good Writing and Writing Coaches." Paper presented at the annual meeting of the Association for Education in Journalism and Mass Communication, Portland, OR, July 1988, ERIC, ED 295206. 25pp.

Ervin, R. Ferrell. "A Matter of Risk: The Police, the Media, and Crime Reporting." Paper presented at the annual meeting of the Association for Education in Journalism and Mass Communication, Portland, OR, July 1988, ERIC, ED 295176. 26pp.

Fry, Don. "Writing Coaching: A Primer." St. Petersburg, FL: The Poynter Institute for Media Studies, 1988. (Revision of materials published in *The Coaches' Corner* and *APME News*.)

Gaudino, James L. "A Predictive Framework for Determining How Journalists Determine News." Paper presented at the annual meeting of the Association for Education in Journalism and Mass Communication, Portland, OR, July 1988, ERIC, ED 297337. 46pp.

Moss, Michael. "Reporting on Literacy: Soft-Selling a Complex Political Story." Paper presented at the national seminar of the Education Writers Association, New Orleans, LA, April 1988, ERIC, ED 296176. 20pp.

"Writing & Editing." Report of the APME Writing and Editing Committee, Boston, MA, Oct. 1988.

Former ASNE Award Winners

1988

Deadline writing: Bob Herbert, New York *Daily News*
Non-deadline writing: Blaine Harden, *The Washington Post*
Commentary: Jimmy Breslin, New York *Daily News*
Editorial writing: James Klurfeld, *Newsday*
Obituary writing: Carl Schoettler, Baltimore *Evening Sun*, and Tom Shales, *The Washington Post*

1987

Deadline writing: Mark Fineman, *Los Angeles Times*, and Craig Medred, *Anchorage Daily News*
Non-deadline writing: Steve Twomey, *The Philadelphia Inquirer*
Commentary: Dave Barry, *The Miami Herald*, and Don Marsh, *The Charleston Gazette*
Obituary writing: Jim Nicholson, *Philadelphia Daily News*

1986

Deadline writing: Bradley Graham, *The Washington Post*
Non-deadline writing: John Camp, *St. Paul Pioneer Press/Dispatch*, and David Finkel, *St. Petersburg Times*
Commentary: Roger Simon, *The Sun*, Baltimore, Md.
Editorial writing: Jonathan Freedman, *The Tribune*, San Diego, Calif.

1985

Deadline writing: Jonathan Bor, *The Post Standard,* Syracuse, NY.
Non-deadline writing: Greta Tilley, *Greensboro News & Record*
Commentary: Murray Kempton, *Newsday*
Editorial writing: Richard Aregood, *Philadelphia Daily News*

1984

Deadline writing: David Zucchino, *The Philadelphia Inquirer*
Non-deadline writing: James Kindall, *The Kansas City Star*
Commentary: Roger Simon, *The Chicago Sun-Times*
Business writing: Peter Rinearson, *The Seattle Times*

1983

Deadline writing: No awards made in this category.
Non-deadline writing: Greta Tilley, *Greensboro News & Record*
Commentary: Rheta Grimsley Johnson, *Memphis Commercial Appeal*
Business writing: Orland Dodson, *Shreveport Times*

1982

Deadline writing: Patrick Sloyan, *Newsday*
Non-deadline writing: William Blundell, *The Wall Street Journal*
Commentary: Theo Lippman Jr., *The Baltimore Sun*
Sports writing: Tom Archdeacon, *The Miami News*

1981

Deadline writing: Richard Zahler, *The Seattle Times*
Non-deadline writing: Saul Pett, Associated Press
Commentary: Paul Greenberg, *Pine Bluff* (Ark.) *Commercial*
Sports writing: Thomas Boswell, *The Washington Post*

1980

Deadline writing: Carol McCabe, *Providence Journal-Bulletin*
Non-deadline writing: Cynthia Gorney, *The Washington Post*
Commentary: Ellen Goodman, *The Boston Globe*

1979

Deadline writing: Richard Ben Cramer, *The Philadelphia Inquirer*
Non-deadline writing—News: Thomas Oliphant, *The Boston Sunday Globe*
Non-deadline writing—Features: Mary Ellen Corbett, *Fort Wayne News -Sentinel*
Grand Prize (Commentary): Everett S. Allen, *New Bedford Standard-Times*

Best Newspaper Writing Order Form

Photocopy or tear out this page to order.

Please send me:

Best Newspaper Writing

_____ copies 1989 edition @ $10.95

_____ copies 1988 edition @ $ 9.95

_____ copies 1987 edition @ $ 9.95

_____ copies 1986 edition @ $ 7.95

Enclosed is $ _____ (check) or

Purchase Order # _____

Name: _____

Company: _____

Department: _____

Street Address: _____

PO Box: _____ City: _____

State: _____ ZIP: _____

---

* **Orders cannot be processed unless remittance or institutional purchase order is enclosed.**

* **Florida residents add 6% state sales tax.**

* **Canadian and overseas residents please make checks payable in U.S. dollars. Overseas orders add $2 per book for surface mailing.**

* **Orders are shipped UPS or USPS 4th class library rate. Expedited shipment available at additional charge. UPS requires street address.**

* **A 20% discount is granted on orders of 20 or more of a single title.**

The Poynter Institute

801 Third Street South

St. Petersburg, FL 33701

(813) 821-9494